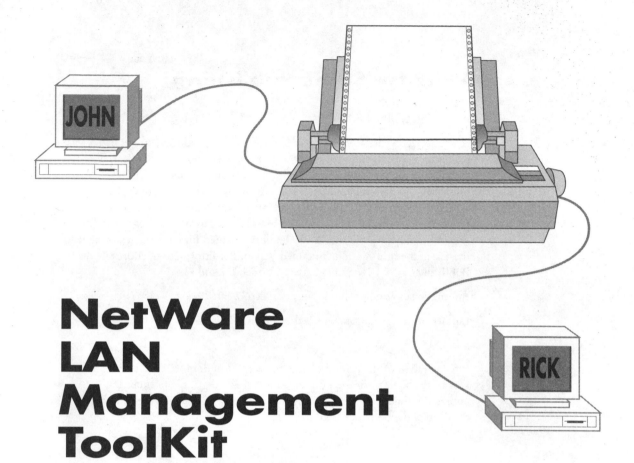

NetWare
LAN
Management
ToolKit

Rick Segal and John T. McCann

SAMS
PUBLISHING
A Division of Prentice Hall Computer Publishing
11711 North College, Carmel, Indiana 46032 USA

Composed in AGaramond and MCPdigital
by Prentice Hall Computer Publishing

Printed in the United States of America

For Michelle Helen Segal. Daddy's done, let's hit the beach. I love you.

Publisher
Richard K. Swadley

Acquisitions Manager
Jordan Gold

Managing Editor
Neweleen A. Trebnik

Acquisitions Editor
Gregg Bushyeager

Development Editor
Gregg Bushyeager

Production Editor
Grant Fairchild

Editor
Mary Corder

Editorial Coordinators
Becky Freeman
William Whitmer

Editorial Assistants
Rosemarie Graham
Lori Keley

Technical Editor
Bill Candow

Formatter
Mary Croy

Cover Designer
Jean Bisesi

Production Director
Jeff Valler

Production Manager
Corinne Walls

Imprint Manager
Matthew Morrill

Book Designer
Michele Laseau

Production Analyst
Mary Beth Wakefield

Proofreading/Indexing Coordinator
Joelynn Gifford

Graphic Image Specialist
Dennis Sheehan

Indexer
Sherri Massey

Production
Katy Bodenmiller
Tim Cox
Lisa Daugherty
Terri Edwards
Mark Enochs
John Kane
Roger Morgan
Juli Pavey
Angela Pozdol
Linda Quigley
Michelle Self
Greg Simsic
Susan Shepard
Angie Trzepacz
Suzanne Tully
Alyssa Yesh

Screen reproductions in this book were created by means of the program Collage Plus from Inner Media, Inc., Hollis, NH.

Overview

Contents

3 Visual Modem: Peekin' and Pokin' Around 95

4 NovBat: Holy Do It in a Batch File, Batman. 113

5 IdleBoot: Knock, Knock, Anything Going On?   161

6 Other Cool Tools 195

Acknowledgments

This is the best part! Please stick with me and read this. I think you should know who the really great people are that made this and other books work.

In the world of books, there is none finer than Gregg Bushyeager. He tops the list because he is tops. Gregg is my mother, rabbi, and resident book expert at Sams. He is also one of my favorite persons and a good friend. Thanks buddy, another one down.

If it were not for John T. McCann, I would have been, well, asleep. John does his best work after 11 p.m. and before 6 a.m. John is an expert, with a passion for getting it right, helping the users, and passing on the gift of knowledge. I am grateful that he and I could work on this project together, and I'm glad we have remained friends over the years. Thanks, John.

Steve Meyer is one of the great ones. An artist who crafts software rather than just programming it. He gave me lots of great feedback and some great software, and you are reading the results of his hard work. He is one of the best. Also, thanks to Bonnie Meyer for letting Steve come out and play and for taking all those "other" calls.

Marc Perkel is one of the last of those true programmers who will get the request by 10 a.m. and have a new version out by 5 p.m. Marc's software is useful and he's an excellent resource.

Thanks to Grant Fairchild and Mary Corder, my editors at Sams. Grant, I'm still learning, and it was a real pleasure to work with you. Your quick, useful edits made my deadlines less painful.

Bill Candow was the technical editor on this project. Bill, you did a great job and I appreciate it. Thanks.

Finally, no book would ever be done without the support of my family. Teresa, Rachel, and Michelle put up with long hours and a Grumpy Gus yet still managed a smile and a hug when I needed it. I love you all.

About the Authors

John T. McCann: John is the author of many commercial and shareware network utilities including Brightwork Development's SITELOCK. He is the author of *The NetWare Supervisor's Guide* (M&T Books, 1989) and has served on Novell's NetWire forum as a lead SysOp. John holds a master's degree in computer science from Texas A&M University.

Rick Segal: Rick is the former vice president of development at Brightwork Development, a network utility software company. Currently a technical evangelist for Microsoft Corporation, Rick authored the *LAN Desktop Guide to Troubleshooting: NetWare Edition* (Sams, 1992), is a frequent speaker at NetWorld and PCExpo, and has served as a NetWire SysOp.

Trademarks

Introduction

It's 9 p.m. The kids are in bed, lights down low, smooth jazz on the radio. There, in the soft light is your better half. Yes, all the hard work is worth it. Then, the phone, the most hated and feared instrument known to a LAN administrator. It's Fred. We all know Fred. Fred is the guy who can't find the on/off switch. His idea of a cold boot is the Tony Lama pair that was left outside. Yes, Fred. . . . Naturally, Fred has a last minute, oh-my-God project that has to be ready to go first thing in the morning. You, kind reader, are the target of Fred's abuse, anger, fear, hopes, dreams, and desires. You have two major issues going on at once. Fred needs some technical help because the LAN has a problem, and you need to be sure that ol' Fred has a very clear understanding of what is going on.

This book is for all of you who know and "love" Fred. For those of you who have missed a kid's play, stood up a date, or put in 100-hour weeks only to have to justify "what you do," this book is for you. This book is for you folks who run around putting out fires with no real set of tools and no real organized way to deal with common problems.

This is a book I've wanted to write for some time. I have been a big fan of some software tools that have helped me and my colleagues over the years. The software developers who wrote these tools are some of the best people in the industry. I am convinced that the right "bag of tricks" solves problems correctly, helps keep your operation running smoothly, and gets you promoted. This book represents my way of helping both the new folks out there who just got this job and for those of you trying to consolidate all that knowledge you have heard about, forgotten, or know you wrote down somewhere.

Finally, this book will give you the chance to get some technical commentary from one of the industry's more colorful players, John T. McCann. John agreed to come along for the ride to provide some technical analysis and the kind of comments that only Big J can offer. More about him shortly.

Objectives

I wrote this book with several objectives in mind. I hope they are on target with why you bought this book!

Getting Your Hands On Some Practical Tools

Today, hundreds of books on almost any networking topic are available, as well as software that covers nearly every problem out there. There are books covering LAN hardware, software, settings, tips, tricks, traps, application installation, security, backup, and so on. With all that stuff, it's easy to lose sight of the big picture when it comes to the basic software tools needed to successfully manage and troubleshoot a LAN. We have selected some of the best software from some of the best developers and we think we are presenting it with a different perspective than other books. Both John and I will guide you through the software and its use with John giving you lots of technical advice, while I provide you with some of the "why" answers—why should you care, why should you do this, and so on. Besides giving you some great software, you should be able to gain a better understanding of the software that is discussed in this book. This, in turn, hopefully makes you a smarter consumer and helps you select software that is appropriate for your needs.

The Technical Information Behind The Tool

My first real job was in the U.S. Air Force. My first boss, T. Sgt. Lee Featherstone, told me on the first day, "Kid [and I was one], knowing stuff is important. If, however, you know where to find out, you'll always have the edge." Featherstone was right and I have followed that advice for many years. For me, knowing a little about a lot, along with knowing where to go for the rest, has helped me to be successful in this crazy field. This book and the accompanying software tools give you lots of information about lots of things in combination with directions on where to get the massive amount of details that you may need. In my view, this gets you past "the monkey see, monkey do" approach. You should understand the tool, the how, and the why.

Hit the Ground Running

After reading this book, you should be able to set up the software and dive into the job much faster. If you are already doing the job, this book/software combination fills in some gaps, provides you with some great software troubleshooting tools, and (hopefully) gets you home a bit earlier.

You're Not Alone

Take heart, you have lots of company. We'll give you enough war stories to make you feel good, and we'll tell you where to go when you need some peer-group help, advice, or sympathy. John and I hope that after reading this book and getting to know some of the people out there who craft excellent software, you'll have yet a few more places to seek help.

Who This Book Is For

This book has several target audiences. Keep in mind that on any given day, you might fit into any or all of these groups.

"Jenkins, handle this LAN thing will ya, just take a sec."

Yeah, my kind of job. You are the lucky person who essentially gets the job tossed at you. In some cases, you volunteer without really understanding what you are getting yourself into. In other cases, you are volunteered. Corporate management at its finest. What you need is information fast, and you need some great software support applications to get you started. Friends, you bought the right book.

"Two years on the job and I still can't find the end of this wire!"

Once into the job, you may find yourself getting buried in the day-to-day stuff and you're never able to really soak up some knowledge, identify problems, or expand your career potential. Well, you too, my friend, have come to the right book. For you, this book represents an attempt to smooth out some of the procedures you have been trying to use by providing you monitoring tools that allow you to get an in-depth understanding of the LAN. You should pay attention to the tools discussed in this book and the way they are used because it tells you a lot about the way problems pop up and can be handled. There are tools here to help your users as well. These kinds of utilities enable you to be more responsive to a user's day-to-day hassles. These pages and the accompanying software can act as a double check on things you think you might have heard or read one late night while waiting for the 300M backup tape to find one stupid file.

"Just call me LANman."

This book can even offer you, the office expert, some good stuff. You'll appreciate the way this book expands your knowledge and verifies or debunks things that you have heard or read. The associated software helps you spend less time watching the small stuff, and allows you to concentrate on the bigger picture. You should pay particular attention to the management notes that are spread throughout the book. These notes are designed to help you translate all the techno-talk into meaningful information the business folks can understand. Finally, this book may inspire you to write your own book. After all, with thousands of new LAN administrators coming on board, they are going to need all the wisdom you can offer. It's like to "boldly avoid where you've gone before!"

What's in the Book

Network Monitoring: You'll find the NetAlarm from Avanti Technologies here, and folks, it's a great little tool. This server monitoring utility is an excellent "smoke detector" for your server. It's great stuff from Steve Meyer and his team.

Menuing: Marc Perkel is a one-of-a-kind guy and MarxMenu is an unbelievable package. With over 750 commands, there's almost nothing you can't do with this tool. If you do find something, call Marc. He'll probably put it in the package.

Modem Hassles: A work of art, Visual Modem will become your ticket to truly understanding what is going on with your modem and how to properly deal with this pesky device.

LAN tools: Idleboot and NovBat are two great products from Phil Case at Horizons Consulting. These tools will help you manage your user's desktop.

The NetWare LAN: Within the bindings of this book is the fastest NetWare technical course ever recorded. Its purpose is to give you a "level set" for the information contained within the rest of the book, to give you something to pass on to others who need instant knowledge (fast reviews are always good for the brain). Fasten your seatbelt, folks, this one is speedy. We'll blow through some history, hardware requirements, software parts, and lots of key facts you should keep in mind when you are dealing with NetWare. Don't skip this. You'll get to see McCann in all his glory.

History: We also present you with the history of Novell and NetWare so you get an idea of where it has been and where it's going. We've added lots of comments, and even the old-timers will enjoy it!

References: There are two interesting approaches to gathering a lot of information and solving a wide range of problems in a quick, effective manner. The first method involves eating, drinking, sleeping, and bathing with books, magazines, conference videos, meeting tapes, and tons of technical junk mail. Trust us, this is no way to get ahead or get a date. The second method is to know where information is and know how to get at it quickly. We have compiled a list of software programs that you can obtain both from the shareware world and the commercial market, along with our opinions as to their usefulness, importance, and so on.

How This Book Was Written

As the lead writer, I used one particular process—survival training! Throughout the book, you'll see my face or John's face beside text boxes that provide you with some additional remarks. I tried to focus on management, high-level stuff, leaving the nuts and bolts to John.

Rick: Although I survived my days in the U.S. Air Force, a "tour of duty" at Aetna Life and Casualty, weird users, crazy bosses, impossible requests, outlandish budgets, unrealistic plans, and much more, I hope that by documenting a lot of the things that I went through, you'll be able to survive as well. I have written this as though you and I were chatting over a couple of brews after a long, hard day. It's my hope that you'll be nodding your head when you recognize something you have been through. I hope that you'll have lots of "Cool!" and "Gee, I didn't know that!" moments, and that you'll enjoy this book.

John: As for me, I've been hacking at this stuff since it first came out. I still live in Texas, still just want to write code, and I'll be riding along here making sure "Joe Corporate" doesn't get you too crazy. Long live bits and bytes!

In addition to the text boxes highlighted by our smiling faces, there are some other elements that the Sams folks use to improve the readability of the book:

Notes: Things you should keep in the back of your mind.

Cautions: Pay attention, there is a problem ahead!

Onward and Upward

We hope you enjoy this book and find it valuable. Please let us know your thoughts on this wild and crazy profession we have chosen. We can be reached in care of the publisher or through a bunch of electronic means. We would love to hear from you. Good luck and continued success.

Rick Segal: Redmond, Washington
CompuServe: 76276,2706
Internet: 76276.2706@COMPUSERVE.COM

John T. McCann: Austin Texas
CompuServe: 70007,3430
Internet: 70007.3430@COMPUSERVE.COM

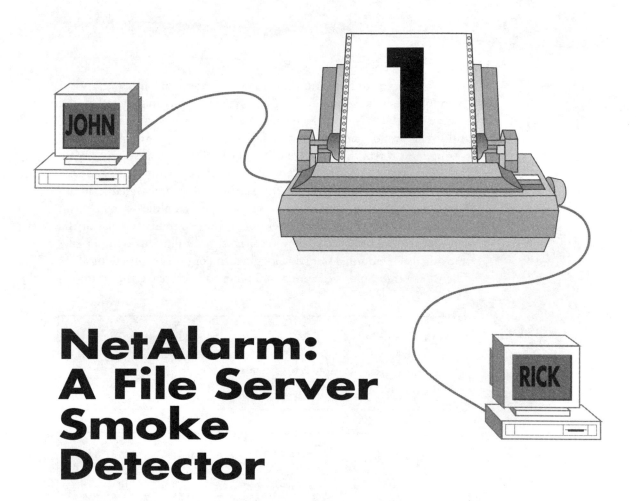

NetAlarm:
A File Server
Smoke
Detector

One of the most important network tools you can have is one that monitors the server's vital signs. NetAlarm is just such a tool. Steve Meyer and the team at Avanti, along with the folks at XTree have provided us with a single-server version of this popular product for use in this book. The reference chapter at the end of this book shows you how to order a full system, multiserver version. First, let's take a look at what NetAlarm is and how it can work for you.

Introduction

This special version of NetAlarm can be used as an unobtrusive terminate-and-stay resident (TSR) program in a "smoke detector" fashion or as a real-time, interactive monitoring process. Those fine folks at Avanti Technology have kindly provided this software so you can get a feel for the features and the use on one server. The multiple-server version is available, and details are located at the end of this chapter if you are interested in getting it. Many of the MONITOR or FCONSOLE statistics NetWare users depend on to isolate the cause of network problems aren't available in NetWare 3.x. Additionally, the statistics that are available under NetWare 2.x are reset when a server is brought back online—after a crash, for example—and thus effectively eliminate the possibility of isolating the cause of the crash. NetAlarm overcomes these limitations by internally tracking the operational statistics, logging, and optionally providing alerts whenever a threshold is exceeded or a potentially critical error occurs.

John: FCONSOLE and MONITOR are Novell Utility programs that enable you to look at a variety of server statistics. Figures 1.1, 1.2, and 1.3 are example screens from NetWare 3.x and the Monitor NLM.

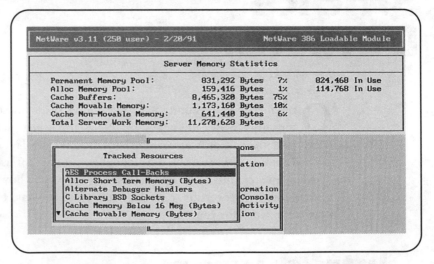

Figure 1.1. A Monitor sample screen showing server statistics.

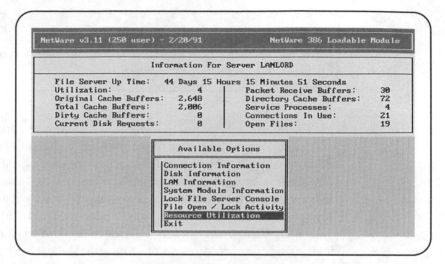

Figure 1.2. A Monitor sample screen showing the opening summary screen and menu options.

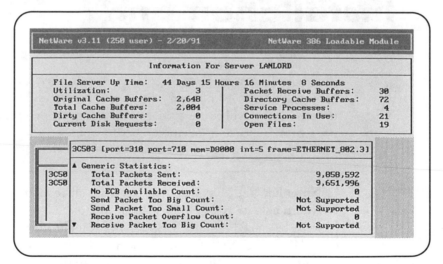

Figure 1.3. A Monitor sample screen showing network interface board statistics.

Rick: One of the key things in the tool, folks, is the logs. Your boss will appreciate these logs and reports that you can provide as status reports regarding system health.

NetAlarm is based on the concept that solutions to problems can be found easily when the source of the problem is determined. NetAlarm, which loosely works like a "smoke detector," logs errors as they occur and identifies the areas requiring immediate attention. Through the alert facilities, network system administrators receive early warnings and take appropriate countermeasures to resolve problems. This is the key to success in any LAN management endeavor. As the network administrator/trouble-shooter, you need to discover the source of the problem as quickly as possible.

Installation and Configuration

You will find that installing NetAlarm is easy. Simply copy the NETALARM.COM file into a directory that is accessible to the workstation on which it will be executed. NetAlarm is not copy-protected and does not require a special installation procedure or key.

 Note: For NetWare 3.x file servers that will be monitored, the Avanti collection NetWare loadable module (AVANTIBK.NLM) must be copied into the SYS:\SYSTEM subdirectory, and the AUTOEXEC.NCF file should be modified to load this NLM at startup (that is, add "load AVANTIBK" to the startup file).

Prior to initial execution, preconfigure each file server to be monitored, with the initial thresholds defined. This procedure is outlined later in this section.

Quick Start Steps

Although NetAlarm is full-featured and complex in its capabilities with broad configuration options, it is simple to install and run. Use the following checklist to initially install and run NetAlarm, then reconfigure and fine-tune this tool to fit a particular environment.

1. Select a monitoring workstation, preferably one with a local hard disk. If a workstation cannot be dedicated to network monitoring, select one that remains attached to the network and is not continuously in use by critical or CPU-intensive processes. Optionally, you can create a subdirectory on the workstation's local hard disk for the distribution files. Copy the files from the distribution disk into the appropriate directory on the workstation local hard disk.

> **Note:** Although dedicated print servers are usually excellent candidates, you should consult the TSR operations section prior to choosing a monitoring workstation.

2. Copy the Avanti Collection NLM (AVANTIBK.NLM) to the SYS:SYSTEM subdirectory on each NetWare 3.x file server to be monitored, then modify the server's AUTOEXEC.NCF startup file to load AVANTI.NLM each time the server is started. Load the Avanti Collection NLM by typing LOAD AVANTIBK from the file server console.

> **Note:** Novell's CLIB NLM must be loaded prior to loading the Avanti Collection NLM.

3. Run NetAlarm with the CONFIG option. When the configured server table appears, use the keyboard arrow keys to position the highlighted bar over the default configuration entry and press Enter.

4. Set the default monitoring thresholds and parameters to be used as the basis for any new configured server table entries and for unconfigured file servers that might be monitored. Use the keyboard arrow keys to position the cursor. Use "00%" to disable thresholds and "N" to disable anomaly events.

NetWare 2.x: Cache ratio is the percentage of cache hits to overall cache operations and should be set above 90 percent.

NetWare 3.x: Cache ratio is the percentage of total cache buffers to total server work RAM and should be set around 50 percent.

Once satisfied with the parameters, press Escape to exit and accept the default configuration.

5. When the configured server table appears, press Insert to enter the name of a file server to be monitored (terminated with the Enter key) or press Escape to exit the configuration process and optionally save the defined parameters.

6. When the configuration parameters screen appears, set the desired monitoring thresholds and parameters for the monitored file server. After you are satisfied with the configuration parameters for this file server, press Escape to return to Step 5.

7. When prompted, if the new configuration information should be saved to disk, reply in the affirmative. NetAlarm saves the new configuration information and then terminates.

8. As SUPERVISOR or equivalent, run SYSCON on each file server to be monitored to ensure that the user associated with the monitoring workstation has been granted file server console operator rights.

9. Confirm that the workstation is attached to the file server to be monitored through a LOGIN that grants file server console operator rights. Although NetAlarm requires that the workstation be attached to the monitored file server, it isn't necessary to have a mapped drive to the monitored server.

10. If NetAlarm runs as a foreground process on a workstation dedicated to network monitoring, you can start by simply executing

the program name from the command line. If it is run as a background task on a workstation used for other tasks, the TSR option must be specified with the program name and option separated by a space.

At this point, NetAlarm begins its monitoring process.

If NetAlarm is running as a foreground process on a workstation dedicated to network monitoring, you can change the configured server parameters by pressing Insert. This suspends the monitoring process and invokes reconfiguration, placing the user at the configured server table (Step 5). You can then enable, disable, and reconfigure the servers with the option to save the new parameters. Upon completion, the workstation returns to its previous monitoring process.

Even if NetAlarm is running as a background TSR on a workstation dedicated to other tasks, it is still possible to reconfigure the memory-resident copy without unloading it. To do so, run NetAlarm using the CONFIG option. You can also unload NetAlarm from memory by using the UNLOAD option.

Configuration

The events that NetAlarm monitors, as well as the threshold levels of some events, can be configured by the user. Some of these events are specific to the version of NetWare in use. Typically, a network system administrator adjusts the configuration several times, or specifically, the threshold levels, to achieve optimum warning with minimal alerts.

> **John:** NetWare 2.x file servers that utilize intelligent/cached disk controllers, for example, may need lower cache ratios and dirty cache buffer thresholds because the enhanced disk management features of such boards tend to reduce the cache efficiency designed into NetWare. Therefore, the alarms that may occur as a result of the default settings may not truly indicate a problem, but rather an offloading of resource management. This is an example of an occasion when the software gurus had no real faith that the hardware folks would ever come up with decent stuff.

You can fine-tune the configuration with Avanti's NetTrack baseline sampling/performance measurement utility, or by periodically reviewing the error log file and adjusting the thresholds. Such reconfiguration or adjustments are accomplished through the NetAlarm configuration screen. The configuration screen allows you to enable or disable the monitoring of individual events and set the appropriate level for threshold alarms. Threshold levels may be set from "00" to "99" ("00" disables the monitoring for the event). You can enable or disable the other alarms by entering either a "Y" or an "N."

Rick: From a management perspective, NetTrack is a very handy tool. It enables you to find out what is appropriate for your environment. For example, my server at home never runs at more than 30 percent average utilization. NetTrack would sample my system and tell me to set an alarm at perhaps 40 percent to indicate that my system was outside its norm. Without NetTrack, I would be guessing. This is cool stuff. Refer to the end of this chapter for NetTrack ordering information.

You can invoke NetAlarm's configuration screen from the command line using the CONFIG option (NetAlarm CONFIG) if NetAlarm is not currently running or is memory resident, or by pressing Insert when NetAlarm is running as a foreground process with real-time screen display.

If NetAlarm is already memory resident, a message indicating this fact will appear. In this event, the configuration information of the memory-resident copy of NetAlarm is retrieved and used as the basis for modification, regardless of how the executed program is actually configured.

The configured server table provides a method for assigning unique configuration parameters to specific file servers. This table shows any preconfigured file servers, as well as those that are enabled or disabled. Using this screen, you can insert, delete, and edit individual file server configurations that may also then be individually enabled or disabled for monitoring.

Upon installation, you should first establish the parameters within the default configuration because the default configuration information is used as base, or default, parameters for any file servers added to the configured server table and for use with file servers for which no configuration is specified. To edit an existing file server entry, position the highlighted bar over the entry to be modified and press Enter. The configuration screen with the parameters defined for that file server then appears, enabling the user to modify the configuration specifics.

To add a file server entry to the table, press Insert, type the file server name, and press Enter. The entry is then automatically inserted in the first available space in the table and the configuration screen appears with the default configuration parameters as the base, enabling you to modify the configuration specifics. A maximum of eight file server entries can be placed in the table.

> **Note:** The version contained on the disk included with this book is a one-server version only. To obtain a full copy, please refer to the ordering information at the end of this chapter.

To delete a file server entry, position the highlighted bar over the entry to be removed and press Delete. This action automatically deletes the entry from the table, and all subsequent entries move up one position to fill its space.

The default monitoring status of each configured server table entry can be toggled between Enabled (+) and Disabled (−) by positioning the highlighted bar over the entry and pressing the space bar. Enabled entries are automatically monitored if the S=[server] option is not specified, provided sufficient access rights exist. Disabled entries are monitored if specified with the S=[server] option, provided sufficient access rights exist. (Note the example server screen in Figure 1.4.)

In Figure 1.5, although each monitored event is listed on this screen, some events are combined into a single configuration setting. For example, the specified dynamic memory threshold is used for Dynamic Memory Pools 1 through 4; the specified disk space usage and directory entry usage threshold monitors all volumes (up to 64) configured on the file server; the specified hot fix usage threshold monitors all physical drives (up to 16) attached to the file server; and specifying "Y" for disk I/O error results in all physical drives (up to 16) attached to the file server being monitored.

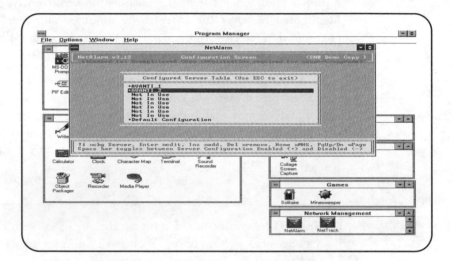

Figure 1.4. A server configuration table.

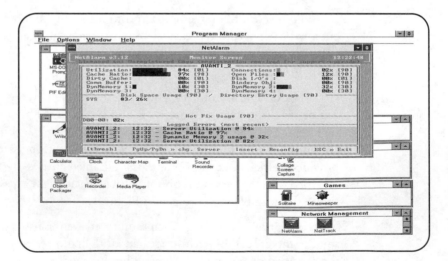

Figure 1.5. The NetAlarm main screen.

Note: Figure 1.5 reflects a NetWare 2.x-based file server. For NetWare 3.x-based file servers, those fields that are not pertinent, such as the dynamic memory fields, do not show statistics or thresholds.

After you enter the configuration screen, you have the following options:

- Accept the displayed value by pressing Enter

- Specify a new value ("00" to "99" for the "%" threshold events and "Y" or "N" for the occurrence events)

- Reposition to another event (through use of the arrow keys)

- Press Escape to optionally update the version of NetAlarm with the new configuration information

As you move through the configuration options, a brief description is displayed on the line titled "Alarm Desc." Once you are satisfied with the configuration, press Escape to return to the configured server table.

When the configured server table reappears, you can resume adding, deleting, or modifying file server entries. After you are finished, press Escape to update.

If NetAlarm is memory resident as a TSR, you are prompted when the memory-resident configuration parameters should be updated with the new information. Pressing "N" bypasses this update and a message to that effect is displayed. Pressing "Y" causes the configuration parameters of the memory-resident copy of NetAlarm to be updated with the new information and a message to that effect is displayed. NetAlarm then proceeds to the next configuration update prompt.

The drive, path, and filename of the executed copy of the reconfigured NetAlarm then appears, and you are prompted if it should be updated with the new configuration parameters. Pressing "N" terminates the configuration process without updating the displayed copy of NetAlarm and a message to that effect is displayed. If you press "Y", the configuration process attempts to update the displayed copy of NetAlarm with the new configuration parameters. If the file cannot be updated because of a write-protect, read-only, or insufficient-rights condition, an appropriate message is displayed. Otherwise, the copy of NetAlarm is updated with the new information and an appropriate message is displayed upon completion.

Options

Several command-line options are available to facilitate the execution of NetAlarm. The options listed in this section are shown in uppercase type to improve readability, but they can be specified in either upper- or lowercase type. The supported options are as follows:

? or HELP	Displays a help screen providing a summary of the information included in this section.
CONFIG	The option for preconfiguring servers and parameters.
MONO	Forces monochrome display mode.
TSR	Forces TSR mode of operation.
UNLOAD	Unloads the memory-resident (TSR) copy of the program.
C=###	Specifies the TSR monitor cycle in ### seconds (range is 1–999; the default is 5).
L=[filename]	Specifies a log file (may include drive/path) for alerts (default is to use the executed program's drive, path, and name, but with an extension of .LOG).
S=[server][,server..]	Specifies up to eight file servers to be monitored. (Default is any configured servers or the current server only if no server has been configured/specified. Use commas to separate servers if two or more are specified.)

Note: Remember that this version is correct only for a single server. See the end of this chapter for information on how to order the full-featured system.

U=[user][,user...]   Specifies user(s) to receive alerts via NetWare 25th line broadcasts (up to 80 bytes maximum; use commas to separate users/log in names if two or more are specified).

These options are discussed in the following sections.

The CONFIG Option

The CONFIG option causes the program to enter the reconfiguration mode of operation. By using this option, specific file servers can be configured and enabled for monitoring. If NetAlarm is already memory resident as a TSR when reexecuted with the CONFIG option, the parameters shown are those of the memory-resident version and you have the option to update the TSR version once the reconfiguration is complete.

The MONO Option

The MONO option forces the NetAlarm screen display into a monochrome mode. While NetAlarm normally auto-detects monochrome display adapters, it cannot detect whether a monochrome monitor is used with a color display adapter or LCD/plasma displays that emulate color monitors. If the displayed information is difficult to read with the adapter/monitor combination in use, the MONO option can be used.

The TSR Option

The TSR option invokes NetAlarm as a TSR program. When running as a TSR, monitoring occurs once per cycle, with a default cycle period of five seconds. The memory-resident copy can be dynamically reconfigured using the CONFIG option or unloaded using the UNLOAD option.

The UNLOAD Option

The UNLOAD option gives you a means to remove a memory-resident (TSR) copy of NetAlarm from memory. The UNLOAD option fails, however, if NetAlarm was not the last memory-resident facility loaded or if NetAlarm was loaded higher than DOS's conventional 640K memory area.

The C=### Option

The C=### option specifies how frequently monitoring activity occurs. Though a range of 1–999 seconds is supported, the default monitor cycle of five seconds normally provides a reasonable balance between monitor with alert notification and normal workstation processing. If TSR has not been specified, the C=### option is ignored because NetAlarm performs its monitoring activity once per second when running as a dedicated, foreground process.

The L=[filename] Option

The L=[filename] option designates a specific file for the logged alerts. You should specify a log file that resides on a local workstation hard disk. This ensures continued alert logging if the workstation detaches from the server or the server goes down. The default log filename consists of the drive, path, and program name of the currently executed copy of NetAlarm with a LOG extension, even if run from a PATH or SEARCH drive. This option overrides the default log file selection with the user-specified file information, which must be a valid DOS filename and must have the workstation armed with sufficient rights to the destination drive/directory.

The S=[server] Option

The S=[server] option is used to selectively enable file server monitoring. If this option is used, any preconfigured file servers not specified in the S=[server] list are disabled. Any file server specified in the S=[server] list for which there is no preconfigured entry is monitored using the default configuration parameters, but only if sufficient space exists to insert it into the server configuration table.

The U=[user] Option

The U=[user] option alerts the user(s)/LOGIN name(s) through NetWare 25th line broadcast messages when an anomaly is detected.

Because NetAlarm uses the file server-based NetWare send-broadcast-message API to notify specified users of detected anomalies, only users who have an active connection with a monitored file server receive NetAlarm alerts pertaining to that file server. You need only be attached to a monitored server to receive NetAlarm alerts.

Rick: For example, a user could be logged into File Server 1 (FS1) and be attached to both File Server 2 (FS2) and File Server 3 (FS3), either manually or through the user's log in script. At this point, although the user may be actively mapped into/working only on FS1 (no mapped drives for FS2 or FS3), the user will receive NetAlarm alerts for FS2 and FS3 because they are attached to these file servers. A user may have up to eight active file server attachments, including their active/logged-in server.

General Overview and Feature Summary

As part of their operational design, NetWare 2.x and NetWare 3.x internally maintain statistics on many network activities. Although most of this data is merely informational, some of these statistics are vital references or hints regarding impending problems.

In NetWare 2.x, much of this information can be viewed through FCONSOLE with some of the statistics reported in a Maximum, Peak Used, and Currently In Use format (most of the information is kept on a historical basis of occurrences since the file server was brought online). The information available in NetWare 3.x, however, is much more limited and can be viewed (whether accessed on the file server console or through RCONSOLE) only with the MONITOR.NLM.

Unfortunately, the various statistics that impact file server operation are spread over several option screens, both in FCONSOLE and MONITOR, and there is no overall critical-operations summary screen. In addition, neither FCONSOLE nor MONITOR provide any anomaly logging or notification. Therefore, both are cumbersome as preventive management tools because you must continuously monitor several screens to manually track the evolution of information in order to detect any anomalies. Now, I am not picking on Novell. They spent lots of time making these statistics available, but they just should have spent a bit more time making them more useful for the troubleshooter.

NetAlarm complements both FCONSOLE and MONITOR by automatically monitoring the critical network statistics, logging, and as an option, broadcasting reports on the occurrence of any critical errors or any instance user-defined threshold violations. Upon receipt of a NetAlarm broadcast, other NetWare compatible utilities can then be used to further isolate and correct detected anomalies. If the file server goes down before the problem is resolved, you can review the error log file to determine potential causes of the network failure.

NetAlarm is written in assembler and optimized so that it occupies approximately 12K of RAM upon TSR installation. It is compatible with upper memory block (UMB) loading techniques such as MS-DOS/PC DOS v5.0 LOADHIGH. Designed using standard MS-DOS/PC DOS function calls and Novell-documented NetWare system calls (also known as application program interfaces or APIs), NetAlarm runs on almost any IBM-compatible MS-DOS/PC-DOS v3.1+, v4.x, and v5.x based workstations that Novell supports with a workstation shell (NETx).

> **Rick:** The simple solution to this assembler techno-whiz stuff is to use either DOS or a third-party memory manager to load the TSR piece into high memory so that less memory is eaten up as part of the base 640K. Steve is a pro at including lots of great stuff into small amounts of code.

NetAlarm intercepts several common 80x86-based interrupts to maintain an active monitoring state, and it is carefully designed to impose minimal overhead on the workstation where it is loaded. This design allows it to be installed on virtually any workstation on the network, even those dedicated to tasks other than network management. In fact, NetAlarm has been tested on print server, remote communications, word processing, and task-accounting workstations, as well as the DOS partition of a non-dedicated NetWare 2.x file server. This capability makes it a tool for nearly any NetWare 2.x v2.1x/v2.2 or NetWare 3.x v3.1x installation.

Caution: In order to monitor the network, NetAlarm must be installed on a workstation that is logged into or attached to every file server to be observed and for which the associated user has been granted file server console operator rights.

Note: The console operator sounds more important and powerful than it really is. File server console operator rights are assigned through the use of the SYSCON utility. See Figure 1.4 for an example of what the screen looks like in SYSCON. File server console operator rights give users the ability to request statistical information from the file server. However, users don't have enough rights to take down a server, modify their own information/rights, or access the disk beyond their normal rights.

When NetAlarm is installed as a TSR, it analyzes the internal LAN I/O, file server, and file system condition on monitoring cycles of between 1 and 999 seconds. This is a user-defined command-line option. The default cycle period is five seconds. If installed as a dedicated workstation process, NetAlarm performs this analysis on every monitored file server once per second. Any detected anomalies are recorded in the error log file (an ASCII text file that can be user specified) and sent to the file server console by the broadcast-to-console API. Optionally, NetAlarm also notifies any specified users by NetWare's send-broadcast-message API. The information in the log file can be used to isolate potential network problems.

Features: The Good Stuff

The following NetAlarm status checks and anomaly alerts occur if the connection to a monitored file server is lost (the <ServerName> is the first eight and last two characters of the monitored file server's name).

Log In Status

NetAlarm first confirms that the workstation has a valid connection to the monitored file server. If the workstation is not actively connected to the monitored file server, the following message appears on the screen at each cycle:

```
[NetAlarm] <ServerName>: No Active Connection!
```

File Server Console Operator Rights

NetAlarm then confirms that the workstation has file server console operator rights for the monitored file server. If not, the following message appears on the screen at each cycle the file server is scheduled to be monitored:

```
[NetAlarm] <ServerName>: No Console Operator rights!
```

Once valid connection and access rights are confirmed, NetAlarm retrieves the following NetWare statistics (<ServerName> is the first eight and last two characters of the monitored file server's name).

Server Utilization

The current file server CPU utilization is retrieved. If the current level is at or above the defined threshold, it is logged with the following alert:

```
<ServerName>: Server Utilization @ ??%
```

Connections In Use

The ratio of concurrent file server connections to the maximum number supported by the version of NetWare in use is calculated. If the current ratio is at or above the defined threshold, it is logged with the following alert:

```
<ServerName>: Connections In Use @ ??%
```

Cache Ratio

The meaning of this statistic is significantly different in NetWare 2.x than in NetWare 3.x. In NetWare 2.x, this statistic reflects the percentage of cache hits as compared to the total cache requests (hit and misses). In NetWare 3.x, this statistic reflects the percentage of memory for total cache buffers as compared to the total server work memory available. If at or below the defined threshold, the current ratio is logged with the following alert:

```
<ServerName>: Cache Ratio @ ??%
```

Open Files

The ratio of concurrently open files to the maximum number configured (NetWare 2.x) or supported (NetWare 3.x allows 100,000) is calculated. If the ratio is at or above the defined threshold, the current ratio is logged with the following alert:

```
<ServerName>: Open Files @ ??%
```

Dirty Cache Buffers

The ratio of currently dirty cache buffers to the total number of cache buffers available is calculated. If the ratio is at or above the threshold, the current ratio is logged with the following alert:

```
<ServerName>: Dirty Cache Buffers @ ??%
```

Disk I/Os Pending

The ratio of currently pending disk I/Os to the maximum concurrent disk cache writes supported is calculated. If the ratio is at or above the defined threshold, the current ratio is logged with the following alert:

```
<ServerName>: Disk I/O's Pending @ ??%
```

Routing Buffers (NetWare 2.x v2.1x/v2.2 only)

The ratio of communication/routing buffers (also called physical receive buffers or communications buffers) in use to the maximum number configured is calculated. If the ratio is at or above the defined threshold, the current ratio is logged with the following alert:

```
<ServerName>: Routing Buffer usage @ ??%
```

Bindery Objects (NetWare 2.x v2.1x/v2.2 only)

The ratio of current bindery objects in use to the maximum number configured is calculated. If the ratio is at or above the defined threshold, the current ratio is logged with the following alert:

```
<ServerName>: Bindery Object usage @ ??%
```

Dynamic Memory 1 (NetWare 2.x v2.1x/v2.2 only)

The ratio of Dynamic Memory Pool 1 in use to that available is calculated. If the ratio is at or above the defined threshold, the current ratio is logged with the following alert:

```
<ServerName>: Dynamic Memory 1 usage @ ??%
```

Dynamic Memory 2 (NetWare 2.x v2.1x/v2.2 only)

The ratio of Dynamic Memory Pool 2 in use to that available is calculated. If the ratio is at or above the defined threshold, the current ratio is logged with the following alert:

```
<ServerName>: Dynamic Memory 2 usage @ ??%
```

Dynamic Memory 3 (NetWare 2.x v2.1x/v2.2 only)

The ratio of Dynamic Memory Pool 3 in use to that available is calculated. If the ratio is at or above the defined threshold, the current ratio is logged with the following alert:

```
<ServerName>: Dynamic Memory 3 usage @ ??%
```

Dynamic Memory 4 (NetWare 2.x v2.2 only)

The ratio of Dynamic Memory Pool 4 in use to that available is calculated. If the ratio is at or above the defined threshold, the current ratio is logged with the following alert:

```
<ServerName>: Dynamic Memory 4 usage @ ??%
```

Hot Fix Usage By Drive:

For each physical hard drive on the file server (up to a maximum of 16 per server), the ratio of used "hot fix" blocks to the configured total for the drive is calculated. If the ratio is at or above the defined threshold, the current ratio for drives that exceed the threshold is logged with the following alert:

```
<ServerName>: Drive # Hot Fix usage @ ??%
```

> **John:** For those of you new to the NetWare game, the term *hot fix* refers to NetWare's ability to automatically detect a problem on the hard drive during a write operation. Once detected, this error is noted and the operating system writes the data to an area reserved for problems. This hot fix area is a percentage of your disk drive space. If you get this alert, it can mean that there are problems on your hard drive with the physical media.

Disk Space Usage By Volume:

For each volume on the file server (up to a maximum of 64 volumes per server), the ratio of allocated disk space to the configured total for the volume is calculated. If the ratio is at or above the defined threshold, the current ratio for those volumes that exceed the threshold is logged with the following alert:

```
<ServerName>: Disk usage @ ??% on <Volume>:
```

Directory Entry Usage By Volume:

For each volume on the file server (up to a maximum of 64 volumes per server), the ratio of allocated directory entries (slots) to the configured (NetWare 2.x) or dynamically allocated (NetWare 3.x) total for the volume is calculated. If the ratio is at or above the defined threshold, the current ratio for volumes that exceed the threshold is logged with the following alert:

```
<ServerName>: Dir. Entries @ ??% on <Volume>:
```

TTS Disabled

The current status of the transaction tracking system (TTS) is checked. If the TTS has been disabled by command or as a result of excessive error, this fact is logged with the following alert:

```
<ServerName>: Transaction Tracking Disabled
```

Hot Fix Disabled

The current status of the file server's automatic disk error remapping ("hot fix") is checked. If it is disabled as a result of failure or excessive error, this fact is logged with the following alert:

```
<ServerName>: Hot Fix Disabled by Server
```

Disk I/O Error

Each physical hard drive on the file server (up to a maximum of 16 per server) is checked for disk drive I/O errors that have occurred since the last monitor cycle. For each drive on which such an anomaly is detected, the following alert is logged:

```
<ServerName>: Drive # Disk I/O error
```

Mirror Failure (NetWare 2.x v2.1x/ v2.2 only)

The status of physical drive mirroring is checked to determine if any drive has gone offline or become unmirrored. If such an anomaly is detected, it is logged with the following alert:

```
<ServerName>: Mirror Failure
```

Cache Physical Read/Write Error (NetWare 2.x v2.1x/v2.2 only)

The cache system is checked for new I/O errors that may have occurred during a cache read or write operation since the last monitor cycle. If such an anomaly is detected, it is logged with the following alert:

```
<ServerName>: Cache Physical Read/Write error
```

Cache Thrashing Error (NetWare 2.x v2.1x/v2.2 only)

The cache system is checked for any thrashing errors that may have occurred since the last monitor cycle. If such an anomaly is detected, it is logged with the following alert:

```
<ServerName>: Cache Thrashing error
```

Fatal File Allocation Table Error (NetWare 2.x v2.1x/v2.2 only)

The file system is checked for any fatal file allocation table (FAT) errors that may have occurred since the last monitor cycle. If such an anomaly is detected, it is logged with the following alert:

```
<ServerName>: Fatal FAT error
```

Write/Scan FAT Error (NetWare 2.x v2.1x/v2.2 only)

The file system is checked for any nonfatal FAT errors that may have occurred since the last monitor cycle. If such an anomaly is detected, it is logged with the following alert:

```
<ServerName>: Write/Scan FAT error
```

Invalid Connection (NetWare 2.x v2.1x/v2.2 only)

The LAN I/O system is checked for any packets with an invalid connection number (0 or greater than the maximum number of connections supported by the NetWare version in use) since the last monitor cycle. If such an anomaly is detected, it is logged with the following alert:

```
<ServerName>: Invalid Connection
```

Packet with Invalid Slot (NetWare 2.x v2.1x/v2.2 only)

The LAN I/O system is checked for any packets with an invalid slot (a connection number not previously allocated through a log in or attach procedure) since the last monitor cycle. If such an anomaly is detected, it is logged with the following alert:

```
<ServerName>: Packet with Invalid Slot
```

Invalid Sequence Number (NetWare 2.x v2.1x/v2.2 only)

The LAN I/O system is checked for any packets with an invalid sequence number (a packet that did not follow the expected sequential packet assignments) since the last monitor cycle. If such an anomaly is detected, it is logged with the following alert:

```
<ServerName>: Invalid Sequence Number
```

Invalid Request Type (NetWare 2.x v2.1x/v2.2 only)

The LAN I/O system is checked for any packets with invalid request types (a request not supported by the version of NetWare in use) since the last monitor cycle. If such an anomaly is detected, it is logged with the following alert:

```
<ServerName>: Invalid Request Type
```

Packet Discarded > 16 Hops (NetWare 2.x v2.1x/v2.2 only)

The LAN I/O system is checked for any packets with more than 16 hops—packets attempting to cross more than 16 bridges/routers in order to arrive at the internet packet exchange (IPX) destination—since the last monitor cycle. If such an anomaly has been detected, it is logged with the following alert:

```
<ServerName>: Packet Discarded for > 16 Hops
```

> **John:** When a packet of information has to go through another device to go from the server to its ultimate destination, this is called a "hop." For example, if you have a bridge between a workstation and the server, the packets of data have "one hop" to get back and forth.

Packet Discarded, Unknown Network (NetWare 2.x v2.1x/v2.2)

The LAN I/O system is checked for any packets with an unknown destination network (an IPX destination network that is not in the file server's routing table) since the last monitor cycle. If such an anomaly is detected, it is logged with the following alert:

```
<ServerName>: Packet Discarded for Unknown Net
```

Incoming Packet, No Buffer (NetWare 2.x v2.1x/v2.2 only)

The LAN I/O system checks for any incoming packets that were discarded because they could not be immediately processed or stored (there are no routing/communications buffers available to hold the packet for future processing) since the last monitor cycle. If such an anomaly is detected, it is logged with the following alert:

```
<ServerName>: Incoming Packet Discarded, No Buffer
```

Outgoing Packet, No Buffer (NetWare 2.x v2.1x/v2.2 only)

The LAN I/O system is checked for any outgoing packets that were discarded because they could not be immediately sent or stored (no

25

routing/communications buffers available to hold the packet for future transmission) since the last monitor cycle. If such an anomaly is detected, it is logged with the following alert:

```
<ServerName>: Outgoing Packet Discarded, No Buffer
```

Parameters

The following section is an overview of the configuration parameters (further information on these items is contained in the troubleshooting section later in this chapter).

Server Utilization

Contrary to widespread belief, NetWare's server utilization level is not based upon the file server's CPU activity, but rather its inactivity. By tracking inactivity, rather than further loading an already busy file server to determine activity, NetWare extrapolates an approximation of the CPU utilization. High server utilization levels can impact network performance by impeding the file server's ability to process service requests, route packets, update cache/disk information, and so on. Generally, this threshold shouldn't be set higher than 90 percent.

Connections in Use

While the number of users (or nodes) that can be configured is a dynamic number limited only by disk space available to the bindery, NetWare has an internal limit on the number of concurrent users that it supports. A concurrent connection to a file server is created upon loading the workstation shell (NETx/EMSNETx/XMSNETx) and may remain active in spite of subsequent ATTACH, LOGIN, and LOGOUT procedures. The monitored percentage of concurrent connections is based on the maximum concurrently supported connections within the version of NetWare running on the file server. This parameter can provide advance warning of concurrent user limitations, and this is especially useful in large, multi-server sites where users may have unintentional file server attachments.

Cache Ratio

This parameter has different meanings for NetWare 2.x versus NetWare 3.x. This factor may compromise monitoring integrity if it is not taken into account. Unlike the other parameters that generate alerts for levels at or above the configured threshold, this parameter is monitored for an "at or below" level condition.

NetWare 2.x: This parameter is the percentage of file I/O requests serviced by the file server's cache system without the need for physical disk I/O. A high cache hit ratio indicates efficient caching (95 to 100 percent is optimum; lower levels degrade performance due to extra disk I/O operations). Although an alert threshold of 90 percent is usually adequate, it may need adjustment if intelligent/cached disk controllers are used.

NetWare 3.x: This parameter is the percentage of total server work memory that is currently allocated to cache buffers. The number of total cache buffers available varies from time to time because directory cache buffers, file service processes (FSP), NetWare loadable modules (NLM), and volume FATs all dynamically allocate memory from this pool. (However, only NLMs release all of their allocated memory back to the pool.) An insufficient allocation of cache buffers can result in indeterminate server problems. Novell's documentation for NetWare 3.x advises against allowing this ratio to drop below 20 percent. Most consultants and certified NetWare engineers (CNEs) recommend 60 percent as a minimum with 65 percent or more as optimal. A threshold of 50 percent may be an appropriate point at which attention is demanded.

Open Files

Although exceeding the maximum number of concurrently open files configured for the file server is not usually associated with network failure, it can cause frustration among users who receive network errors and experience application failure. A threshold of 90 percent is usually appropriate, but this may need adjustment depending upon the configuration and the applications in use.

Dirty Cache Buffers

When any part of a cache buffer changes, such as through a file write or update, the buffer is "dirty" because it needs to be flushed to update the disk. It is not unusual for dirty cache buffers to fluctuate during network operations, especially as a result of network-wide E-mail and backup operations. Novell's documentation for NetWare 3.x recommends parameter adjustment if more than 70 percent, which seems to be a reasonable threshold, of the total cache buffers become dirty. However, slower disk drives/controllers may cause bottlenecks that require a higher threshold.

Disk I/Os Pending

NetWare queues dirty cache buffers to the elevator mechanism so they can be flushed to the disk. Although the efficiency of NetWare's elevator mechanism allows several buffers to be written in a single disk I/O operation, concurrent file I/O operations can compromise this ability and result in numerous requirements for disk I/Os. It's not unusual for the disk I/O's pending level to fluctuate during network operations, especially as a result of network-wide E-mail and backup operations. If the disk I/Os pending exceeds 70 percent of the maximum concurrent disk writes, a serious bottleneck may be developing. However, slower drives/controllers may cause bottlenecks that require a higher threshold.

Routing Buffer Usage (NetWare 2.x only)

NetWare uses routing buffers as temporary storage for incoming packets that cannot be immediately processed due to a lack of file service processes (FSP); to queue up outgoing request replies that cannot be immediately sent; and for any other packets that are being routed. Severe network degradation, and the possibility of file server lockup, can occur if a file server exhausts all of its configured routing buffers. This threshold should not be set higher than 90 percent to provide sufficient response time.

> **John:** This elevator mechanism stuff is loosely defined as the way NetWare gets data onto the disk drive as efficiently as possible. NetWare tries to organize disk requests so that the access to the drive is done in an organized, logical manner. One problem with low server memory, for example, is that the cache system doesn't get enough to handle the drive. The term *thrashing* will come up because the operating system will begin to bounce all over the drive in an attempt to service data requests.

Bindery Objects (NetWare 2.x only)

If the version of NetWare 2.x running on the file server is configured to limit the amount of disk space available to users, a maximum number of bindery objects must also be set and the current number of objects in the bindery should be tracked. Because bindery objects can be many different types of entities, such as users, groups, file servers, bridges, job servers/queues, print servers/queues, and so on, this count grows over time. This parameter can be set to issue a warning if growth approaches the maximum configured level.

Dynamic Memory (NetWare 2.x only)

The Dynamic Memory Pools (1–3 for v2.1x and 1–4 for v2.2) manage users, file service requests, mapped drives, open files, record/file/semaphore locks, server/router tables, and virtually all resources associated with the file server. Insufficient dynamic memory in any group can cause application and log in problems, and file server lockups are possible when Dynamic Memory Pool 1 is exhausted. Because this threshold monitors all the dynamic memory pools, it should not be set higher than 90 percent.

Hot Fix Usage

NetWare monitors data physically written to the disk to ensure its accuracy compared to that in cache. Discrepancies found here indicate potential disk problems, and the data is redirected to another area on the disk (the hot fix area). The disk block is then marked to avoid reuse. If enough errors occur to fill the hot fix, data is lost and catastrophic disk failure may occur. Therefore, use a threshold level of 90 percent or less to ensure that you are given ample warning of the problem. Hot fix usage is monitored by disk for up to 16 disks per file server.

Disk Space Usage

Running out of disk space can be extremely frustrating if you are trying to save several hours of work. Because a file server is a disk resource for many users, disk space usage levels often vary widely. NetAlarm monitors the disk space usage of each configured volume (up to the 64 volumes per server). A threshold level of 90 percent is usually adequate, but this may need to be adjusted depending upon the amount of disk space configured for each volume and the application/user's file needs. The threshold level should be appropriate to the usage level of the most active volume on the file server to avoid excess alerts.

Directory Entry Usage

An insufficient directory entry (also known as directory slot) configuration can result in the failure of applications that dynamically create temporary files or applications that tend to retain numerous files, such as E-mail programs. NetAlarm monitors the directory entry usage of each configured volume (up to 64 volumes per server). Because this threshold level is used for all volumes, it should be appropriate to the usage level of the most active volume on the file server to avoid excess alerts, yet it should be low enough to ensure that alerts are issued in advance of application program failures. A threshold level of 90 percent is usually adequate. However, this may need to be adjusted depending on the number of directory entries configured for each volume and the permanent/temporary file activity level.

Transactional Tracking System (TTS) Disabled

NetWare monitors the status of the TTS operations and sets a flag if the file server must disable TTS because it cannot compensate for the number of errors that are occurring. This monitor should be enabled because data integrity may be compromised by the lack of expected TTS support (some NetWare internal operations utilize TTS).

Hot Fix Disabled

NetWare monitors the status of the hot fix operations and sets a flag if the file server must disable the hot fix because it cannot compensate for the level of disk I/O errors. This monitor should be enabled because disk failure is possible. (A disabled hot fix table is monitored by NetAlarm for up to 16 disks per file server.)

Disk I/O Error

NetWare monitors data physically written to the disk to ensure its accuracy against that in cache. If a disk I/O error is detected (even if corrected by the hot fix), this internal counter is incremented. This monitor should be enabled because frequent occurrences indicate a higher probability of disk failure. Disk monitors disk I/O errors for up to 16 disks per file server.

Mirror Failure (NetWare 2.x only)

NetWare maintains a table for cross-referencing logical drives to their physically mirrored pairs, plus a flag to indicate both the availability and status of disk mirroring. Mirrored disk failures can be detected using this information. This monitor should be enabled because a mirrored disk failure compromises data integrity.

Cache Physical Read/Write Error (NetWare 2.x only)

NetWare internally maintains statistics on the physical read/write operations by the cache system. If a disk read/write request by the cache system fails, this internal counter is incremented. This monitor should be enabled because frequent occurrences indicate upcoming disk/controller problems.

31

Cache Thrashing Error (NetWare 2.x only)

Cache thrashing occurs if NetWare needs to allocate a cache buffer but can't because all the cache buffers are marked as actively in use. This type of error usually occurs only on machines with a minimal number of cache buffers. However, this monitor should be enabled because frequent occurrences can cause severe performance degradation.

Fatal File Allocation Table Error (NetWare 2.x only)

Like DOS, NetWare maintains both an original and a mirrored FAT linking noncontiguous blocks in a file. If a disk write operation indicates a sector is corrupt in both the original and the mirrored FATs, this internal counter is incremented. This monitor should be enabled because it indicates when data integrity is compromised (you need to back up the system before taking it down).

Write/Scan File Allocation Table Error (NetWare 2.x only)

NetWare maintains both an original and a mirrored FAT linking noncontiguous blocks in a file. If a disk write or scan operation indicates a sector is corrupt in either the original or the mirrored FAT, this internal counter is incremented. This monitor should be enabled to ensure data integrity.

Invalid Connection (NetWare 2.x only)

NetWare stores workstation node addresses and connection information in a table, based upon the logical (sequential) order in which the workstations attach to the file server. If the file server receives a workstation request that contains a logical connection identification (ID) not previously allocated, or if the packet's source address does not match the corresponding entry in the connection table, the packet is discarded and this internal counter is incremented. This monitor should be enabled because such events create additional file server overhead and may indicate that a workstation or router needs attention.

Packet with Invalid Slot (NetWare 2.x only)

NetWare stores workstation node addresses and connection information in a table based upon the logical (sequential) order in which the workstations attach to the file server. If the file server receives a request with an invalid slot (a logical connection of 0 or greater than the maximum number of users supported by the NetWare version in use), it is discarded and this internal counter is incremented. This monitor should be enabled because such events create additional file server overhead and may indicate that a workstation or router needs attention.

Invalid Sequence Number (NetWare 2.x only)

NetWare core protocol (NCP) workstation file service requests are sequenced and acknowledged to ensure delivery. If the file server receives a request that is out of sequence, it is discarded and an internal counter is incremented. This monitor should be enabled because such events create additional file server overhead and may indicate that a workstation or router needs attention.

Invalid Request Type (NetWare 2.x only)

Each version of NetWare supports a specific set of request types. As NetWare evolves, some request types become obsolete and return an error code indicating they are no longer supported. If the file server receives an invalid or unknown request, the packet is discarded and an internal counter is incremented. This monitor should be enabled because it may indicate an incompatible workstation shell or other connection problems that create additional file server overhead.

Packet Discarded > 16 Hops (NetWare 2.x only)

IPX packets include a hop count indicating the number of times the packet was routed. If the file server receives a packet that it determines will exceed 16 routing hops before reaching its destination, the server assumes that the packet is lost. The server then discards the packet and an internal counter is incremented. This monitor should be enabled because such events may indicate bridge/router problems, a downed file server across a bridge, or misconfigured peer-to-peer software, such as E-mail programs routing messages to an invalid server.

Packet Discarded, Unknown Net (NetWare 2.x only)

IPX packets contain a media access control (MAC) destination address for routing and an IPX destination address for ultimate delivery. An internal counter is incremented if the file server receives an IPX packet that contains an unknown or invalid IPX destination network address. This monitor should be enabled because packets with unknown destination network addresses may indicate bridge/router problems, a downed file server across a bridge, or misconfigured peer-to-peer software, such as E-mail programs routing messages to an invalid server.

Incoming Packet, No Buffer (NetWare 2.x only)

NetWare stores incoming requests that can't be immediately processed in temporary storage (routing) buffers for later retrieval. If a packet must be discarded because no temporary storage buffer is available, this internal counter is incremented. This monitor should be enabled because such events may indicate either an insufficient routing buffer configuration or an overloaded file server.

Outgoing Packet, No Buffer (NetWare 2.x only)

NetWare stores request replies and routed packets in temporary storage (routing) buffers until delivery is ensured. If a packet must be discarded because no temporary storage buffer is available, this internal counter is incremented. This monitor should be enabled because such events may indicate either an insufficient routing buffer configuration or an overloaded file server.

Usage

NetAlarm provides two modes of operation: In the default mode, NetAlarm executes as a dedicated, foreground process with real-time display of the statistics associated with the monitored file servers; optionally, it can be executed as a TSR program that monitors the file servers as a background task on a workstation used for or dedicated to other tasks. In either mode of operation, up to eight file servers can be actively monitored from a single workstation with detected anomalies logged and broadcasted to the affected file server console. NetAlarm also provides the option of having alerts routed to other destinations.

> **Rick:** NetAlarm has quite a few options and settings that you can use to fine-tune it. These options are covered in an upcoming section.

During the initial program load, the workstation rights are checked for all configured/specified file servers to be monitored. If insufficient rights exist, the monitoring for that file server is disabled. Once the monitoring process begins (whether as a dedicated, foreground process or as a TSR), any change in these access rights affects the monitoring ability of the program and results in alerts.

When NetAlarm runs as a dedicated, foreground process, each specified/configured file server is monitored approximately once per second. A real-time screen also displays the statistics associated with the primary monitored server. If you wish to view the statistics associated with a different server, a single key sequence toggles among the monitored servers.

When NetAlarm is loaded as a TSR, it monitors each specified/configured file server once per cycle. Although the default cycle is five seconds, it can be changed through a command-line option. The memory-resident (TSR) copy can also be dynamically reconfigured and unloaded using command-line options.

Once per monitor cycle, NetAlarm checks the workstation shell's file server connection table to ensure that a valid connection exists for each monitored file server. If a valid connection no longer exists with a monitored file server (perhaps caused by the workstation logging into another file server or the file server going down), NetAlarm displays the following error message on the workstation screen, writes the message to the error log file, and broadcasts an alert through the default file server (if a connection still exists):

```
[NetAlarm] <ServerName>: No Active Connection!
```

NetAlarm then issues a NetWare system call to reconfirm file server console operator rights for the monitored file server. If unable to confirm file server console operator rights, NetAlarm displays the following error message on the workstation screen, writes the message to the error log file, and broadcasts an alert using the default file server (if a connection still exists):

```
[NetAlarm] <ServerName>: No Console Operator rights!
```

NetAlarm then collects and analyzes the statistics associated with the monitored file server. If any anomalies are detected or any of the statistics exceed predefined thresholds, NetAlarm issues alerts.

By default, anomaly reports are broadcast to the affected file server console and written to the log file. Optionally, you can also route alerts to selected users at each connection where they are logged in by NetWare 25th line broadcast messages. The format of the file server console message is:

```
[NetAlarm] hh:mm - {message}
```

The format of the log file entry is:

```
<ServerName>: hh:mm - {anomaly message}
```

The format of the NetWare 25th line broadcast message is:

```
>> [NetAlarm] <ServerName>: {msg.}(CTRL-ENTER to clear)
```

In all formats, the {anomaly message} is appropriate to the anomaly detected or the threshold exceeded.

Note: Alerts sent by NetWare's internal broadcasting mechanism display the message on the bottom line of the screen and require the user to press <Ctrl-Enter> to clear the message. Because this mechanism has a limited receive buffer, it's possible only the first alert message may appear. Therefore, it's advisable to check the log file whenever an alert is received. Alerts are not broadcast to the monitoring workstation's connection to avoid any conflict with the operation of other software on the workstation.

Caution: If a specified user-alert broadcast recipient is also used for network backup or other critical operations, use NetWare's CASTOFF/CASTON utilities to enable/disable the receipt of NetWare broadcast messages. Prior to the execution of any such operations, execute CASTOFF to prevent alert messages from interrupting the critical operations. Upon completion, use CASTON to reenable the receipt of NetWare broadcast messages.

How you terminate the program depends on the mode of execution. If NetAlarm runs as a TSR, you must use the UNLOAD option to remove the program from memory. If it runs as a dedicated, foreground process, press Escape to terminate the monitoring activity.

Examples

Here are a couple of examples to help you understand how NetAlarm can be loaded.

NETALARM [mono | MONO]

With sufficient access rights, NetAlarm runs as a dedicated, foreground process that monitors either the preconfigured file servers or the current/ default file server. Monitoring occurs approximately once per second with detected anomalies logged into the default error log file (same drive, directory, and filename as the program, but with a LOG extension) and broadcast to the affected file server console. The active statistics associated with the monitored file server are displayed on the screen. If mono or MONO is specified, the screen display is in monochrome mode.

NETALARM S=AVANTI_1 L=AVANTI_1.ERR U=SYSOP [MONO]

NetAlarm runs as a dedicated, foreground process monitoring AVANTI_1 if sufficient access rights exist. Monitoring occurs approximately once per second with detected anomalies written to AVANTI_1.ERR located in the default directory and broadcast to AVANTI_1's file server console, with NetWare 25th line broadcast messages sent to each connection where the system operator (SYSOP) is logged into at the time the anomaly is detected. The active statistics associated with the monitoring of AVANTI_1 are displayed on the screen. If mono or MONO is specified, the screen display is in monochrome mode.

NETALARM TSR C=15 L=C:\SERVER.LOG S=AVANTI_1,AVANTI_2

NetAlarm runs as a memory-resident (TSR) program monitoring AVANTI_1 and AVANTI_2 once every 15 seconds, if sufficient access rights exist. Detected anomalies are written to C:\SERVER.LOG and broadcast to the affected file server console (AVANTI_1 or AVANTI_2, as appropriate).

TSR Operational Notes

You can load NetAlarm as a memory-resident program by specifying the TSR option on the command line. When loaded, it occupies approximately 12K of workstation RAM and can be loaded high, above DOS's conventional 640K of RAM.

Note: The UNLOAD option does not work if NetAlarm is loaded higher than DOS's conventional RAM.

In this mode of operation, NetAlarm performs its monitoring tasks as a background process, allowing the workstation to be used for other purposes.

As a TSR, NetAlarm attempts to activate and perform its monitoring tasks once per cycle. However, NetAlarm has been carefully designed not to activate during disk, screen, communications, and other timing-critical hardware interrupts, or if the workstation is in the midst of critical applications or DOS systems-level operations. If such activities are detected, NetAlarm defers action until the next CPU clock tick, which occurs approximately 18.2 times per second. If the scheduled task must be deferred several times due to workstation activity, NetAlarm resets the monitoring activity to occur after another cycle period has passed. After NetAlarm determines that it is safe to do so, it assumes temporary control of the workstation in order to perform its tasks. When this activity is completed, control is returned to the process at the exact point where it was interrupted. NetAlarm can perform its tasks so quickly that, in most cases, there is no noticeable interruption in workstation processing.

Although NetAlarm is designed to impose minimal CPU overhead on the workstation, it's still important for you to consider the background tasks that NetAlarm performs when you select a monitoring workstation. NetAlarm is compatible with workstations using technology as old and slow as an Intel 8088. However, it's not practical to use such a workstation to monitor eight file servers on one-second cycles as a background task, while a foreground task is actively involved in other processing. Even though NetAlarm has been used as a background task on workstations dedicated as communications gateways that host high levels of activity, it is more commonly used behind print servers and data collection workstations. Ideally, you should try to strike a balance between foreground activity, including the monitoring cycle associated with NetAlarm, and workstation processing power.

Foreground or Dedicated Operational Notes

NetAlarm provides its highest level of monitoring when run in a foreground mode of operation on a dedicated workstation. In this mode, NetAlarm can poll monitored file servers approximately once per second and display real-time statistics associated with a monitored server without conflict.

The configured file servers are monitored and the statistics updated approximately once per second. The numbers enclosed in brackets reflect the threshold levels configured for the currently displayed file server. By pressing Alt-Escape, the user can toggle among monitored file servers to view the statistics associated with each server.

If you press Insert, NetAlarm enters the configuration mode, which allows you to enable, disable, insert, and delete file servers in the configured server table. In this mode you can modify the configuration parameters associated with each file server. After completing the reconfiguration process and exiting by pressing Escape, NetAlarm returns to real-time screen display and monitoring activity.

Pressing Escape terminates the program. If NetAlarm is already memory resident, the foreground copy retrieves the configuration and log information from the memory-resident copy. The foreground copy displays a message indicating that NetAlarm is memory resident and then assumes the monitoring responsibility for the configured file servers. Upon termination, the memory-resident copy is updated with the foreground information and the TSR portion resumes its cyclical monitoring.

Troubleshooting with NetAlarm

This section is intended to give you an overview of potential causes and possible actions for NetAlarm alerts. Where applicable, separate notes are included with references to differences between NetWare 2.x and NetWare 3.x.

Server Utilization @ ??%

Contrary to widespread belief, NetWare's server utilization level is not based on the file server's CPU activity, but rather its inactivity. By tracking inactivity, instead of further loading a busy file server to determine activity, NetWare extrapolates an approximation of the CPU utilization. It's not unusual for server utilization to climb during peak network activity or even network backups. On occasion, however, server utilization may climb even when activity on the network is minimal.

Many troublesome cases can be attributed to problems with the PSERVER NLM/VAP or PSERVER misconfiguration. The most common problem areas are the definition of interrupt-driven printers in PSERVER (typically not necessary), or older versions of the NLM/VAP that were known to cause problems. If you are running PSERVER, confirm that you are using the latest release and consult the documentation to ensure that printers are properly configured.

On NetWare 3.x file servers, some third-party NLMs steal CPU idle time in a manner that fails to compensate the internal counters. This occurs more often when the MONITOR NLM is also loaded. As a result, the accepted CPU idle-time algorithm (also used by the MONITOR NLM) reflects an inaccurate level of CPU utilization. In most cases, merely unloading and then reloading the MONITOR NLM resynchronizes these counters.

However, a continuous, high level of server utilization may indicate that the file server can't service the current network load, or that insufficient FSP exists in the file server for the current network load. Possible solutions include upgrading the file server to a faster processor or adding/reconfiguring for additional FSP.

41

> **Note:** FSP is directly proportionate to NetWare's ability to concurrently service NCP file service requests.

NetWare 2.x: This is possible only through careful recon-figuration. Consult the notes following the dynamic memory usage section in this chapter for suggestions.

NetWare 3.x: Increasing the maximum service processes value may help (at the console or through AUTOEXEC.NCF, default is 20, supported values range from 5 to 40), but only if NetWare 3.x is peaking at the maximum number of service processes. The CPU utilization of different processes and NLMs can be checked by loading the MONITOR NLM with the -P option. This option provides a processor utilization selection on the MONITOR menu from which CPU utilization can be viewed by process.

Connections In Use @ ??%

NetWare licensing is based on the maximum number of concurrent users supported. Once the maximum number of concurrent users is attached, even if not currently logged into a file server, NetWare prevents further attachments until a connection slot is free. Although this is not necessarily a critical error, it is frustrating when you know fewer users are logged in than the maximum allowed and NetWare is preventing further attachments.

NetWare allocates a workstation connection slot whenever the shell (NETx) is loaded, whether or not the user ever logs in. The connection is not cleared even if the user runs LOGOUT. The connection is cleared only when the user logs into another file server or turns off the workstation, and then only after the watchdog time-out period (up to 15 minutes), as NetWare attempts to keep the connection open in case the user tries to reestablish a connection. The result is that although only a few users may be logged in, everyone who has loaded the workstation shell (NETx) occupies a file server connection slot.

The long-term solution to this problem is to upgrade to a version of NetWare with a higher concurrent user count. Though you can use the following temporary solutions, they are *not* recommended because they may force the cleared workstations into a network error from which the only recovery is to reboot and potentially compromise data. The following solution also results in one or more packets with invalid slots being sent to the file server due to the workstation connection information being cleared, and then possibly replaced, in the server connection table.

Rick: As a general rule, use care when "cleaning house" like this. Timing and other network events make this a risky deal, at best.

NetWare 2.x:	By either using FCONSOLE connection information or USERLIST, make a note of those connection numbers (from 1 to the maximum concurrent user support) where no user is logged in. Go to the file server console and type Clear Station ## (where ## is a connection number without a logged-in use). One connection slot is freed for each station cleared.
NetWare 3.x:	As SUPERVISOR, run FCONSOLE connection information. Position the highlighted bar over a connection showing NOT-LOGGED-IN and then press Delete. You will be prompted to clear the connection. Answering affirmatively causes the connection to be cleared. Repeat this procedure as many times as necessary. One connection slot is freed for each NOT-LOGGED-IN connection cleared.

Cache Ratio @ ??%

This alert has a significantly different meaning in NetWare 2.x than it does in NetWare 3.x. For NetWare 2.x, it reflects the ratio of cache hits to total cache operations. Although NetWare's documentation lists 90 percent and greater as acceptable, the optimum is at 95 percent or greater. However, the cache ratio of hits to operations is immediately lower following the file server initially being brought online, as the cache buffers are filled and cache management is optimized.

NetWare 2.x: The number of available cache buffers can be increased by adding RAM to the file server. Optimum cache size for NetWare 2.x is between 800–1,000 buffers for an Intel 80286-based file server; 1,000–1,250 for an Intel 80386-based file server; and 1,250–1,500 for an Intel i486-based file server. Due to the caching algorithm used by NetWare, an imbalance among cache buffer count, CPU speed, and RAM speed may result in the cache response time being slower than access would be with some drive/controller combinations.

For NetWare 3.x, this alert reflects the percentage of total server work RAM allocated to total cache buffers. When NetWare 3.x first loads, it determines the total server work RAM and allocates it, less the kernel requirements, to cache buffers. This initial allocation is what the MONITOR NLM refers to as original cache buffers (the size of each cache buffer is based upon the largest configured block size for any volume on the file server, plus a small percentage for cache management overhead).

The number of original cache buffers decrements, yielding the total cache buffers for each NLM loaded, each additional service process, each directory cache buffer or receive packet buffer allocated, and several other NetWare tasks that require dynamically allocated memory blocks. Although NetWare's documentation warns that indeterminate results may occur if this cache ratio drops to 20 percent or less, problems have been noted with the ratio at 45 percent. Most consultants and NetWare system operators recommend a ratio of 65 percent or greater.

NetWare 3.x:	You can increase the number of total cache buffers by unloading/not loading NLMs, reducing minimum allocations (such as the minimum directory cache buffers and minimum packet receive buffers, though it does not take effect until the server is rebooted), or ideally, by adding RAM to the server. At minimum, total cache buffers should comprise 50 percent or more of total server work RAM.

Open Files @ ??%

NetWare manages each open file to coordinate user and cache access. Memory for this management is allocated dynamically in NetWare 3.x, and from the DGroup dynamic memory pool in NetWare 2.x. Therefore, NetWare imposes a maximum concurrently open file limit. Once this limit is reached, subsequent file opens may result in network errors. The DGroup memory pool is a section of server memory reserved for various operations such as file opens. One of the most notable differences between the 2.x and the 3.x version of the OS is the way in which memory is used. In 3.x, memory is allocated to different operations as required. The system can stay pretty flexible about throwing memory at a particular operation. 2.x is more problematic because the OS divides the memory. Sometimes you can have a situation in which a lot of memory is in the server, but the group or section of memory you are using runs out.

NetWare 2.x:	Run NETGEN and allocate more Open Files/Index File support
NetWare 3.x:	Fixed at 100,000 (not user configurable)

Dirty Cache Buffers @ ??%

When any part of a cache buffer is modified, it is marked as "dirty" because it needs to be flushed to the disk. If an entire cache buffer is changed, it's marked for immediate updating to disk. Otherwise, a cache buffer is flushed only after it has been dirty for a specific period of time. Although an occasional dirty-cache-buffers to total-cache-buffers ratio of up to 70 percent can be attributed to operations such as file server backup or an E-mail broadcast to a large number of users, consistently high ratios may indicate a disk/controller I/O latency problem.

NetWare 2.x: The dirty cache buffer latency is set to 3.3 seconds (60 timer ticks) and is not adjustable.

NetWare 3.x: Adjust the dirty disk cache delay time value (at the console or through AUTOEXEC.NCF; default is 3.3 seconds, supported values range from .01 seconds to 10 seconds) or the maximum concurrent disk cache writes value (at the console or through AUTOEXEC.NCF; default is 50, supported values range from 10 to 100) may need to be adjusted.

Caution: Lowering the dirty disk cache delay time impacts performance because caching becomes less optimized. The higher the maximum concurrent disk cache writes value, the more efficient file write requests become. Conversely, a lower maximum concurrent disk cache writes value makes file read requests more efficient.

Disk I/Os Pending @ ??%

NetWare queues dirty cache buffers to the elevator mechanism to optimize disk I/O so that a single head sweep can update numerous disk blocks. Though extremely efficient, concurrent file I/O operations can compromise this ability and result in numerous disk I/Os requirements. Although occasional disk I/Os pending to maximum concurrent disk writes ratio of up to 70 percent can be attributed to operations such as file server backup or an E-mail broadcast to a large number of users, consistently high ratios may indicate a disk/controller I/O latency problem.

NetWare 2.x:	The dirty cache buffer latency and maximum concurrent disk write operations are not configurable. The only option is to install a faster disk/controller combination.
NetWare 3.x:	Adjust the dirty disk cache delay time value (at the console or through AUTOEXEC.NCF; default is 3.3 seconds, supported values range from .01 seconds to 10 seconds) or the maximum concurrent disk cache writes value may need to be adjusted (at the console or through AUTOEXEC.NCF; default is 50; supported values range from 10 to 100).

> **Caution:** Lowering the dirty disk cache delay time impacts performance, because caching becomes less optimized. The higher the maximum concurrent disk cache writes value, the more efficient file write requests become. Conversely, a lower maximum concurrent disk cache writes value makes file read requests more efficient.

Check the drive/controller in use to see if it automatically does a read verify after each write. If so, set `Enable Disk Read After Write Verify=OFF` to disable the internal read verify after write logic and reduce disk I/O overhead. The other option is to install a faster disk/controller combination.

Routing Buffer Usage @ ??%

Routing buffers are temporary storage areas for network packets from servers, workstations, network printers, and other network devices. In NetWare 2.x, the routing buffer size is based on the largest maximum packet size of any file server installed network interface card (NIC) driver. In NetWare 3.x, you can define the size with the maximum physical receive packet size parameter. A rule of thumb is to configure ten routing buffers for each NIC in the file server, one for each workstation on the network, and two for each network printer, remote printer, or gateway/router on the network, with the total rounded up to the next base of ten.

NetWare 2.x: Run NETGEN and increase communications buffers (part of configuration procedure; the recommended minimum is 40, the maximum supported is 150).

NetWare 3.x: Adjust the minimum packet receive buffers (only configurable at file server boot through STARTUP.NCF; the default is 10, supported values range from 10 to 1,000) and the maximum packet receive buffers (at the console or through AUTOEXEC.NCF; the default is 100; supported values range from 50 to 2,000).

Verify that the maximum physical receive packet size is equal to or greater than the maximum packet size used on the network. (This is configurable only at file server boot through STARTUP.NCF; the default is 1,130; supported values range from 618 to 4,202.) This parameter should be set to the largest packet size (plus the packet header) on the network. This ensures that network packets do not require more than a single packet receive buffer each.

Bindery Objects Usage @ ??%

Bindery objects include file servers, gateways, users, groups, job servers/queues, print servers/queues, and so on. In NetWare 2.x, it's possible during the configuration process to limit the number of bindery objects that can be created on a file server, but only if you also set the limit disk space configuration option.

NetWare 2.x: Run NETGEN and disable the limit disk space option or increase the number of bindery objects (the default varies depending upon the file server configuration; supported values range from 500 to 5,000). Other options include deleting inactive users, groups, or other unused bindery objects.

NetWare 3.x: Not supported under NetWare 3.x.

Dynamic Memory 1 Usage @ ??%

This message, along with the other dynamic memory messages, usually indicates a need for prompt attention to the file server. On all NetWare 2.x v2.1x/v2.2 versions, the Dynamic Memory Pool 1 stores disk drive/ volume information, print queue service requests, file service requests (temporarily), and, on NetWare 2.x v2.1x only, user drive mappings, among other NetWare configuration/operation items. Less than optimum configurations may cause Dynamic Memory Pool 1 shortages resulting in a loss of print queue jobs, lost file service request, and, on NetWare 2.x v2.1x only, user drive-mapping errors, as well as other network anomalies that may cause a file server lockup.

Dynamic Memory Pool 1 is a part of NetWare 2.x's fixed 64K DGroup of memory from which FSP is also based. Although the amount of memory assigned to Dynamic Memory Pool 1 (which ranges from 16K– 21K) is not directly user configurable, its definition can be optimized by user-configured parameters. This memory pool is consumed as follows: each physical drive attached to the file server requires 612 bytes; the auto remirror queue consumes 4 bytes per mirrored drive; VAPs consume 128 bytes each for stack space; each mounted volume consumes up to 16 bytes; each workstation consumes 8 bytes at log in; each open Macintosh file consumes 4 bytes; each print spool queue consumes 28 bytes with 5 additional bytes used per queue server; each spool queue print job consumes 44 bytes; and disk storage tracking requires 960 bytes if NetWare 2.x accounting is enabled.

In v2.1x, an additional 14 bytes is consumed for every user-mapped drive (v2.2 uses the Dynamic Memory Pool 4 for drive mapping). A potential way to reclaim memory for this pool is to adjust one or more of the previously mentioned parameters (that is, disable accounting, don't load VAPs, reduce spooled printers/jobs, minimize mapped directories, and so on). Another way is to reconfigure NetWare 2.x so that more DGroup memory is available.

Dynamic Memory 2 Usage @ ??%

This message, along with the other dynamic memory messages, usually indicates a need for prompt attention to the file server. The Dynamic Memory Pool 2 is used for open file, file lock, record lock, and semaphore tracking. Typically, a high Open Files @ ??% alarm accompanies this message. You can adjust this memory pool by running NETGEN and allocating more open files/index file support (part of the installation procedure).

Dynamic Memory 3 Usage @ ??%

This message, along with the other dynamic memory messages, usually indicates a need for prompt attention to the file server if the reported threshold is greater than 90 percent. The Dynamic Memory Pool 3 tracks file server and routing information.

Dynamic Memory Pool 3 is a part of NetWare 2.x's fixed 64K DGroup of memory and is not user configurable. The only way to increase the memory allocation assigned to this pool is to reconfigure NetWare 2.x so that more DGroup memory is available.

Dynamic Memory 4 Usage @ ??%

This message, along with the other dynamic memory messages, usually indicates a need for prompt attention to the file server if the reported threshold is greater than 90 percent. The Dynamic Memory Pool 4 is used for the tracking of user drive mappings. This memory pool cannot be adjusted through NETGEN but can be optimized through better drive mapping management and menu design.

> **Note:** You can improve Dynamic Memory Pool 1 and 3 (plus Dynamic Memory Pool 4 on NetWare 2.x v2.2) allocations by increasing the amount of available DGroup memory. NetWare 2.x configuration options that can accomplish this are disabling TTS, reducing the configured maximum number of volumes and directory entries per volume, reducing the number of NICs in the file server, changing the type of NIC(s) in the file server, and/or changing the NIC driver software.

Hot Fix Usage @ ??%

This error indicates existing, as well as oncoming, disk problems. Because NetWare attempts to alleviate any disk problems by remapping the affected blocks into the hot fix, a high usage factor indicates the occurrence of numerous unrecoverable errors and the potential for insufficient resources to overcome future disk problems. It is prudent for you to carefully check the hard disk drive and controller.

Disk Space Usage @ ??%

Temporary solutions to this problem include backup/removal of inactive files, deletion of unnecessary files, reallocation of disk resources, or an increase in the amount of allocated space for the affected volume.

	Caution: Do not attempt any disk changes without a full, verified backup.

NetWare 2.x:	Run PURGE to release files that have been deleted but not yet purged by the system or NETGEN to reallocate volume resources (part of the installation procedure) or add another drive (part of the configuration procedure).
NetWare 3.x:	Review the minimum file delete wait time (at the console or through AUTOEXEC.NCF; the default is 1 minute, 5.9 seconds; supported periods range from 0 seconds to 7 days) or the file delete wait time (at the console or through AUTOEXEC.NCF; the default is 5 minutes, 29.6 seconds; supported periods range from 0 seconds to 7 days).

Directory Entry Usage @ ??%

Temporary solutions to this problem include backup/removal of inactive files, deletion of unnecessary files, or an increase in the amount of supported directory entries for the affected volume.

> **Caution:** Do not attempt any volume changes without a full, verified backup.

NetWare 2.x: Run NETGEN and increase the number of directory entries supported for the affected volume (part of the installation procedure).

NetWare 3.x: As directory entries reach 85 percent of the available count, NetWare 3.x automatically allocates additional directory entries, up to the maximum percent of volume used by directory limit. Possible adjustments include: maximum percent of volume used by directory (at the console or through AUTOEXEC.NCF; the default is 13 percent; supported percentages range from 5 to 50 percent); the minimum file delete wait time (at the console or through AUTOEXEC.NCF; the default is 1 minute, 5.9 seconds; supported periods range from 0 seconds to 7 days); or the file delete wait time (at the console or through AUTOEXEC.NCF; the default is 5 minutes, 29.6 seconds; supported periods range from 0 seconds to 7 days).

TTS Disabled

This error indicates that excess TTS errors were more than NetWare could track and compensate for, so the system disabled TTS.

> **Caution:** Give immediate attention to this error because data integrity is at risk! This is really bad stuff, especially if you are doing intense database work because you have no protection. This reminds me of a night of shore leave while in the navy . . .

Hot Fix Disabled

This error indicates that excess disk I/O problems were more than NetWare could compensate for through hot fix remapping, so the system disabled hot fix.

> **Caution:** Give immediate attention to this error because data integrity is at risk! This is even worse than the TTS problem because this is the disk drive itself. Don't let this go for long and get users off the systems as soon as possible. All of your drive data is at risk.

Disk I/O Error

This error indicates that a problem occurred during physical disk I/O. Although hot fix attempts to compensate for this type of error, persistent recurrences indicate potential hard disk drive and/or controller problems.

Mirroring Failure

This error indicates that one or more mirrored disk drives are no longer online (this is often due to a disk crash).

Cache Physical Read/Write Error

This error indicates that an error occurred during cached disk I/O. Although hot fix attempts to compensate for this type of error, persistent recurrences indicate potential hard disk drive and/or controller problems.

> **Caution:** Give immediate attention to this error because data integrity is at risk! Lots of you folks out there are using mirroring as a "lazy man's" disk backup. Pay attention to this alert if you are—this one means your "shorts are exposed to the breeze," so to speak.

Cache Thrashing Occurred

This error indicates that a cache block was needed to service a request, but none was available. As a result, the file server had to issue a standby message to the requester, causing network degradation.

NetWare 2.x:	The number of available cache buffers can be increased by adding RAM to the file server. Optimum cache size for NetWare 2.x is between 800 and 1,000 buffers. Due to the caching algorithm, more than 1,000 cache buffers may result in the cache response time being slower than access would be with some drive/controller combinations.
NetWare 3.x:	Adjust the minimum file cache buffers value (at the console or through AUTOEXEC.NCF; the default is 20; supported values range from 20 to 1,000). File server RAM may need to be added to allocate sufficient buffers.

Fatal FAT Error

Fatal FAT errors indicate an unrecoverable inconsistency occurred between the live and the mirrored FAT information on the file server disk. Normally, the mirrored FAT can compensate for any FAT read/scan errors. However, a fatal FAT error indicates a disk and/or cache memory problem prevented such recovery from occurring. When users receive this message, they should be advised to not use any applications that access and/or update the data on the affected disk until the disk can be fully backed up and the problem corrected.

> **Caution:** Do not take down the server prior to backing up because irretrievable data damage can occur. You may need to reinitialize the hard disk or replace it. If you can, get critical data to another server, or at least to a local hard drive, if you can't get a backup going.

Write/Scan FAT Error

This error indicates that an inconsistent state exists between the live and the mirrored FAT information. Although the mirrored FAT information alleviates most problems of this type, recurrence of this error could indicate disk and/or cache memory problems.

Invalid Connection

This message indicates a that workstation tried to communicate with the file server by using a logical connection ID not currently active in the connection table.

This error may be caused by a workstation that had a valid logical connection to a file server before the server went down and was brought back online. In this event, the user needs to reboot the workstation and reattach it to the file server. Other possible causes of this error include a failing workstation NIC adapter, a loose cable connection, or electrical interference. Problems in software that communicate directly between PCs by IPX, such as E-mail or remote printing software, can also cause this type of error.

Packet with Invalid Slot

This message indicates that a workstation tried to communicate with the file server by using a logical connection ID greater than that supported by the NetWare version in use (for example, ID 0, 1001, and so on).

This type of error is usually caused by a failing workstation NIC adapter, a loose cable connection, or electrical interference. However, problems in software that communicate directly between PCs via IPX, such as E-mail or remote printing software, can also cause this error.

Invalid Sequence Number

This message indicates that the file server received a packet that was numerically out of sequence from the workstation. All packet exchanges between workstation and file server are sequenced to ensure accurate delivery of the data. If an out-of-sequence packet is received, for example, and the packet sequence jumps from 10 to 12, this message appears.

This type of error may be caused by a bad boot ROM on a diskless workstation, the use of several different versions of workstation shells within the same network, bridge/router delays, or network saturation. If this error occurs regularly and it can't be traced to workstation shell or network saturation problems, it's possible that an NIC adapter is going bad, a cable connection is loose, a router/bridge has a problem, or electrical interference is present.

Invalid Request Type

This message indicates that a workstation sent a request that the file server could not recognize. For example, this error results from a bad boot PROM on a diskless workstation, software that was specifically designed for a different version of NetWare (an older or newer API support set), or workstations running shells that are older, newer, or incompatible with the file server's capability to service.

Packet Discarded for > 16 Hops

This message indicates that a packet attempted to cross more than 16 bridges and, therefore, is assumed to be lost or bad. This type of error most often occurs on large internetworks and can indicate that a problem exists within a bridge/router on the network or that an NIC is sending out corrupted packets. However, problems in software that communicate directly between PCs through IPX, such as E-mail or remote printing software, can also cause this type of error.

Packet Discarded for Unknown Net

This message indicates that the file server received a packet with an invalid destination network address. This type of error is most common when a file server in a multiserver environment is taken down while attached workstations are actively accessing it. It can also signify a problem within a bridge/router on the network or in software that communicates directly between PCs through IPX, such as E-mail or remote printing software.

Incoming Packet Discarded, No Buffer

This message indicates that the file server discarded a packet because of insufficient buffers to temporarily store the packet until it could be serviced. Typically, a high Routing Buffer usage @ ??% alarm accompanies this message.

This type of error is often corrected by increasing the resources available to the file server for temporarily storing incoming packets. As a rule of thumb, configure ten routing buffers for each NIC in the file server and two for each workstation, network printer, remote printer, or gateway server on the network, with the accumulated total rounded up to the next base of ten. However, you should also check the file server to ensure that the file server utilization is not abnormally high, that sufficient FSP exists, and that the dynamic memory pools are within tolerances (NetWare 2.x only).

NetWare 2.x:	Run NETGEN and increase communications buffers (part of configuration procedure; the recommended minimum is 40, the maximum supported is 150).
NetWare 3.x:	Adjust the minimum packet receive buffers value (only configurable at file server boot through STARTUP.NCF; the default is 10; supported values range from 10 to 1,000) and the maximum packet receive buffers (at the console or through AUTOEXEC.NCF; the default is 100; supported values range from 50 to 2,000).

Outgoing Packet Discarded, No Buffer

This message indicates that the file server discarded a packet because of insufficient buffers to temporarily store the packet while the file server sent the packet and awaited acknowledgment of receipt. Typically, a high `Routing Buffer Usage @ ??%` alarm accompanies this message.

This type of error is often corrected by increasing the resources available to the file server for temporarily storing outgoing packets. As a rule of thumb, configure ten routing buffers for each NIC in the file server and two for each workstation, network printer, remote printer, or gateway server on the network, with the accumulated total rounded up to the next base of ten. You should also check the file server to ensure that the file server utilization is not abnormally high, that sufficient FSP exists, and that the dynamic memory pools are within tolerances (NetWare 2.x only).

NetWare 2.x: Run NETGEN and increase communications buffers (part of configuration procedure; the recommended minimum is 40; maximum supported is 150).

NetWare 3.x: Adjust the minimum packet receive buffers value (only configurable at file server boot through STARTUP.NCF; the default is 10; supported values range from 10 to 1,000); the maximum packet receive buffers (at the console or through AUTOEXEC.NCF; the default is 100; supported values range from 50 to 2,000); or the maximum alloc short-term memory value (at the console or through AUTOEXEC.NCF; the default is 2,097,152; supported values range from 50,000 to 16,777,216).

NetAlarm Load Sequence

Upon execution, NetAlarm first checks to ensure that its code has not been altered by a virus or an incomplete/invalid copy process. If the test indicates potential alteration, NetAlarm aborts with an appropriate message. NetAlarm then processes the command line. If any invalid or erroneous options are detected, NetAlarm aborts with the following message along with the original command line specified:

```
ERROR - Invalid Command Line Option!

Specified command line options were:
```

NetAlarm checks if it has already been loaded memory resident. If a copy exists in memory and the TSR option was specified, NetAlarm aborts with the following message:

```
Monitoring program already memory resident.
```

If memory resident, the currently executed version is compared with the one in memory. If the two are incompatible, NetAlarm aborts with the following message:

```
This version is incompatible with Memory Resident
copy!
```

NetAlarm determines if it is compatible with the operating system in use. If an incompatible operating system is in use, it aborts with the following message:

```
ERROR - Unable to recognize the DOS version in use!
```

NetAlarm then confirms that IPX is loaded on the workstation. If IPX is not present, it aborts with the following message:

```
ERROR - IPX must be loaded and a log in connection estab-
lished with File Server Console Operator rights before
this program can load!
```

NetAlarm verifies that a NETx workstation shell is loaded on the workstation. If a NETx workstation shell is not present, it aborts with the following message:

```
ERROR - NETx must be loaded and a log in connection estab-
lished with File Server Console Operator rights before
this program can load!
```

NetAlarm searches for a valid file server attachment. If no active file server connection exists, it aborts with the following message:

```
ERROR - No File Server attachment exists! Run NETx and log
in with File Server Console Operator rights before running
this program.
```

NetAlarm then retrieves the version of NetWare to check for compatibility. If an incompatible NetWare version is in use, it aborts with the following message:

```
ERROR - NetWare 2.x v2.1+/v2.2 -or- NetWare 3.x/v3.1x
required!
```

NetAlarm finally verifies that the workstation has file server console operator rights. If unable to confirm these rights, it aborts with the following message:

```
ERROR - Workstation must be logged in with File Server
Console Operator rights for this program to be able to
monitor the network!
```

At this point, NetAlarm begins to monitor the server.

Summary

This chapter covers the basics of NetAlarm, including instructions on how you can set it up and use it to help manage your servers. NetAlarm is a great product. Thanks to Steve Meyer and his team for allowing us to bring this special version to you. If you like it and want to expand on it, give these great folks at Avanti a call at the following address. Onward!

Avanti Techology
13740 Research Boulevard, Suite R-1
Austin, Texas 78750

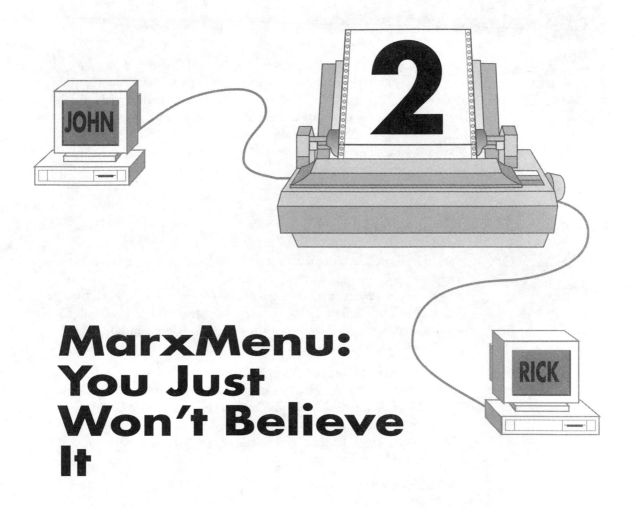

MarxMenu: You Just Won't Believe It

It's difficult to do justice to MarxMenu. The list of things this software tool can do is so long with such an extensive number of options (750 at last count) that we could do an entire book on MarxMenu alone. Well, maybe next time. For the moment, however, suffice it to say that MarxMenu is without exception one of the most powerful menu programming systems on the market today. MarxMenu is a language that enables you to create menus to do things you wouldn't imagine menus were supposed to do. It's a world-class piece of code written by Marc Perkel (in my estimation, a programming artist) of Computer Tyme.

Before you turn to the next chapter, stick around. This tool really is a neat piece of work. As a menu, MarxMenu is as simple or complex as you want it to be. If you want something simple, MarxMenu was made just for you. If you want power, if you want to get really weird, or if you want the menu to remind you to go vote, MarxMenu may be the perfect tool for you. If you're into astrology and you want certain menu items to appear only if Mars is in a certain place in the sky, MarxMenu can calculate the orbit of Mars for you. This tool does a ton of things you wouldn't normally associate with a menu system.

Introduction

MarxMenu is not just another fill-in-the-blank menu system. It is a menu programming language and a job control language. It gives you the freedom to do whatever you want. Total freedom, however, has a price. You need to know and understand how to use a text editor (this shouldn't be difficult if you're able to use a word processor competently), and you need to have a basic understanding of DOS and batch files.

With a text editor, you can create a menu file that is a text file with a .MNU extension. Or you can copy and then modify the text file QUICK.MNU, which displays the menus you see when MarxMenu is executed. This text file contains a set of instructions for MarxMenu to follow. MarxMenu then reads your menu file and runs the instructions. A menu file may look like this:

```
DrawBox 31 5 18 4
UseArrows
Writeln ' W - WordStar'
Write ' L - Lotus'
OnKey 'W'
     CD\WORDSTAR
     WS
OnKey 'L'
     CD\LOTUS
     LOTUS
```

This is an example of a fully working MarxMenu program. Just because MarxMenu has 700 commands doesn't mean you have to use them all. The reason there are so many commands is that people kept calling Marc Perkel asking him to add such and such. In almost every case, he did it.

Installing MarxMenu

Before you install MarxMenu, create a directory just for this program. This makes life a lot easier when you're trying to sort things out. To install MarxMenu:

1. Create a directory named Marx for the software.

2. Copy the Marx.zip file to this directory.

3. Unzip the file.

You'll end up with a lot of sample menu commands, an online help system, and the program itself.

Getting Started Quickly

The fastest way to get started with MarxMenu is to run it with the sample menu. The sample is set up to let you build on or customize it. To get rolling quickly, first install the system as described above and then get into the menu system by typing:

```
Marx Sample
```

> **Note:** You must use the MARX.BAT batch file to run stuff. Don't run things as MarxMenu <menu>; it won't work properly.

Figure 2.1 shows what the screen looks like—a simple menu. At this point you can try out the two menu options. They are two utilities that are included on the disk, and they fire off as you select the menu option.

The third menu option is the most interesting one because it's the one that enables you to drop in and customize this sample. If you select C, you should see what comes up in Figure 2.2.

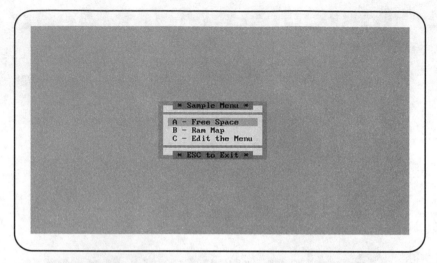

Figure 2.1. A sample MarxMenu.

```
                                                        <F10> for menus
     SAMPLE MNU   B:   Line 1   Col 1        Insert Indent Wrap
;----- To run this menu type: MARX SAMPLE

TextColor Red Brown
ClearScreen '█'

;----- Here we set up colors!

BoxBorderColor Green Blue
BoxInsideColor Yellow Blue
BoxHeaderColor White Cyan
InverseColor Yellow Mag

UseArrows
BoxHeader ' * Sample Menu * '
BoxFooter ' * ESC to Exit * '
DrawBox 28 10 23 7

;----- Here we display our choices!

DrawBar
Writeln
Writeln '  A - Free Space'
Writeln '  B - Ram Map'
```

Figure 2.2. Inside MarxEdit.

You are now in the famous MarxEdit program. You can invoke this separately by typing ME at the DOS prompt. As shown in Figure 2.2, you can see the "source" for the sample menu. There's not much to it, and it's quite readable. You can next add a new menu item.

Rick: This editor can be painful if you have never used WordStar. If you're coming from the WordStar world, well, guess what? Marc is too. As you can see in Figure 2.3, the <CTRL K> stuff is alive and well! The WordStar command set is pretty much intact within this editor. Remember that any text editor can be used to create these .MNU files. For now, however, try to live through this so you can understand how to build the menus.

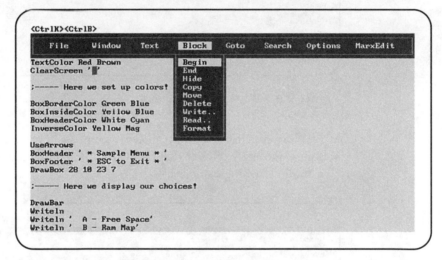

Figure 2.3. MarxEdit menu options.

Note: Source files are *.mnu and the compiled, ready-to-run files are *.mrx. The text editor is now working on the sample.mnu file.

With more than 700 items to choose from, it's difficult to pick. To make it simple, you can first add the ability to run Syscon from the menu system. First add the command to the set of choices that the menu displays by adding option D (see Figure 2.4).

```
                                                    <F10> for menus
    SAMPLE.MNU   88%  Line 40   Col 17      Insert Indent Wrap
;----- Here we display our choices!

DrawBar
Writeln
Writeln '   A - Free Space'
Writeln '   B - Ram Map'
Writeln '   C - Edit the Menu'
Writeln '   D - Run Syscon'
DrawBar

;----- OnKey statements are just like writing batch files!

OnKey 'A'
   Free
   Pause

OnKey 'B'
   RamMap
   Pause

OnKey 'C'
   ME SAMPLE.MNU
```

Figure 2.4. Adding a menu choice.

Next, you need to add an OnKey section. As shown in Figure 2.5, this is done quite easily. Notice that the pause command is also included and that the D is in single quotes.

```
                                                    <F10> for menus
    SAMPLE.MNU   88%  Line 46   Col 17      Insert Indent Wrap
Writeln '   C - Edit the Menu'
Writeln '   D - Run Syscon'
DrawBar

;----- OnKey statements are just like writing batch files!

OnKey 'A'
   Free
   Pause

OnKey 'B'
   RamMap
   Pause

OnKey 'C'
   ME SAMPLE.MNU

OnKey 'D'
   Syscon
   Pause

;----- Yes, it can be this simple!
```

Figure 2.5. Adding the OnKey section.

John: Marc has enough sense to deal with case sensitivity, so don't worry about upper- or lowercase letters. This is internal to the program. Upper- and lowercase letters are treated in the same way.

The OnKey command is the place where you actually create the temporary batch file that the menu system fires off. In this case, the file that runs is:

```
SYSCON
PAUSE
```

When you exit the editor, you are asked whether you want to save the file or not. If you respond with "yes," you are back with a new menu item. The behind-the-scenes work that takes place is the compiling of the new menu source file. MarxMenu then runs the new compiled sample menu. As shown in Figure 2.6, the menu now shows the option to run Syscon. Assuming you have a search path to the public directory, you can select D and Syscon pops up.

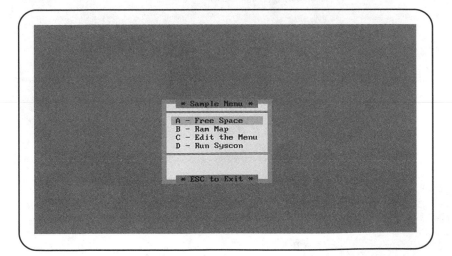

Figure 2.6. An updated sample menu.

Okay, so that was a bit boring, but let's face it, that was no barn-burning feat. But wait, there's more.

> **Rick:** I spent lots of late nights writing this stuff and half-listening to infomercials for things like Ginsu knives and all kinds of real-estate courses, and they all say "but wait there's more." Sorry, folks, it just creeps in.

Put up the default server you are attached to on the menu screen, and select option C from the sample menu to get back to the editor. Next, add one of those 700 or so commands to the system. As shown in Figure 2.7, you can see that the following line is added:

```
Writeln ' Default:'NovDefaultServer
```

```
                                                    <F10> for menus
    SAMPLE.MNU   58%   Line 26     Col 12      Insert Indent Wrap

BoxBorderColor Green Blue
BoxInsideColor Yellow Blue
BoxHeaderColor White Cyan
InverseColor Yellow Mag

UseArrows
BoxHeader ' * Sample Menu * '
BoxFooter ' * ESC to Exit * '
DrawBox 28 10 23 10

;----- Here we display our choices!

DrawBar
Writeln
Writeln '   A - Free Space'
Writeln '   B - Ram Map'
Writeln '   C - Edit the Menu'
Writeln '   D - Run Syscon'
Writeln '   Default:' NovDefaultServer
DrawBar

;----- OnKey statements are just like writing batch files!
```

Figure 2.7. The menu with changes.

This is the command to get the default file server you are currently logged into. There's nothing to it. The Writeln command does what you would expect—it writes the line to the screen. This line is underneath the menu options so that's where it shows up. After saving this file and getting back to the menu illustrated in Figure 2.8, you see the results.

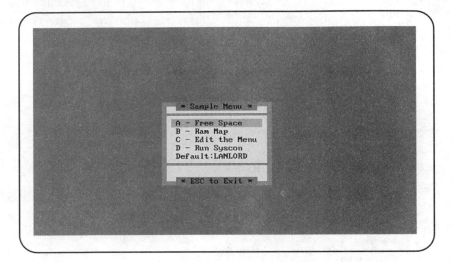

Figure 2.8. A menu with default server information.

That's pretty much it. You can add lots of things to this menu or you can start with any of the other sample menus that are included with MarxMenu. Simple stuff, folks, but incredibly powerful.

Running MarxMenu

For MarxMenu to work, you need to create a MARX.BAT file by typing INSTALL. INSTALL unpacks the compressed menu files and documentation files, and then brings up the installation menu.

The MARX.BAT file looks like this:

```
@ECHO OFF
C:\MARX\MARXMENU.EXE %1
%MXCMD%
%0 %1
```

The first line of MARX.BAT turns off the echo (you may change this to ECHO ON for debugging purposes). You can also insert Pause commands to debug a menu. This enables you to see what's going on.

The second line of MARX.BAT runs MARXMENU.EXE. The second parameter, %1, is the name of the menu file to run. A third parameter (%2) may be added to tell MarxMenu to use a specific directory to create temporary batch files. Otherwise, MarxMenu creates temporary batch files in the same directory as MARXMENU.EXE.

When you select a program to run, MarxMenu writes a temporary batch file that contains the commands that run the program. MarxMenu then writes a command to the MXCMD environment variable to execute the temporary batch file and exits.

The Commands

The next few figures show some of the 750 commands within this program. As you go through this material remember that this software is classified as menuing software. As you will see, it is really much more, depending on how you use the product.

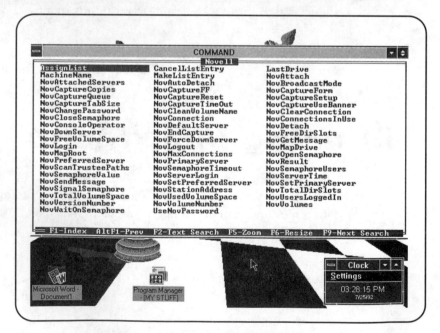

Figure 2.9. The MarxMenu commands.

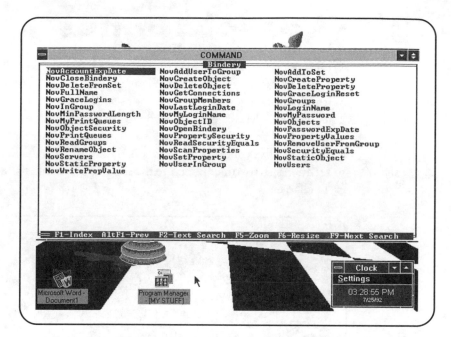

Figure 2.10. The MarxMenu commands.

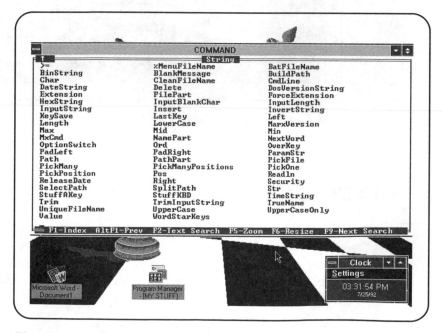

Figure 2.11. The MarxMenu commands.

The Console Bonus

While inside MarxMenu, you and your users have use of short, built-in pop-up functions. As shown in Figure 2.12, you get four handy items. With Blank Screen, you can blank your screen while you head out for a bit. The "Set Blank Message" enables you to put up the "out to lunch" message. You can lock the keyboard as well so that only your secret code gets you back in. Finally, you'll see a "Set Blank Time" function. This enables you to set an inactivity timeout before the screen goes blank; handy stuff at no extra charge.

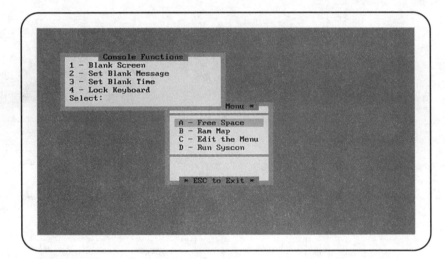

Figure 2.12. A console menu pop up.

Feature List

The following list contains the commands available within MarxMenu. Complete details for each command are contained online. At the C prompt, simply type MarxHelp and you have a complete help system available to you. Figure 2.13 is an example of the help system.

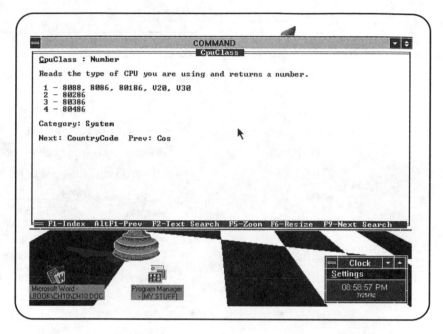

Figure 2.13. A sample help system screen.

The following table is a listing of commands that you will find within the walls of MarxMenu. The online help system contains the complete reference and some samples.

Table 2.1. The MarxMenu commands.

Command	Action
Abs	Returns the absolute value of a number.
Actual	Special command to write variables.
Alias	Compiler level text substitution.
AllowAbort	Control flow command.
AllowEsc	Allows to ignore/test for Escape key.
And	Boolean expression.
AppendArray	Array processing.

continues

Table 2.1. continued

Command	Action
ApplicationMemory	Test for memory available to run applications.
ArcTan	Returns the arc tangent of a number.
AssignList	Gets Network Assign list.
BadDate	Boolean to test for valid date conversion.
Bat	Used to write lines for batch files.
BatFileName	Returns names of batch files MarxMenu creates.
BigShadow	Display option.
BinString	Converts a number into base 2.
Blanked	Boolean for testing the screen blank function.
BlankMessage	Message you can display when screen is blank.
BlankScreenProgram	Customize what program you want to blank screen.
BlankTime	When to blank screen.
Blink	Boolean for blinking colors.
BlockBox	Border formatting.
BootDrive	Returns boot drive (DOS v4+).
BoxBorderColor	Border formatting.
BoxHeader	Centers header message for boxes.
BoxHeaderColor	Colors for box headers/footers.
BoxHeaderLeft	Flushes the header message left.
BoxHeaderRight	Flushes the header message right.
BoxFooter	Centers footer message.
BoxFooterLeft	Flushes message left.
BoxFooterRight	Flushes message right.
BoxInsideColor	Color for inside box.

Command	Action
Break	Stops processing.
BrightBackground	Color command.
BuildPath	Gets path information and builds array.
CancelListEntry	Kills a network redirection.
CapsColor	Allows uppercase letters to be displayed in a different color.
CapsLock	Boolean if CapsLock on/off.
Chain	Allows for new menu loading.
Char	Converts number to character.
ChDir	Changes directory.
CleanFileName	Gets full pathname of a file.
ClearLine	Clears current line on-screen.
ClearScreen	Take a wild guess. Don't cheat!
ClearScreenFirst	Allows you to clear the screen before execution.
ClearScreenOnExit	Like ClearScreenFirst except only upon return.
ClockColor	Change color of screen clock.
ClockMode	Sets how you want the clock displayed.
ClockPos	Where to position the clock.
ClosePrinter	Printer control.
ClusterSize	Drive cluster size. (I told you everything is in here.)
CmdLine	Get command line screen.
CMOS	Writing to the CMOS. (Be careful!)
ColdBoot	Allows you to cold boot the PC.
ColorScreen	Boolean. Determines screen type.
Comment	Comment marker for comments in your menu source file.
Console	Determines access to the console.

continues

75

Table 2.1. continued

Command	Action
ConsoleBorderColor	Colors for console.
ConsoleHeaderColor	Colors for console.
ConsoleInsideColor	Colors for console.
ConsolePos	Where to put it.
Const	Creates a constant.
Cos	Generates the cosign of a number.
CpuClass	Type of CPU in machine.
CountryCode	Where the PC thinks it is.
CurrentEnvironment	Not the weather report. Environment Var selection.
CurrentWindow	Number of current window.
Cursor	Turns cursor on/off.
CustomBox	Box drawing command.
DateSeparator	Date manipulation stuff.
DateString	Date in string format.
Day	Returns a day of the month.
DayOf	Returns the day of a date.
DayOfWeek	Returns day of the week.
DayOfWeekOf	Returns day of the week from any date.
DecimalSeparator	Returns the decimal separator from the country information.
Delete	Deletes characters from a string.
DelFile	Kills a file.
DisplayType	Gets video card.
DirectoriesOnly	On/off switch for reading directories or files.
DiskType	Returns disk type: floppy, hard, Novell, and so on.
Dispose	Memory reclamation command.

Command	Action
DosVersion	Shows major DOS version number.
DosVersionString	Shows complete version number.
DosWindow	Gets a DOS window to execute simple commands.
DoubleLineBox	Box drawing stuff.
DrawBox	What it says.
Drives	Gets last drive information from config.sys.
DvAppNumber	DESQview command.
DvFrame	DESQview command.
DvFreeze	DESQview command.
DvHide	DESQview command.
DvKillTask	DESQview command.
DvLastHandle	DESQview command.
DvLoaded	DESQview command.
DvMoveWindow	DESQview command.
DvMyHandle	DESQview command.
DvPifExecute	DESQview command.
DvResizeWindow	DESQview command.
DvSetBottom	DESQview command.
DvSetTop	DESQview command.
DvUnFreeze	DESQview command.
DvUnHide	DESQview command.
Else	Conditional.
ElseIf	Conditional.
EndComment	End of comment block.
Endif	Conditional.
EndLoop	Conditional.
EndOfFile	Checks for end-of-file marker. Boolean.

continues

Table 2.1. continued

Command	Action
EndProc	Ends a procedure.
EndWhile	Conditional. End of a While loop.
EnvFree	Free space in the selected environment.
EnvSize	Size of current environment.
EraseTopWindow	Screen drawing command.
EraseWindow	Screen drawing command.
Execute	Executes a command without leaving MarxMenu.
ExistDir	Checks for directory existence. Boolean.
ExistFile	Checks for file existence. Boolean.
ExistOnPath	Looks for command on path.
ExitCode	ErrorLevel that can be set upon leaving MarxMenu.
ExitMenu	That's all folks. Exits MarxMenu.
Exp	Exponential of a real number.
Explode	Exploding Windows on/off.
ExplodeDelay	Exploding Windows delay time.
Extension	Gets file extension.
FileAppend	Opens a file for writing and goes to the end of file.
FileAssign	Variable name to filename.
FileAttr	Gets file attributes.
FileClose	Closes file.
FileCreate	Creates a file. If it exists, it's overwritten.
FileDate	Gets the date from a file as a 32-bit integer.
FileFlush	Flushes any buffers.
FileLog	Opens a file, goes to end, and writes a string.

Command	Action
FileOpen	Opens a file.
FilePart	Gets part of a file.
FilePos	Returns the current file position.
FileReadln	Reads one line in an open file.
FileRename	Renames a file. Bonus: you can move a file as well.
FileResult	Returns the results of a file operation.
FileSeek	Moves a file pointer to a specific place in the file.
FileSize	Returns a file size.
FileTime	Gets the timestamp from a file.
FileWrite	Writes text to a file with no CR/LF.
FileWriteln	Writes text to a file with CR/LF.
FixPath	Checks station's path and fixes as required.
Floppies	Number of floppy drives on the system.
ForceExplosion	Force a window to blow up.
ForceExtension	Attach an extension to a file.
Fraction	More math stuff.
FreeDiskSpace	Disk space left.
FreeEms	Free LIM EMS memory.
FreeMem	Frees any memory that was allocated.
FreeMemory	How much memory you have left.
GetMem	Memory allocation function.
GotoXY	Position stuff.
HexString	Conversion.
HiddenAndSystem	Yes/no for reading hidden or system files.
HighWord	Gets upper 16 bits of a number.
Hour	Current hour in 24-hour format.

continues

Table 2.1. continued

Command	Action
HourOf	Returns hour of a specific time input.
Hundredth	Returns the 1/100 of a second from system clock.
IdleProgram	Procedure that runs while waiting for keyboard input.
If	Conditional.
InactiveBox	Border color of box not active.
InactiveBoxColor	Border color of inside box.
InactiveShadow	Border color for Shadow.
Include	Conditional. Inserts another menu inside the existing menu.
IncludeDirectories	On/off for reading directories and files.
InFile	Input/output conditional.
InputBlankChar	Screen formatting command.
InputLength	Screen formatting command.
InputString	Screen formatting command.
Insert	Inserts a string into another string.
InsertMode	On/off for Readln command.
Int	Yet more math. Integer part of a real number as a real number.
Integer	Yawn. Integer part of a real number as an integer.
Intr	Used to call system interrupts. Use with care!
InverseColor	Makes the screen pretty.
InvertString	Flips a string around. ABC becomes CBA. Slick, eh?
Jump	Conditional. Jumps to another menu with no return.
KbdReady	Boolean. Has a key been pressed?

Command	Action
KeySave	Command to store keystrokes.
KeyFromMouse	Boolean. Did this come from the rat?
KillMusic	Stops the music.
LastDrive	Last drive as reported from config.sys.
LastKey	Last key typed at keyboard.
Left	Gets characters from another string. Left from position.
Length	How long is the string.
Ln	Natural logarithm of a real number.
Loc	Positional location inside a procedure.
LockWord	Default to lock up the keyboard.
Logoff	Log off the network, immediately.
LogoffTime	Same as above except you set inactivity timeout.
Logout	Same as logoff.
Loop	Conditional.
LoopIndex	Returns the number of the loop you are in.
LoopLevel	How many loops deep you are.
LoopLimit	Upper level of the loop limit.
LowerCase	Makes characters lowercase.
LowWord	Low value (16 bits) of a number.
MachineName	Environment variable name of machine.
MakeListEntry	Adds entry to network redirection table.
MarxVersion	Version number of MarxMenu.
MasterEnvironment	Selects the Master Environment (used with other commands).
Max	Returns the greater of two numbers.
MatrixInvert	Used with array processing.

continues

Table 2.1. continued

Command	Action
Mem	Returns the byte at a memory location.
MemL	Gets memory information.
MemSize	Gets memory information.
MemW	Gets memory information.
MenuKeyBuffer	Internal menu variable.
MhsDirectory	Novell message-handling system command.
MhsMailDirectory	Novell message-handling system command.
MhsReadFile	Novell message-handling system command.
MhsSendDirectory	Novell message-handling system command.
MhsUserDirectory	Novell message-handling system command.
Mid	String manipulation.
Min	Smallest of two numbers.
MinorDosVersion	Gets the minor or point release of DOS.
Minute	Returns the current minute.
MinuteOf	Pass a time and you get the minute as an integer.
MkDir	Make a directory.
Mod	Returns division remainder.
ModifyPath	Modify system path.
Month	Gets current month.
MonthOf	Gives you month number of any date.
Mouse	On/off for using the mouse.
MouseHorizontal	Mouse sensitivity.
MouseVertical	Mouse sensitivity.

Command	Action
MoveWindow	Window movement.
MsDos	Calls Int21. Takes registers as input. Watch out!
MxCmd	Internal variable.
NamePart	Gets the name part of a filename.
NetworkVersion	Boolean. Are you running the network version of MarxMenu?
NextWord	Gets next logical word in a string.
Nil	Empty return for any data type.
NoBoxBorder	Screen stuff.
NoExit	Prevents using Escape key to leave menu system.
Not	Boolean.
NotesLeft	Music numbers left.
NotesPlayed	Notes played.
NovAccountExpDate	NetWare specific command.
NovAddUserToGroup	NetWare specific command.
NovAddToSet	NetWare specific command.
NovAttach	NetWare specific command.
NovAttachedServers	NetWare specific command.
NovAutoDetach	NetWare specific command.
NovBroadcastMode	NetWare specific command.
NovCaptureCopies	NetWare specific command.
NovCaptureFF	NetWare specific command.
NovCaptureForm	NetWare specific command.
NovCaptureQueue	NetWare specific command.
NovCaptureReset	NetWare specific command.
NovCaptureSetup	NetWare specific command.
NovCaptureTabSize	NetWare specific command.

continues

83

Table 2.1. continued

Command	Action
NovCaptureTimeOut	NetWare specific command.
NovCaptureUseBanner	NetWare specific command.
NovChangePassword	NetWare specific command.
NovCleanVolumeName	NetWare specific command.
NovClearConnection	NetWare specific command.
NovCloseBindery	NetWare specific command.
NovCloseSemaphore	NetWare specific command.
NovConnection	NetWare specific command.
NovConnectionsInUse	NetWare specific command.
NovConsoleOperator	NetWare specific command.
NovCreateObject	NetWare specific command.
NovCreateProperty	NetWare specific command.
NovDefaultServer	NetWare specific command.
NovDeleteFromSet	NetWare specific command.
NovDeleteObject	NetWare specific command.
NovDeleteProperty	NetWare specific command.
NovDetach	NetWare specific command.
NovDownServer	NetWare specific command. (Be careful, you "kill" everyone when downing an active server.)
NovEndCapture	NetWare specific command.
NovFreeDirSlots	NetWare specific command.
NovFreeVolumeSpace	NetWare specific command.
NovForceDownServer	NetWare specific command.
NovFullName	NetWare specific command.
NovGetConnections	NetWare specific command.
NovGetMessage	NetWare specific command.
NovGraceLoginReset	NetWare specific command.

Command	Action
NovGraceLogins	NetWare specific command.
NovGroupMembers	NetWare specific command.
NovGroups	NetWare specific command.
NovInGroup	NetWare specific command.
NovLastLoginDate	NetWare specific command.
NovLogin	NetWare specific command.
NovLoginName	NetWare specific command.
NovLogout	NetWare specific command.
NovMapDrive	NetWare specific command.
NovMapRoot	NetWare specific command.
NovMaxConnections	NetWare specific command.
NovMinPasswordLength	NetWare specific command.
NovMyLoginName	NetWare specific command.
NovMyPassword	NetWare specific command.
NovMyPrintQueues	NetWare specific command.
NovObjectID	NetWare specific command.
NovObjects	NetWare specific command.
NovObjectSecurity	NetWare specific command.
NovOpenBindery	NetWare specific command.
NovOpenSemaphore	NetWare specific command.
NovPasswordExpDate	NetWare specific command.
NovPreferredServer	NetWare specific command.
NovPrimaryServer	NetWare specific command.
NovPrintQueues	NetWare specific command.
NovPropertySecurity	NetWare specific command.
NovPropertyValues	NetWare specific command.
NovReadGroups	NetWare specific command.
NovReadSecurityEquals	NetWare specific command.

continues

Table 2.1. continued

Command	Action
NovRemoveUser-FromGroup	NetWare specific command.
NovRenameObject	NetWare specific command.
NovResult	NetWare specific command.
NovScanProperties	NetWare specific command.
NovScanTrusteePaths	NetWare specific command.
NovSecurityEquals	NetWare specific command.
NovSemaphoreTimeout	NetWare specific command.
NovSemaphoreUsers	NetWare specific command.
NovSemaphoreValue	NetWare specific command.
NovServerLogin	NetWare specific command.
NovServers	NetWare specific command.
NovServerTime	NetWare specific command.
NovSendMessage	NetWare specific command.
NovSetPreferredServer	NetWare specific command.
NovSetPrimaryServer	NetWare specific command.
NovSetProperty	NetWare specific command.
NovSignalSemaphore	NetWare specific command.
NovStaticObject	NetWare specific command.
NovStaticProperty	NetWare specific command.
NovStationAddress	NetWare specific command.
NovTotalDirSlots	NetWare specific command.
NovTotalVolumeSpace	NetWare specific command.
NovUsedVolumeSpace	NetWare specific command.
NovUserInGroup	NetWare specific command.
NovUsers	NetWare specific command.
NovUsersLoggedIn	NetWare specific command.
NovVersionNumber	NetWare specific command.
NovVolumeNumber	NetWare specific command.

Command	Action
NovVolumes	NetWare specific command.
NovWaitOnSemaphore	NetWare specific command.
NovWritePropValue	NetWare specific command.
NumberOfElements	Returns number of elements in array.
Now	Returns current moment or sets system clock.
NumLock	Boolean. Set or not?
Offset	Returns memory offset where string is located.
OnKey	This is the command that creates the batch file to execute.
OnScreenOnly	Selection restriction.
OpenPrinter	Opens a printer device.
OptionSwitch	Boolean. Tests for options on strings.
Or	Boolean.
Ord	Returns numeric value of an ASCII character.
OutFile	Output switch for standard I/O settings.
OverKey	Variable used with UseArrows command.
Overlay	Loads another menu. After it runs, back to calling menu.
PadLeft	Fill string with spaces on left.
PadRight	Same as above, to the right.
ParallelPorts	Number of parallel ports.
ParamStr	Returns parameter string from the command line.
ParentEnvironment	Environment selection command.
Password	Passwords for inside MarxMenu.
Path	Returns current path.
PathPart	Gets a part of the path.

continues

Table 2.1. continued

Command	Action
PauseAfterExecute	On/off. If on, press any key message after command.
Pi	In case you're still with me, this returns Pi to 18 digits.
PickFile	Array manipulation command.
PickMany	Array manipulation command.
PickManyPositions	Array manipulation command.
PickOne	Array manipulation command.
PickPosition	Array manipulation command.
Port	Returns or writes port value.
Pos	String manipulation.
PosInList	String manipulation.
PosInSortedList	String manipulation.
Power	Raises a real to a given power.
Pred	Returns a number minus one.
Print	Does what it says to the printer.
PrinterName	Selects Printer Name.
Println	Sends text with CR/LF to the printer.
PrintScreen	Hmm . . .
Procedure	Conditional for programming your own procedures.
PullMenu	Menu behavior.
Qualifier	Array handling.
Random	Creates random number.
ReadAscTextFile	Reads comma delimited file into an array.
ReadDirectory	Reads directory into array.
ReadEnv	Returns environment string.
ReadEnvironment	Reads environment into an array.
ReadFileBlock	Reads file information into a memory buffer.

Command	Action
ReadKey	Reads a key from the keyboard.
Readln	Reads a line of text from the keyboard.
ReadSqDirectory	Like ReadDirectory only gets all information into second array.
ReadTextFile	Reads text file into an array.
Real	Returns the real equivalent of an integer.
Reboot	Soft boot of PC.
ReleaseDate	MarxMenu release date.
Repeat	Conditional for programming.
ResizeWindow	Windows control command.
Return	Conditional for programming.
ReturnCode	When using the execute command, a code is returned.
Right	String manipulation.
RmDir	Kill a directory.
RollWindow	Scroll through to the next window in the menu stack.
Run	Runs a procedure stored in a variable.
SavePosition	Screen control option.
ScreenHeight	Returns number of lines on the screen.
ScreenWidth	Width of screen.
ScrollLock	Boolean. Is it set?
ScrollMove	Controls screen movement.
Second	Current second.
SecondOf	Returns second of any given time. Acts as a parser command.
Security	Allows you to hide what the user is typing. Boolean.
Segment	Returns memory segment where a string is located.

continues

Table 2.1. continued

Command	Action
SelectPath	Ext. command used with other Computer Tyme programs.
SerialPorts	Number of serial ports.
SetArraySize	Sets array size boundary.
SetEnv	Used to set environment strings.
SetTopWindow	Selects a window by making it current.
SetWindowUnder	Moves one window underneath another.
Shadow	Boolean. Shadows on/off.
ShadowColor	Shadow color setting.
ShadowPosition	Shadow positioning.
Shared	Sets variables as shared between menu overlays.
ShellEnvironment	Selects last command.com as environment.
Shl	Shift left. Binary.
Shr	Shift right. Binary.
Sin	Returns the sine of a real.
SingleLineBox	Box drawing command.
SmallShadow	Shadow command.
SortArray	As it says, array sorting command.
Sound	Sound effects on/off. Boolean.
SplitPath	Yet another command to get the path and put it into an array.
Sqr	Square roots.
StandardIO	On/off tells the menu to use/not use standard I/O.
Str	Number into a string.
StuffAKey	Stuff a single key into the DOS keyboard.
StuffKBD	Stuffs a 16-character string into the keyboard.

Command	Action
StuffKeyboardNow	Stuffs upon quitting MarxMenu. Sort of a going away gift.
Succ	Returns a number plus one.
Suggest	Allows to position arrow selection on menu.
TaskNumber	Current task number of DESQview or Carousel.
TextBackground	Color command.
TextColor	Color command.
TextMode	Sets the video text mode.
TextPos	Returns current position in a text file.
TextSeek	Moves to a specific byte in a text file.
Then	Conditional for programming.
TimeOf	Converts a string representing a date to time number.
Timer	System timer.
TimeSeparator	Returns time separator from country information.
TimeString	Returns time as a string.
TMaxActiveTasks	Returns the number of active tasks started under TaskMax.
TMaxCreateTask	Creates a task and executes it.
TMaxCut	Activates TaskMax data cutting function.
TMaxDeleteTask	Kills task.
TMaxDirectSwitching	On/off. Determines direct switching ability.
TMaxEMSMemLim	Max amount of LIM EMS memory for a task.
TMaxGetPasteBuffer	Reads paste buffer into an array of strings.
TMaxInstalled	Boolean. Is TaskMax installed?
TMaxMaxTasks	TaskMax amount of tasks.

continues

91

Table 2.1. continued

Command	Action
TMaxNameTask	Get the name of current task.
TMaxPaste	Activates TaskMax data pasting function.
TMaxReadTaskInfo	Task information into an array.
TMaxResult	Variable for results status.
TMaxReturnCount	Timer ticks.
TMaxSetPasteBuffer	Buffer for pasting.
TMaxSwitchTasks	Task switching.
TMaxSwitchToManager	Switch to the task manager.
TMaxTakeOver	Allows your menu to take over task manager. On/off.
TMaxTaskOpenFiles	Returns number of open files in a task.
TMaxThisTask	Task ID of current task.
TMaxVersion	Version of TaskMax.
Today	Returns the current day as a date.
Tomorrow	Returns the time of the day after midnight.
Tone	Plays a note.
TotalDiskSpace	Gets disk space.
TotalEms	Gets EMS in bytes.
Trim	Trims whitespace from both ends of a string.
TrimInputString	On/off. Determines if you want the trim to happen on input.
TrueName	Undocumented DOS feature to get real filenames.
UnBlank	Boolean. Is the screen finished?
UniqueFileName	Used to create unique filenames.
Until	Conditional control.
UpperCase	String conversion.

Command	Action
UpperCaseOnly	Converts input to all uppercase. Boolean.
UseArrows	Menu selection command. On/off.
UseCommand	On/off. Whether to use command.com for batch files.
UsedDiskSpace	How much is in use.
UseNovPassword	Forces the user to use Novell password with screen blanker.
Value	Converts string to number.
Var	Used to create variables.
VarType	Returns variable type.
VideoMode	Returns current video mode.
VideoPage	Returns current video page.
ViewArray	Allows you to view an array of strings.
ViewTextFile	Allows you to view a text file.
VinCheckService	Banyan Vines command network operating system command.
VinesInt	Banyan Vines special command.
VinesLoaded	Banyan Vines special command.
VinUserName	Banyan Vines special command.
VinSerialNumber	Banyan Vines special command.
Volume	Returns the label of the specified drive.
Wait	Delay for 1/100th of a second.
WaitOrKbdReady	As above or until somebody hits a key.
WhereX	Horizontal cursor positioning in a window.
WhereXAbs	Horizontal cursor positioning on the screen.
WhereY	Vertical cursor positioning in a window.
WhereYAbs	Vertical cursor positioning on the screen.
While	Conditional. Program execution.

continues

Table 2.1. continued

Command	Action
WholeFileNames	On/off. Will ReadDirectory and return whole filenames.
Window	Window sizing.
WindowHeight	Returns number of rows in current window.
WindowWidth	Returns number of columns in current window.
WinX	Returns the horizontal location of left corner of window.
WinY	Returns the vertical location of left corner of window.
WordStarKeys	On/off. Allows to get real scan codes and not WordStar stuff.
Write	Writes string on the screen at the current cursor position.
WriteCenter	Writes string centered in current window.
WriteError	Writes to DOS error-handling device.
WriteFileBlock	Writes buffered data to disk file.
Writeln	Writes string on screen with CR/LF.
WritelnError	Writes string on DOS error-handling device with CR/LF.
WriteTextFile	Writes string array to text file.
WriteVertical	Takes a string and prints it one letter per line, hence, vertical.
Xor	Operator.
Year	Returns the current year.
YearOf	Returns the current year of any date.

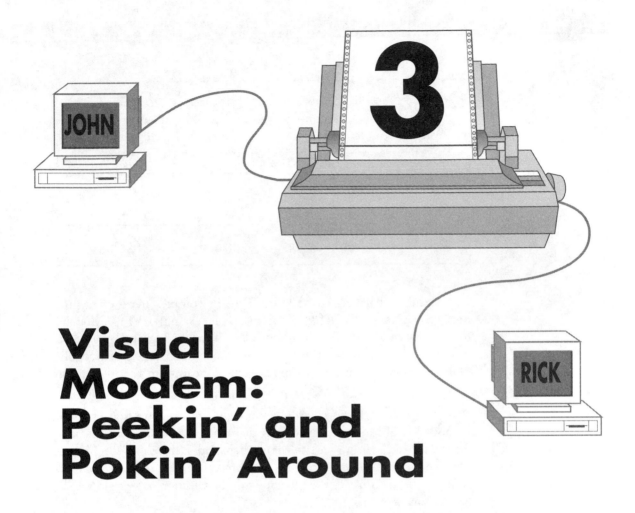

Visual Modem: Peekin' and Pokin' Around

Visual Modem is a particularly good piece of software for dealing with the never-ending battle of modems and proper settings. If you've ever tried to figure out where the correct modem code goes or what the heck the last guy did with the modem manual, this software is a lifesaver.

Visual Modem provides you with a simple way to examine and alter your modem settings. While full functionality is geared toward use with the US Robotics HST (USRHST) modem, any modem can take advantage of the custom modem command creation facility to create, save, and send modem commands tailored to a particular modem.

John: The best part about this is the fact that you can create a storehouse of modem configuration files under real names like "AutoAns" or "Xtrwait". Don't you just love this eight-character DOS limitation? Hey Segal, make yourself useful and fix this.

 Rick: Uh, yeah right, big guy, I'll get right on it.

Instead of having to wade through the complex maze of cryptic modem commands (ATB1&S0=0E1F0&F, for example), Visual Modem offers a collection of screens that display all the setting options in text format, enabling you to comfortably scroll through the listing of available modem commands and change or reset any of the modem's configuration settings.

Visual Modem also acts as a tutor (just in case you find yourself without Visual Modem someday) by displaying the actual modem commands for each setting sent to the modem and each response received. Once the desired modem settings are set, you can send the entire set of new configuration settings to the modem with the selection of a single Visual Modem menu item.

 Rick: From a technical support perspective, Visual Modem is helpful when you are asked to provide modem information to someone on the other end of the phone. If you hear some mumbling about setting a register, you'll appreciate this software.

For those occasions when you prefer to send individual modem commands to the modem, Visual Modem also is equipped with a Build-A-Command feature. With this feature, you can scroll through the entire command library and select any combination that you want, building the command string as you go. Visual Modem also enables you to save your configured settings to a file at any time.

Installation

To get rolling with Visual Modem, simply go into Windows and run the program Setup.exe from the Run option within the program manager. This will install Visual Modem on your system.

When you enter Visual Modem, you are at the main menu from which you may either open a previously saved Visual Modem settings configuration file or simply configure a new settings file from the default values provided at startup. As shown in Figure 3.1, you set up the basic configuration settings here. The three items you'll deal with are the communications port the modem is connected to, the length of time you want to wait until you get a response from the modem after sending a command, and the option to tell Visual Modem to display the commands that are returned (you should always select this option as a fail-safe review point).

In addition, a full help system is ready to assist you at any point. Clicking on the help button gets you into the help system. Figure 3.2 shows an example screen. As you can see, some real work was put into this and it shows.

Features

After the initial screen (shown in Figure 3.1), you are dropped off at the main screen, and nothing much happens until you select an item from the menu bar. Several options are available to you (File, Configure, Modem, and Help), and each item is discussed in the following section.

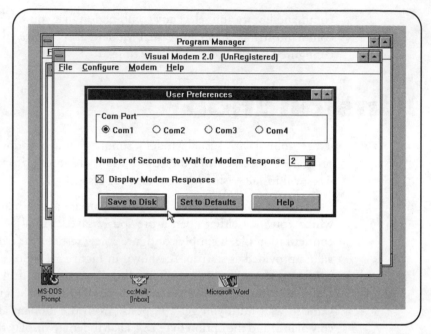

Figure 3.1. The user configuration screen.

The File Menu Option

The New file command immediately resets all current settings to their default values. This command also indicates that you want Visual Modem to disregard any configuration file you may have been building at the time. In order to save your current settings, you need to use the Save As... menu option to establish a new filename. Thereafter, use the Save menu option to save any updates. Any subsequent use of the New file menu option again resets all the current settings.

Note: The resetting of default values that occurs when the New file menu option is selected occurs only in the computer's memory. No settings are altered in the modem's memory or NRAM.

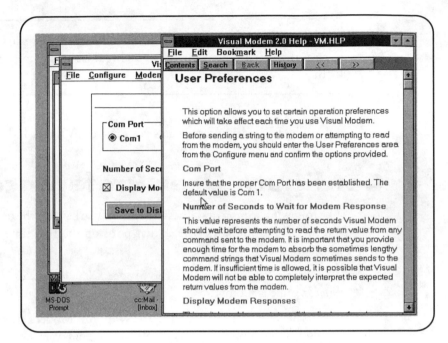

Figure 3.2. A sample help screen.

The Open option enables you to select any existing Visual Modem configuration files that you may have created and saved previously. Opening a file does not send the configuration settings contained in that file to the modem. It only loads those values into the computer's memory. To actually set the values contained in the opened file to the modem, you need to use the Send Current String to Modem or Write Settings to NRAM option from the Modem file menu. In this way, you can browse the existing settings for any Visual Modem-saved settings file without altering your modem's current settings.

The Save option saves the current settings in the file designated at the time the Save As... file menu option is selected. This option is available only after the file has already been saved at least once during the current Visual Modem session.

The Save As... option enables you to save all of the current Visual Modem settings in a file that you can then reload into Visual Modem at a later date using the Open file menu command. You are given a dialog box in which to specify the name of the file you wish to save.

Note: Regardless of the file extension you specify, Visual Modem uses the ".VM" extension when saving the settings configuration file.

The Exit option terminates your current Visual Modem program.

Configure User Preferences

The following section describes the options you have on the user preference screen. This is the same screen that pops up the first time you run the program.

Com Port ensures that the proper Com Port is established. The default value is Com 1.

The Number of Seconds to Wait for Modem Response value represents the number of seconds Visual Modem waits before attempting to read the return value from any command sent to the modem. It's important that you provide enough time for the modem to absorb the sometimes lengthy command strings that Visual Modem occasionally sends to the modem. If insufficient time is allowed, it's possible that Visual Modem won't be able to completely interpret the expected return values from the modem.

The Display Modem Responses switch enables you to turn off the display of modem commands sent and received from the modem. Although it's quite informative to be able to see exactly what is transpiring between you and your modem, turning off this option makes interaction much faster.

The bulk of Visual Modem's functionality is found in the Modem Menu Commands. The main set of menu options is shown in Figure 3.3, and all of these items are discussed below.

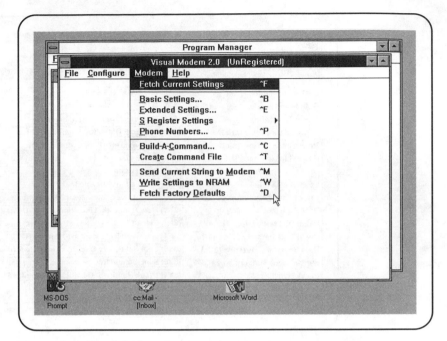

Figure 3.3. The Modem menu options.

To retrieve the settings currently contained in your modem and place them into Visual Modem for inspection and subsequent alteration (Fetch Current Settings):

1. Select Modem from the main window menu.

2. From the Modem menu, select Fetch Current Settings.

The Basic Settings option provides you with a simple and accurate means to alter your modem's current basic settings. By scrolling through the various list boxes, you can alter the current basic subsequent write to your modem or a file, or you may cancel any changes made during the dialog. You may also set the values to factory default specifications.

John: You really need to bring up every screen in this system to fully appreciate this software. Figures 3.4 and 3.5 are just two of the screens that are chock-full of information. Cool stuff, eh?

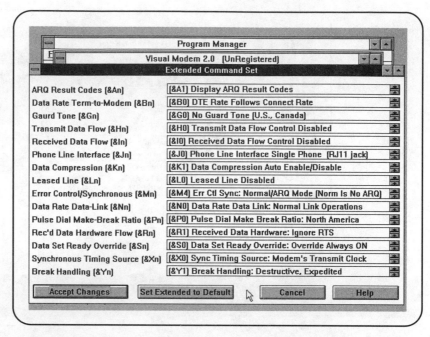

Figure 3.4. The Extended Command Set options window.

The Extended Settings option provides you with a simple and accurate means to alter your modem's current extended settings. By scrolling through the various list boxes, you can alter the current extended settings options in any combination. You may either save the settings for subsequent write to your modem or a file, or you may cancel any changes made during the dialog. You may also set the values to factory default specifications.

S Register Settings are a set of memory areas in your modem that contain values which tell the modem how to operate under certain conditions. Most of the registers contain values ranging from 0 to 255. A few of the registers are bitmapped (that is, their values are set by combining several values together, resulting in a single value). The S Register settings are spread across several screens. Each screen is accessible from the other.

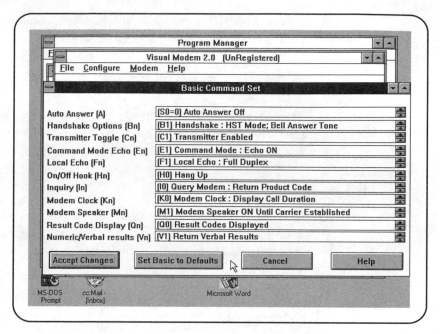

Figure 3.5. The Basic Command Set options window.

The following S Register screens are provided:

S Registers 0 through 12: From this screen you can alter the current S register values, set the values to their factory defaults, or access other S Register screens. Alteration of the S Register values does not take effect until you Send Current String to Modem or Write Settings to NRAM.

S Register 13: From this screen you can alter the current S register values, set the values to their factory defaults, or access other S Register screens. Alteration of the S Register values does not take effect until you Send Current String to Modem or Write Settings to NRAM.

S Register 15: From this screen you can alter the current S register values, set the values to their factory defaults, or access other S Register screens. Alteration of the S Register values does not take effect until you Send Current String to Modem or Write Settings to NRAM.

S Registers 19 through 38: From this screen you can alter the current S register values, set the values to their factory defaults, or access other S Register screens. Alteration of the S Register values does not take effect until you Send Current String to Modem or Write Settings to NRAM.

Phone Numbers: Your modem can store up to four phone numbers in its NRAM. With this screen, you can browse the numbers currently stored and change any or all of the numbers.

Usage

The Build-A-Command dialog enables you to send any combination of commands to the modem. This feature is especially helpful for trouble-shooting and for users who have nonstandard, non-USRHST modems.

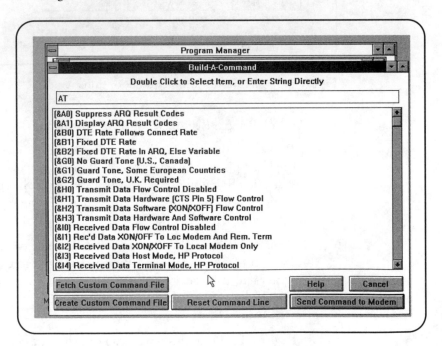

Figure 3.6. The Build-A-Command option window.

To build a command, double-click on the list box selection of the command you wish to send to the modem. The list box contains all of the allowable commands. Any item you double-click is automatically appended to the starting command string of "AT".

Since the USRHST maximum length allowable for a command line is 40 characters (including the AT prefix), Visual Modem automatically detects and informs you when that limit has been reached. Some other modems may allow less, so check your modem manual in the section that talks about command strings. Visual Modem also detects and informs you of any attempt to add a command that is already a part of the existing command string.

A special feature of Visual Modem is its ability to retrieve custom modem commands saved to disk with the Create Command File function and display those custom commands for use in the Build-A-Command dialog. If you haven't created a custom modem command file, you may do so by invoking the Create Command File option from this dialog.

Rick: This comes in handy if you have to set modems up for different command packages manually. For example, I use a program called TAPCIS, and it is great except that I like the modem to be in a certain state just prior to running it. While I can use an option in TAPCIS, this program allows me to walk through and, in plain English, set up a decent command string so I know exactly what I am doing. This also allows me to talk in plain English to the technical-support person if I have to walk through the modem commands.

The command string that you build is not sent to the modem until you select the "Send Command to Modem" button located in the bottom-left area of the dialog box. When you select this option, the entire command string that you have built is sent to the modem and the modem response is displayed for you. The command line is left intact after being sent to the modem.

You may reset the command line at any time to its original value of "AT" by selecting the "Reset Command Line" button in the bottom-middle area of the dialog box. This resets the command line without sending the existing command line to the modem.

If you created a file with custom modem commands using the Create Command File function, you can retrieve the commands contained in the file and display them for use by the Build-A-Command dialog with the Fetch Custom Command File.

If you need to create additional modem commands not contained in the Build-A-Command list, you can use the Create Custom Command File option to create and store the commands to disk. This feature is particularly useful for those with non-USRHST modems that may not recognize the modem commands contained in Visual Modem.

When you wish to send the whole of the various configuration options to the modem (Basic Settings, Extended Settings, and so on), use the Send Current String to Modem option to send each of the commands to the modem, thus updating the modem's current setting memory with the new values.

> **Caution**: The modem's current settings memory is lost when the modem is turned off. To save the current settings from power-off to power-on, you must use the Write Settings to NRAM option.

The Write Settings to NRAM option writes the current Visual Modem settings to your modem's NRAM memory. This enables you to save the modem's settings even after the modem is turned off.

At any time, you can fetch the factory defaults into your modem (and into Visual Modem as well) with the following procedure:

1. Select Modem from the main window menu.

2. From the Modem menu, select Fetch Factory Defaults.

Visual Modem Procedures

The following section explains how to carry out various procedures using Visual Modem.

Save Current Modem Settings to Disk

You can save the modem settings that you create and alter in Visual Modem by storing them in a file. To save the settings to disk:

1. Select File from the main window menu.

2. From the File menu, select Save or Save As....

3. Specify the filename under which you wish to save the current settings.

    If you are saving the file for the first time, select the Save As... menu option from the File menu. Otherwise, just use the Save option.

> **Note**: Regardless of the file extension you provide to the Save dialog, Visual Modem always uses a ".VM" extension.

Retrieve Previously Saved Modem Settings

Once you have saved settings to disk, you can retrieve those settings back into Visual Modem and subsequently send the settings to your modem. To retrieve a settings file from disk:

1. Select File from the main window menu.

2. From the File menu, select Open.

3. Specify the file you wish to retrieve into Visual Modem.

Fetch Current Modem Settings into Visual Modem

This option loads the current settings of your modem into Visual Modem. The current settings area of your modem's memory is not saved each time the modem is turned off. To save the settings of your modem between power-off and power-on, you must write the settings to your modem's NRAM.

Fortunately, with Visual Modem you can store several different settings configurations in the form of a file that can be reloaded at a later date and sent to the modem. In this way you can quickly, easily, and accurately configure your modem to fit individual calling needs.

Send Customized Command String to Modem

Visual Modem enables you to create a custom string to send to the modem. When you are presented with a list box of all available commands, simply click on the commands you wish to send to the modem and the appropriate command string is built. To build and send your own command strings:

1. Select Modem from the main window menu.

2. From the Modem Menu, select Build-A-Command.

Create Customized Modem Command File

The Create Command File option enables you to create and maintain your own set of custom modem commands. This feature is particularly useful for those with modems other than USRHST-type modems.

With this ability, you can still invoke the Build-A-Command dialog to send individual commands to the modem. Create Command File enables you to build any number of modem commands, save the commands to disk, retrieve a previously created custom command file, and delete existing commands from an existing command file. The functions available from this dialog box are:

- Add: Use this command to add the custom command you've just built to the command listing. Visual Modem checks to ensure that you made a valid entry in the command field and that the command is not already in the command listing.

- Delete: Use this command to delete any selected item from the custom command listing. When you've selected the items you wish to delete, click on the delete button to remove those items.

Note: The deleted items are not actually deleted from the custom command file until you save the new listing with the Save File option.

- Get File: Use this option to retrieve a previously saved Custom Command File. Custom Command Files are denoted with the extension of ".VMC". Once you've selected the file and it's been read into the Create Command File dialog, the filename that you selected is displayed in the upper-left corner of the screen.

- Save File: This option enables you to save to disk the custom commands you've entered or changed.

Note: Regardless of the extension you assign to the filename to save, Visual Modem always assigns a ".VMC" extension to all Custom Command Files.

- Clear Current Commands: With this option, you can immediately erase the custom commands listed in the display area.

Note: The commands erased in the display area are not erased from any existing disk file. To delete a Custom Command File, you must use the DOS delete command.

- Build-A-Command: This option takes you directly to the Build-A-Command dialog, from which you may either build commands based on the USRHST commands contained in the Build-A-Command list box or retrieve any of the custom command files you build in the Create Command File function.

- Send Current Settings to Modem: When you are satisfied with the settings within Visual Modem, you can send the entire settings string to the modem with the following procedure:

1. Select Modem from the main window menu.

2. From the Modem menu, select Send Current String to Modem.

Note: This option sends the current settings to your modem's memory, not to your modem's NRAM. To send the settings to your modem's NRAM, use the Write Settings to NRAM option from the Modem Menu.

- Write Current VM Settings to Modem's NRAM: When you're satisfied with the settings within Visual Modem, you can send the entire settings string to your modem's NRAM with the following procedure:

1. Select Modem from the main window menu.

2. From the Modem menu, select Write Settings to NRAM.

- Fetch Factory Settings into VM and Your Modem: This option enables you to recall the factory default configuration settings into your modem's current setting memory. It does not, however, fetch the settings into your modem's NRAM. The factory settings are lost when you turn off your modem unless you Write Settings to NRAM after loading the factory defaults.

- Define Visual Modem Startup Parameters: You can define and alter the startup parameters that Visual Modem uses each time the program is invoked using the following procedure (such items as Com Port and display options are configurable by you):

  1. Select Configure from the main window menu.

  2. Select User Preferences from the Configure menu.

> **Note:** Visual Modem stores your startup parameters in a file called "VM.PRF".

- Inhibit Display of Modem Response in VM: To increase performance and reduce distraction, you can turn off the modem responses received by Visual Modem that are displayed on the screen by selecting Configure from the main window menu. At this point, the User Preferences Screen comes up.

Keyboard Hot Keys

A number of hot keys are available for you to use to go directly to the screen or function you wish. Hot keys are invoked by pressing Control and the appropriate corresponding keyboard letter simultaneously. The following hot keys are available:

^A   About Visual Modem

^B   Basic Settings

^C   Build-A-Command

^D	Defaults
^E	Extended Settings
^F	Fetch Current Settings
F1	Can be pressed at any time to obtain HELP
^I	Visual Modem Registration Information
^M	Send Current String to Modem
^N	New File
^O	Open File
^P	Phone Numbers
^R	Register Visual Modem
^S	Save As...
^T	Create Command File
^U	User Preferences
^V	Save File
^W	Write Settings to NRAM
^X	Exit Program

Summary

This excellent piece of software is brought to you by:

Mark Findlay
8717 31st Ave N.W.
Seattle, WA 98117.

For full registration information, click on the Help menu item and select the Registration option.

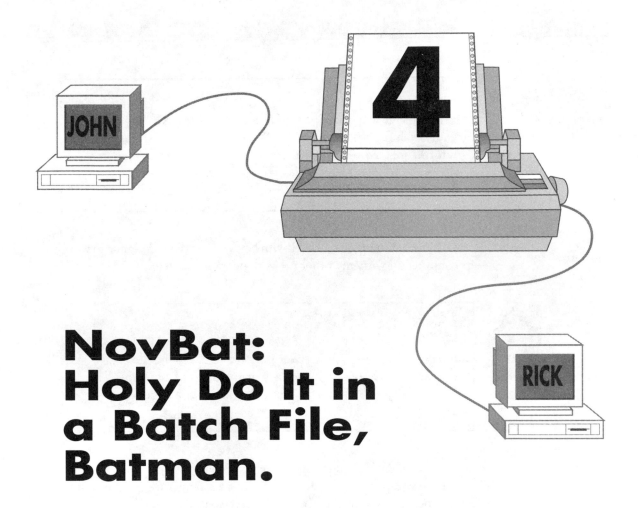

NovBat:
Holy Do It in
a Batch File,
Batman.

D esigned by Horizons Consulting's Phil Case, NovBat is a unique set of tools for the Novell Network. These tools enable you to gain some control over your Novell Network from within a batch file.

Case developed NovBat in the fall of 1991 from his NetWare experience and what he felt was a surprising lack of support available from batch files. After he saw several statements from other NetWare users to that effect on Novell's NetWire forum, being a take-action kind of guy, Phil decided to do something about it. He then crafted an easy method of allowing batch files to ask NetWare for information about the operating environment.

Note: Although you can execute NovBat from the DOS command line, it was developed for use in batch files. NovBat allows your batch files to query the NetWare operating system for information. You can use the results of these queries to modify a user's environment, an application configuration, or whatever your environment requires.

NovBat is designed to work with NetWare. It is not designed to work in conjunction with any other network operating system.

John: NovBat is not compatible with NetWare Lite, which is the limited peer-to-peer connectivity product from Novell. At the time of this writing, Novell has not offered developers access to the NetWare Lite internals, which are required in order to give Phil and guys like him (and me) a shot at making compatible products.

NovBat enables you to ask Novell NetWare for specific information about many aspects of the network. This data ranges from information about the user, group memberships, servers, and network addresses to local, hardware-specific information. With NovBat, you can develop network intelligent batch files. In many instances, using NovBat saves time and effort.

Rick: If you can think of a command or something else you want to see in this product, give Phil and the Horizons team a call. They're interested in ensuring that NovBat is a package that network users want to use.

Usage

Using NovBat is a snap. This tool has 47 commands that address a specific type of query from NetWare. Many of these commands have command-line parameters that enable you to be quite specific.

The NovBat commands are divided into two groups: ERRORLEVEL and ENVIRONMENT. The first group is called ERRORLEVEL because these commands return an ERRORLEVEL status code to your batch file. The second group is called the ENVIRONMENT group because these commands place their results into the environment space for later reference by either your batch files or other applications.

The ERRORLEVEL commands all return a standard set of ERRORLEVEL codes. When a given NovBat query is processed, there are three possible ERRORLEVEL codes: 1 for True, 0 for False, and 255 for Error Condition. These are the only ERRORLEVEL codes that NovBat generates.

In addition to placing their results into the environment area, the Novbat ENVIRONMENT commands exit with an ERRORLEVEL code of 0 unless an error occurred, in which case an ERRORLEVEL of 255 is generated.

Because both groups of commands always return an ERRORLEVEL code of 255 in the event of problems, you should design your batch files to trap an ERRORLEVEL 255. Some errors are important enough for NovBat to display its own error messages in addition to returning the 255 error code.

The ENVIRONMENT commands normally place their results into an environment variable called NOVBAT=, but you can override this default and specify your own environment variable by simply adding the name of the desired environment variable as an extra parameter at the end of any NovBat ENVIRONMENT command. The legal syntax for using NovBat is:

```
NOVBAT command [parameter1] [parameter2]
```

in which command is one of the legal NovBat commands. The parameter elements of a command vary according to which command is used. Some commands do not need any parameters; in some cases parameters are required and at other times they are optional. No more than two parameters are ever required. NovBat commands and parameters are not case sensitive; that is, the expressions "NOVBAT SizeOfGroup everyone" and "NOVBAT sizeofgroup EVERYONE" are considered as the same command.

John: You can generate a list of all the NovBat commands at any time by typing NOVBAT /? or NOVBAT HELP.

Although most of the commands that make up NovBat are Novell NetWare specific, a few are not. These commands provide information about such things as your DOS version, memory sizes and usage, video type, processor, and other system-specific parameters (see Table 4.1).

Table 4.1. Command summary.

Command	Parameter(s)	Return Type
DoesGroupExist?	<Group>	ERRORLEVEL
DoesGroupHave-Member?	<Group> <UserName>	ERRORLEVEL
DoesUserExist?	<UserName>	ERRORLEVEL
IsAttached?	<ServerName>	ERRORLEVEL
IsDefaultServer?	<ServerName>	ERRORLEVEL
IsCPU?	<8088, 286, 386, 486>	ERRORLEVEL
IsDOSVer?	<DosVer> {Less the <.>}	ERRORLEVEL
IsDosVerSince?	<DosVer> {Less the <.>}	ERRORLEVEL
IsFreeEMS@Least?	<Number> {Expressed in K}	ERRORLEVEL

IsFreeRAM@Least?	<Number> {Expressed in K}	ERRORLEVEL
IsFullName?	<FullUserName>	ERRORLEVEL
IsMailID?	<MailIDCode>	ERRORLEVEL
IsMaxUsers?	<Number>	ERRORLEVEL
IsMessageMode?	<ALL, SERVER, or NONE>	ERRORLEVEL
IsNetNum?	<Number>	ERRORLEVEL
IsNetWareVer?	<Number> {Less the <.>}	ERRORLEVEL
IsNodeNum?	<Number>	ERRORLEVEL
IsPrimaryServer?	<ServerName>	ERRORLEVEL
IsSecurityEquiv?	<Group/User>	ERRORLEVEL
IsStationAddress?	<Number>	ERRORLEVEL
IsTotalEMS@Least?	<Number> {Expressed in k}	ERRORLEVEL
IsTotalRAM@Least?	<Number> {Expressed in k}	ERRORLEVEL
IsUserDuplicated?	<UserName>	ERRORLEVEL
IsUserLoggedIn?	<UserName>	ERRORLEVEL
IsUserName?	<UserName>	ERRORLEVEL
IsUsers@Least?	<Number>	ERRORLEVEL
IsVideo?	<MGA, CGA, MCGA, EGA, VGA,or PGA>	ERRORLEVEL
SetCPU	= No Parameters =	ENVIRONMENT
SetDefaultServer	= No Parameters =	ENVIRONMENT
SetDOSVer	= No Parameters =	ENVIRONMENT
SetFreeEMS	= No Parameters =	ENVIRONMENT
SetFreeRAM	= No Parameters =	ENVIRONMENT
SetFullName	= No Parameters =	ENVIRONMENT

continues

Table 4.1. continued

Command	Parameter(s)	Return Type
SetMailID	= No Parameters =	ENVIRONMENT
SetMaxUsers	= No Parameters =	ENVIRONMENT
SetMessageMode	= No Parameters =	ENVIRONMENT
SetNetNum	= No Parameters =	ENVIRONMENT
SetNetWareVer	= No Parameters =	ENVIRONMENT
SetNodeNum	= No Parameters =	ENVIRONMENT
SetNumberLog-ged In	= No Parameters =	ENVIRONMENT
SetPrimaryServer	= No Parameters =	ENVIRONMENT
SetSizeOfGroup	<Group>	ENVIRONMENT
SetStationAddress	= No Parameters =	ENVIRONMENT
SetTotalEMS	= No Parameters =	ENVIRONMENT
SetTotalRAM	= No Parameters =	ENVIRONMENT
SetUserName	= No Parameters =	ENVIRONMENT
SetVideo	= No Parameters =	ENVIRONMENT

Features

DoesGroupExist?

Function: Verifies the existence of a specified NetWare group

Syntax: NOVBAT DoesGroupExist? NameOfGroup

Response Type: ERRORLEVEL (Codes: 1=True, 0=False, 255=Error)

Remarks: Sometimes it's useful to verify the existence of a given Group, and the DoesGroupExist command accomplishes this. You must be logged into the server to use this command.

See Also: DoesGroupHaveMember?, SetSizeOfGroup

Example:

```
:Start
    @ECHO OFF
    NOVBAT DoesGroupExist? %1
    IF ErrorLevel 255 GOTO Error
    IF ErrorLevel 1 GOTO GotGroup
:NoGroup
    ECHO sorry, Group does not exist.
    GOTO End
:GotGroup
    ECHO yes, that Group does exist.
    GOTO End
:Error
    ECHO you got a problem here. Try logging in first!
:End
```

DoesGroupHaveMember?

Function: Verifies that a user is a member of a specified group

Syntax: NOVBAT DoesGroupHaveMember? NameOfGroup NameOfUser

Response Type: ERRORLEVEL (Codes: 1=True, 0=False, 255=Error)

Remarks: This command has one required and one optional parameter. The first parameter, NameOfGroup, is required and should be a valid group name. The second parameter, NameOfUser, is optional. If absent, NOVBAT assumes the current user as the name to look up. You must be logged in to use this command.

See Also: DoesGroupExist?, SetSizeOfGroup

Example:

```
:Start
     @ECHO OFF
     NOVBAT DoesGroupHaveMember? ACCOUNTING %name%
     IF ErrorLevel 255 GOTO Error
     IF ErrorLevel 1 GOTO IsMember
:NotMember
     ECHO only accounting Dept. can access this function!
     GOTO End
:IsMember
     ECHO ACCOUNTING ACCESS GRANTED.
     map k:=f:\ACCOUNTING
     GOTO End
:Error
     ECHO sorry, but you are not logged in I'm Afraid!
:End
```

DoesUserExist?

Function: Verifies that a given name has a user account

Syntax: NOVBAT DoesUserExist? NameOfUser

Response Type: ERRORLEVEL (Codes: 1=True, 0=False, 255=Error)

Remarks: This command verifies the existence of a given user. The parameter NameOfUser is required. The user you are searching for does not need to be logged in; however, you must be logged in to use this command.

See Also: IsUserLoggedIn?, IsUserDuplicated?

Example:

```
:Start
     @ECHO OFF
     NOVBAT DoesUserExist? %1
     IF ErrorLevel 255 GOTO Error
     IF ErrorLevel 1 GOTO Exists
:NotExist
     ECHO sorry, but no user by that name on this net.
```

```
     GOTO End
:Exists
     ECHO yes, that user has an account.
     GOTO End
:Error
     ECHO sorry, but you are not logged in I'm Afraid!
:End
```

IsAttached?

Function: Verifies that a user is attached to a specific server

Syntax: NOVBAT IsAttached? ServerName

Response Type: ERRORLEVEL (Codes: 1=True, 0=False, 255=Error)

Remarks: Being "attached" to a file server does not mean that a user is logged into that server. The IsAttached? command indicates if a user is attached to any given server name. The ServerName parameter is required and is not case sensitive. You do not need to be logged into the server you are checking, but you do need to have IPX and your Net Shell loaded to avoid an error.

Rick: This one has some value in that being attached to a server is good information to know if you are launching a program that has specific server attachment requirements.

See Also: IsDefaultServer?, IsPrimaryServer?, SetDefaultServer, SetPrimaryServer

Example:

```
:Start
     @ECHO OFF
     NOVBAT IsAttached? ACCOUNTING
     IF ErrorLevel 255 GOTO Error
     IF ErrorLevel 1 GOTO FoundAccounting
```

```
:NoAccounting
     ECHO you are not attached to the ACCOUNTING server.
     GOTO End
:FoundAccounting
     ECHO you are attached to the ACCOUNTING server.
     GOTO End
:Error
     ECHO ERROR: try loading your IPX & Net Shell!
:End
```

IsCPU?

Function: This command confirms your processor type

Syntax: NOVBAT IsCPU? CPUName

Response Type: ERRORLEVEL (Codes: 1=True, 0=False, 255=Error)

Remarks: In some instances, it's useful to confirm a user's processor type. For example, you might want to install QuarterDeck's QEMM memory manager on all the 386 systems on the network. The IsCPU? command returns a true response only when the CPUName parameter matches the CPU type of the system. The legal options for CPUName are 8088, 286, 386, and 486. Any other string generates an error result code. If you're using a V20, 8086, or other clone-type XT processor, it's interpreted as an 8088. The CPUName parameter is required. (Note that this command does not require NetWare and can be used in a non-network environment.)

See Also: SetCPU

Example:

```
:Start
     @ECHO OFF
     NOVBAT IsCPU? 386
     IF ErrorLevel 1 GOTO GoQEMM
     NOVBAT IsCPU? 486
     IF ErrorLevel 1 GOTO GoQEMM
```

```
:NoQEMM
     GOTO End
:GOQEMM
     CALL GOQEMM.BAT
:End
```

IsDefaultServer?

Function: This command verifies your default server

Syntax: NOVBAT IsDefaultServer? ServerName

Response Type: ERRORLEVEL (Codes: 1=True, 0=False, 255=Error)

Remarks: Sometimes it's useful to confirm that your default server is a specific server. This is especially important in a multiserver environment. The use of the IsDefaultServer? command makes this possible. The ServerName parameter is required.

See Also: IsAttached?, IsPrimaryServer?, SetDefaultServer, SetPrimaryServer

Example:

```
:Start
     @ECHO OFF
     NOVBAT IsDefaultServer? ENGINEERING
     IF ErrorLevel 255 GOTO Error
     IF ErrorLevel 1 GOTO Confirmed
:NotConfirmed
     ECHO ENGINEERING isn't your current default server.
     GOTO End
:Confirmed
     ECHO yes, ENGINEERING is your current default server.
     GOTO End
:Error
     ECHO ERROR: try loading your IPX & Net Shell!
:End
```

IsDOSVer?

Function: Verifies your DOS version number

Syntax: NOVBAT IsDOSVer? VersionNum

Response Type: ERRORLEVEL (Codes: 1=True, 0=False, 255=Error)

Remarks: If you operate in an environment that supports multiple versions of DOS, it may be useful to verify your DOS version. The IsDOSVer? command does this. The VersionNum parameter requires that the version number be expressed without use of the period. For example, if you are testing for DOS 3.30 then you must express VersionNum as 330. This command returns True only when you have an exact match on the DOS version number. (Note that this command does not require NetWare and can be used in a non-network environment.)

Rick: Remember that working in a multiversion of DOS world is a pain in the royal rump because it is one more variable to deal with when troubleshooting. All versions should be the same if possible.

John: Right, from the Microsoft guy. Send him the check. Okay, he has a point.

See Also: IsDOSVerSince?, SetDOSVer

Example:

```
:Start
    @ECHO OFF
    NOVBAT IsDOSVer? 401
    IF ErrorLevel 255 GOTO Error
    IF ErrorLevel 1 GOTO Running401
```

```
:Opps
     ECHO sorry, you need DOS 4.01 for this option.
     GOTO End
:Running401
     ECHO DOS 4.01 Confirmed. Please hold for access.
     ; access to application goes here!
     GOTO End
:Error
     ECHO ERROR: Illegal parameter syntax!
:End
```

IsDOSVerSince?

Function: Confirms DOS version is as recent as specified version

Syntax: NOVBAT IsDOSVerSince? VersionNum

Response Type: ERRORLEVEL (Codes: 1=True, 0=False, 255=Error)

Remarks: Some applications require that your version of DOS be at least as recent as a specific version. In a multi-DOS environment, it's sometimes important to ensure that a user is running a version of DOS that is at least as new as a specified version. The VersionNum parameter requires that the period be dropped (see the IsDOSVer? command). This command returns True if the current version of DOS is equal to or newer than the specified version. (Note that this command does not require NetWare and can be used in a non-network environment.)

See Also: IsDOSVer?, SetDOSVer

Example:

```
:Start
     @ECHO OFF
     NOVBAT IsDOSVerSince? 300
     IF ErrorLevel 255 GOTO Error
     IF ErrorLevel 1 GOTO AtLeast3
:NotRightDos
     ECHO sorry, you need DOS 3.00 or newer for this option.
     GOTO End
```

```
:AtLeast3
     ECHO DOS 3.00 or newer confirmed, hold for access.
     ; access to application goes here!
     GOTO End
:Error
     ECHO ERROR: illegal parameter syntax!
:End
```

IsFreeEMS@Least?

Function: This command confirms the amount of available EMS RAM

Syntax: NOVBAT IsFreeEMS@Least? NumberOfK

Response Type: ERRORLEVEL (Codes: 1=True, 0=False, 255=Error)

Remarks: Because some applications need to use EMS memory, it's useful to ensure that enough EMS RAM is currently available for certain programs. This command returns True if the amount of available EMS RAM is at least equal to the NumberOfK parameter.

> **John:** This command does not require NetWare and can be used in a non-network environment. You can use it before running applications that have specific EMS requirements.

See Also: IsTotalEMS@Least?, SetFreeEMS, SetTotalEMS

Example:

```
:Start
     @ECHO OFF
     NOVBAT IsFreeEMS@Least? 145
     IF ErrorLevel 255 GOTO Error
     IF ErrorLevel 1 GOTO GotEMS
:NotEnoughEMS
     ECHO Sorry, you need more EMS memory to use SwapSK.
     GOTO End
```

```
:GotEMS
     ECHO Sufficient EMS confirmed, hold for SWAPSK.
SwapSK ;Puts Sidekick into EMS memory! GOTO End
:Error
     ECHO ERROR: illegal parameter syntax!
:End
```

IsFreeRAM@Least?

Function: This command confirms the amount of unused system RAM

Syntax: NOVBAT IsFreeRAM@Least? NumberOfK

Response Type: ERRORLEVEL (Codes: 1=True, 0=False, 255=Error)

Remarks: With heavy use of TSR programs, sometimes the amount of unused system RAM is inadequate for larger programs to function properly. The IsFreeRAM@Least? command verifies that sufficient RAM is available before you execute a given application. This command returns True if the amount of unused RAM is at least equal to the NumberOfK parameter.

John: Like the EMS command, this one can also be used in normal operations. Attaboy, Phil!

See Also: IsTotalRAM@Least?, SetFreeRAM, SetTotalRAM

Example:

```
:Start
     @ECHO OFF
     NOVBAT IsFreeRAM@Least? 512
     IF ErrorLevel 255 GOTO Error
     IF ErrorLevel 1 GOTO GotRAM
:NotEnoughRAM
     ECHO not enough memory, try unloading some TSRs!
     GOTO End
```

```
:GotRAM
     ECHO Loading... please wait..
     BigProgram.exe ;Execute Application
     GOTO End
:Error
     ECHO ERROR: illegal parameter syntax!
:End
```

IsFullName?

Function: This command verifies your full Novell user name

Syntax: NOVBAT IsFullName? FullNameString [UserName]

Response Type: ERRORLEVEL (Codes: 1=True, 0=False, 255=Error)

Remarks: This command verifies the full name of any user. There are two possible parameters for this command. The first parameter, FullNameString, is required and is the full Novell name of a user as defined by SYSCON. The second parameter is optional and specifies which user to check the full name against; if absent, then the current user <Self> is assumed. When specifying the full name, replace any embedded spaces with the underline ("_") character. For example the name "George Bush" is expressed as "George_Bush". This command returns True only if the full name compared is an exact match. The name compare is not case sensitive.

See Also: SetFullName

Example:

```
:Start
NOVBAT IsFullName? "George_Herbert_Walker_Bush"
     IF ErrorLevel 255 GOTO Error
     IF ErrorLevel 1 GOTO Confirmed
:NotThePresident
     ECHO Access restricted to the President's Eyes Only!
     GOTO End
:Confirmed
     ECHO Thank you Mr. President.
     PORKBARL.EXE ;Execute Application
     GOTO End
```

```
:Error
     ECHO ERROR: illegal parameter syntax!
:End
```

IsMailID?

Function: This command verifies your Novell Mail User ID

Syntax: NOVBAT IsMailID? MailIDString UserName

Response Type: ERRORLEVEL (Codes: 1=True, 0=False, 255=Error)

Remarks: This command verifies the Novell Mail ID of any user. The two possible parameters for this command are MailIDString, which is required and is the actual Mail ID of a user, and the second parameter, which is optional, specifies which user to check the Mail ID String against. If absent, then this user <Self> is assumed. This command returns true only if the MailID string compare is an exact match. The name compare is not case sensitive.

See Also: SetMailID

Example:

```
:Start
     NOVBAT IsMailID? 1
     IF ErrorLevel 255 GOTO Error
     IF ErrorLevel 1 GOTO Confirmed
:NotTheSupervisor
     ECHO sorry, Supervisor Access Only!
     GOTO End
:Confirmed
     SYSCON.EXE ;Execute Application
     GOTO End
:Error
     ECHO ERROR: illegal parameter syntax!
:End
```

IsMaxUsers?

Function: Verifies maximum number of users allowed by NetWare

Syntax: NOVBAT IsMaxUsers? Number

Response Type: ERRORLEVEL (Codes: 1=True, 0=False, 255=Error)

Remarks: This command enables you to determine the maximum number of users your version of NetWare concurrently supports. NetWare is sold in versions that support a wide number of users. With this NovBat command you can conveniently check this limit. The Number parameter is required.

See Also: IsUsers@Least?, SetMaxUsers, SetUsersLoggedIn

Example:

```
:Start
     NOVBAT IsMaxUsers? 250
     IF ErrorLevel 1 GOTO WayToGo
     NOVBAT IsMaxUsers? 100
     IF ErrorLevel 1 GOTO NotBad
:CouldBeBetter
     ECHO next time get a bigger network!
     GOTO End
:WayToGo
     ECHO all right! Now that's real power!
     GOTO End
:NotBad
     ECHO looks like a pretty good situation.
:End
```

IsMessageMode?

Function: Verifies your current Message Receive Mode

Syntax: NOVBAT IsMessageMode? ModeType

Response Type: ERRORLEVEL (Codes: 1=True, 0=False, 255=Error)

Remarks: The NetWare SEND command enables users to send messages to each other and gives receiving users the ability to block incoming messages. The IsMessageMode? command verifies which receive mode you are in. The modes are ALL, where all messages are displayed, SERVER, where only server messages are accepted, and NONE, where no messages are accepted. The ModeType parameter must be set to either ALL, SERVER, or NONE.

See Also: SetMessageMode

Example:

```
:Start
     @ECHO OFF
     NOVBAT IsMessageMode? ALL
     IF ErrorLevel 1 GOTO ModeAll
     NOVBAT IsMessageMode? SERVER
     IF ErrorLevel 1 GOTO ModeServer
:ModeNone
     ECHO no messages are currently being accepted.
     GOTO End
:ModeAll
     ECHO All messages are being accepted.
     GOTO End
:ModeServer
     ECHO Only SERVER messages are being accepted.
     GOTO End
:End
```

IsNetNum?

Function: Verifies which network number you are connected to

Syntax: NOVBAT IsNetNum? Number

Response Type: ERRORLEVEL (Codes: 1=True, 0=False, 255=Error)

Remarks: The IsNetNum? command verifies the network number you are connected to. Many large companies have multiple networks with a common backbone. In this environment, you might want to restrict users to accessing certain functions from some networks and not others. The Number parameter must be from 1 to 255.

Rick: This feature is valuable, for example, if you wanted to restrict someone from running an application on a particular segment, but not lock them out from the network as a whole.

See Also: IsNodeNum?, IsStationAddress?, SetNetNum, SetNodeNum, SetStationAddress

Example:

```
:Start
    @ECHO OFF
    NOVBAT IsNetNum? 254
    IF ErrorLevel 255 GOTO Error
    IF ErrorLevel 1 GOTO HomeNet
:NotOnHomeNet
    ECHO please return to your home net for this option.
    GOTO End
:HomeNet
    EMAIL
    GOTO End
:Error
    ECHO ERROR: try logging in first.
:End
```

IsNetWareVer?

Function: Verifies your Novell NetWare version number

Syntax: NOVBAT IsNetWareVer? VersionNum

Response Type: ERRORLEVEL (Codes: 1=True, 0=False, 255=Error)

Remarks: In a large multi-LAN environment, it's possible to be attached to several servers with multiple versions of Novell NetWare. At times it might be convenient to verify which version of NetWare you are currently using. The IsNetWareVer? command does this. Please note that the VersionNum parameter is a NetWare version number expressed without any periods. For example, NetWare 3.11 is expressed as 311.

See Also: SetNetWareVer

Example:

```
:Start
    @ECHO OFF
    NOVBAT IsNetWareVer? 311
    IF ErrorLevel 1 GOTO Best
    NOVBAT IsNetWareVer? 215
    IF ErrorLevel 1 GOTO Better
:ModeOK
    ECHO Running NetWare.
    GOTO End
:Better
    ECHO Running NetWare 2.15.
    GOTO End
:Best
    ECHO Running NetWare 386 Ver 3.11.
:End
```

IsNodeNum?

Function: This command verifies your station's node number

Syntax: NOVBAT IsNodeNum? Number

Response Type: ERRORLEVEL (Codes: 1=True, 0=False, 255=Error)

Remarks: For security reasons, there may be times when you want to verify that a user is logged into a specific workstation. The IsNodeNum? command provides you with a mechanism to accomplish this. The Number parameter is the node number to test. Please note that the Number parameter is a hexadecimal number, not a decimal.

See Also: IsNetNum?, IsStationAddress?, SetNetNum, SetNodeNum, SetStationAddress

Example:

```
:Start
    @ECHO OFF
    NOVBAT IsNodeNum? 15
```

```
        IF ErrorLevel 255 GOTO Error
        IF ErrorLevel 1 GOTO HomeStation
:NotAtHome
        ECHO you must be at YOUR workstation to access EMAIL.
        GOTO End
:HomeStation
        EMAIL.EXE ;Access Application
        GOTO End
:Error
        ECHO ERROR: invalid Parameter.
:End
```

IsPrimaryServer?

Function: This command verifies the name of your primary server

Syntax: NOVBAT IsPrimaryServer? ServerName

Response Type: ERRORLEVEL (Codes: 1=True, 0=False, 255=Error)

Remarks: In larger multiserver corporations, some users access several file servers in a single operating session. It's useful to be able to verify that their primary server is the expected server. The required ServerName parameter is the Name string of the server to test; if absent, an error results.

See Also: IsAttached?,   IsDefaultServer?,   SetDefaultServer, SetPrimaryServer

Example:

```
:Start
        @ECHO OFF
        NOVBAT IsPrimaryServer? HORIZONS
        IF ErrorLevel 255 GOTO Error
        IF ErrorLevel 1 GOTO OnHorizons
:NotHorizons
        ECHO primary Server isn't HORIZONS. Please correct.
        GOTO End
:OnHorizons
        ECHO thank you. You are on server: HORIZONS.
        GOTO End
```

```
:Error
    ECHO ERROR: invalid Parameter(s)!
:End
```

IsSecurityEquiv?

Function: This command compares your security equivalences

Syntax: NOVBAT IsSecurityEquiv? GroupOrUser UserName

Response Type: ERRORLEVEL (Codes: 1=True, 0=False, 255=Error)

Remarks: It may be useful to verify that a user has a particular security equivalence. You might want only supervisor-equivalent users to have a menu option to run SYSCON, for example. This command enables you to verify if a user is equivalent to another user or a group. This command has one required parameter, GroupOrUser, and one optional parameter, UserName. If the UserName parameter is missing, NovBat assumes the current user <Self>.

See Also: None

Example:

```
:Start
    @ECHO OFF
    NOVBAT IsSecurityEquiv? Supervisor %1
    IF ErrorLevel 255 GOTO Error
    IF ErrorLevel 1 GOTO GoSup
:NotSup
    ECHO no, that user is not Supervisor Equivalent.
    GOTO End
:GoSup
    ECHO yes, that user is Supervisor Equivalent.
    GOTO End
:Error
    ECHO ERROR: are you logged in?
:End
```

IsStationAddress?

Function: This command verifies your computer's station address

Syntax: NOVBAT IsStationAddress? AddressString

Response Type: ERRORLEVEL (Codes: 1=True, 0=False, 255=Error)

Remarks: The IsStationAddress? command verifies your workstation's address against the address specified in the parameter AddressString. The syntax for this required parameter is Network number:Node number. The Node number portion of the argument must be expressed as a hexadecimal number. For example, if you are connected to Network number 250 and your Node number is 100 decimal, then the proper syntax for AddressString is 250:64.

See Also: IsNetNum?, IsNodeNum?, SetNetNum, SetNodeNum, SetStationAddress

Example:

```
:Start
    @ECHO OFF
    NOVBAT IsStationAddress? 254:5
    IF ErrorLevel 255 GOTO Error
    IF ErrorLevel 1 GOTO AtHome
:NotAtHome
    ECHO please return to your desk before using EMAIL.
    GOTO End
:AtHome
    EMAIL.EXE ;Execute Application
    GOTO End
:Error
    ECHO ERROR: please Login before sending EMAIL!
:End
```

IsTotalEMS@Least?

Function: Confirms the amount of workstation EMS RAM

Syntax: NOVBAT IsTotalEMS@Least? NumberOfK

Response Type: ERRORLEVEL (Codes: 1=True, 0=False, 255=Error)

Remarks: Because some applications can take advantage of EMS memory, it's useful to verify if a given workstation contains enough EMS to execute certain applications. This command returns True if the amount of EMS RAM installed is at least equal to the NumberOfK parameter. This command does not ensure that the EMS memory is currently unused by other applications.

John: Like other memory commands, this does not require NetWare and can be used in a non-network environment.

See Also: IsFreeEMS@Least?, SetFreeEMS, SetTotalEMS

Example:

```
:Start
    @ECHO OFF
    NOVBAT IsTotalEMS@Least? 1
    IF ErrorLevel 255 GOTO Error
    IF ErrorLevel 1 GOTO GotEMS
:NoEMS
    ECHO sorry, you need EMS memory to use this program.
    GOTO End
:GotEMS
    ECHO EMS Memory Present, please hold.
    EMSAPP.EXE ;Application requiring EMS
    GOTO End
:Error
    ECHO ERROR: illegal parameter syntax!
:End
```

IsTotalRAM@Least?

Function: Confirms the amount of system RAM

Syntax: NOVBAT IsTotalRAM@Least? NumberOfK

Response Type: ERRORLEVEL (Codes: 1=True, 0=False, 255=Error)

Remarks: Because some applications require large amounts of system RAM, it's useful to verify if a given workstation has enough RAM before attempting to execute these programs. The IsTotalRAM@Least? command returns True if the amount of system RAM installed is at least equal to the NumberOfK parameter. This command does not ensure the system RAM is currently unused by other applications.

See Also: IsFreeRAM@Least?, SetFreeRAM, SetTotalRAM

Example:

```
:Start
     @ECHO OFF
     NOVBAT IsTotalRAM@Least? 512
     IF ErrorLevel 255 GOTO Error
     IF ErrorLevel 1 GOTO GotLotsOfRam
:NotEnoughRam
     ECHO you need at least 512k of RAM for this program.
     GOTO End
:GotLotsOfRam
BIGPRGM.EXE ;App requiring at least 512k of RAM.
     GOTO End
:Error
     ECHO ERROR: illegal parameter syntax!
:End
```

IsUserDuplicated?

Function: Indicates if a user is logged into more than one station

Syntax: NOVBAT IsUserDuplicated? UserName

Response Type: ERRORLEVEL (Codes: 1=True, 0=False, 255=Error)

Remarks: You can use this command to restrict users from logging into multiple workstations without first logging off their previous systems. The security risks associated with a user leaving workstations logged in is obvious. The UserName parameter is optional, but if present should be a valid user name. If absent the current user <Self> is assumed. This command returns True if the user in question is currently logged into two or more workstations.

Example:

```
    ; Portion of a possible login Script
    NOVBAT SetUserName Name
    NOVBAT IsUserDuplicated? %Name%
    IF ErrorLevel 255 GOTO Error
    IF ErrorLevel 1 GOTO TwoMany
:AllsFine
    GOTO ExitScript
:TwoMany
    ECHO sorry, already logged into another computer.
    ECHO you must logoff the previous system before logging
    ECHO into this system.
    GOTO ExitScript
:Error
    ECHO NOVBAT Error: report it to system supervisor!
:ExitScript
```

IsUserLoggedIn?

Function: Indicates if a particular user is currently logged in

Syntax: NOVBAT IsUserLoggedIn? UserName

Response Type: ERRORLEVEL (Codes: 1=True, 0=False, 255=Error)

Remarks: This command determines if the user indicated by the UserName parameter is currently logged into the network. If this parameter is missing, the current user <Self> is assumed.

See Also: IsUserDuplicated?

Example:

```
:Start
    @ECHO OFF
    NOVBAT IsUserLoggedIn? %1
    IF ErrorLevel 255 GOTO Error
    IF ErrorLevel 1 GOTO YesGotUser
```

```
:NoUserIsNotOnLine
    ECHO sorry, that user is not available at this time.
    GOTO End
:YesGotUser
    send %1 %2
    GOTO End
:Error
    ECHO Error: you must be logged in to use this command.
:End
```

IsUserName?

Function: This command verifies your user name

Syntax: NOVBAT IsUserName? UserName

Response Type: ERRORLEVEL (Codes: 1=True, 0=False, 255=Error)

Remarks: The UserName parameter is required. This command returns True only if the user name of the current user and the parameter are an exact match. The name compare is not case sensitive.

See Also: SetUserName

Example:

```
:Start
    @ECHO OFF
    NOVBAT IsUserName? FAX
    IF ErrorLevel 255 GOTO Error
    IF ErrorLevel 1 GOTO IsFax
:NotFax
    ECHO sorry, this program can be executed only by the
    ECHO automatic Fax server.
    GOTO End
:IsFax
    FAXPURGE.EXE ;Application Goes Here
    GOTO End
:Error
    ECHO NovBat Error: report it to system supervisor!
:End
```

IsUsers@Least?

Function: Confirms number of users currently logged into network

Syntax: NOVBAT IsUsers@Least? Number

Response Type: ERRORLEVEL (Codes: 1=True, 0=False, 255=Error)

Remarks: This command confirms that the number of users logged in to the network is above a minimum threshold. By starting with a larger threshold and working down, network usage can be categorized. This condition returns True whenever the number of users logged in to the network is at least equal to the Number parameter.

See Also: SetUsersLoggedIn

Example:

```
:Start
     NOVBAT IsUsers@Least? 200
     IF ErrorLevel 1 GOTO Heavy
     NOVBAT IsUsers@Least 100
     IF ErrorLevel 1 GOTO Moderate
:Light
     ECHO network usage is currently light. (< 100 Users)
     GOTO End
:Heavy
     ECHO network usage is heavy. ( 200 and >)
     GOTO End
:Moderate
     ECHO network usage is moderate. (100-200 Users)
     GOTO End
:End
```

IsVideo?

Function: This command verifies your graphics adapter type

Syntax: NOVBAT IsVideo? VideoType

Response Type: ERRORLEVEL (Codes: 1=True, 0=False, 255=Error)

Remarks: Because different workstations on the network have varying display adapters, it's useful to determine which adapter type a particular system has for the purpose of selecting the correct software drivers for that system. This command compares the adapter type to the current system, returning true if there is a match. The legal options for the VideoType parameter are MGA or HERC, CGA, MCGA, EGA, VGA, and PGA. Any other string generates an error.

> **Rick:** So John doesn't get all the glory, I'll point out that you can use this command on stand-alone or non-network machines.

See Also: SetVideo

Example:

```
:Start
    @ECHO OFF
    NOVBAT IsVideo? MGA
    IF ErrorLevel 255 GOTO Error
    IF ErrorLevel 1 GOTO Mono
:Color
SPREADC.EXE ;Color Configured Version of Program.
    GOTO End
:Mono
SPREADM.EXE ;Mono Configured Version of Program.
    GOTO End
:Error
    ECHO NovBat Error: illegal parameter!
:End
```

SetCPU

Function: Sets an environment variable to the type of CPU

Syntax: NOVBAT SetCPU [VarName]

Response Type: ENVIRONMENT

Remarks: This command stores your processor type into the specified environment variable. The possible result strings are 8088, 286, 386, and 486. (Note that this command does not require NetWare and can be used in a non-network environment.)

See Also: IsCPU?

Example:

```
:Start
    @ECHO OFF
    NOVBAT SetCPU CPU
    IF ErrorLevel 255 GOTO Error
    NOVBAT SetName
    IF ErrorLevel 255 GOTO Error
    ECHO ---------------------------------------------
    ECHO User: %NovBat% - Using a %CPU%.
    ECHO ---------------------------------------------
    set CPU=
    set NovBat=
    GOTO End
:Error
    ECHO NovBat Error: alert your system supervisor!
:End
```

SetDefaultServer

Function: Sets environment variable to name of default server

Syntax: NOVBAT SetDefaultServer [VarName]

Response Type: ENVIRONMENT

Remarks: This command reads the name of your default server and places it into an environment variable called NOVBAT unless you have specified the optional VarName parameter, in which case the variable name matches the parameter. Sufficient environment space must be available to avoid an error. If enough environment space is not available, NovBat displays a warning indicating so and aborts the command without attempting to write the new data into the environment. Any previous data in the environment with the same name is lost.

See Also: IsDefaultServer?, IsPrimaryServer?, SetPrimaryServer

Example:

```
:Start
     NOVBAT SetUserName Name
     IF ErrorLevel 255 GOTO Error
     NOVBAT SetDefaultServer
     IF ErrorLevel 255 GOTO Error
     ECHO ----------------------
     ECHO User: %Name% - Attached to server: %NovBat%.
ECHO ----------------------
     set Name=
     set NovBat=
     GOTO End
:Error
     ECHO NovBat Error: alert your system supervisor!
:End
```

SetDOSVer

Function: Sets environment variable to current DOS version number

Syntax: NOVBAT SetDOSVer [VarName]

Response Type: ENVIRONMENT

Remarks: This command places your current DOS version number into an environment variable. Note that the period in the version number is dropped. If your DOS is version 5.00, then the environment variable is set to 500. (Note that this command does not require NetWare and can be used in a non-network environment.)

See Also: IsDOSVer?, IsDOSVerSince?

Example:

```
:Start
     @ECHO OFF
     NOVBAT SetDosVer
     IF ErrorLevel 255 GOTO Error
     ECHO -----------------------------------
```

```
        ECHO you are using DOS Version %NovBat%.
        ECHO --------------------------------------
        set NovBat=
        GOTO End
:Error
        ECHO NovBat Error: alert your system supervisor!
:End
```

SetFreeEMS

Function: Sets environment variable to amount of unused EMS RAM

Syntax: NOVBAT SetFreeEMS [VarName]

Response Type: ENVIRONMENT

Remarks: This command determines how much unused K of EMS RAM exists in the workstation and sets an environment variable accordingly.

See Also: IsFreeEMS@Least?, IsTotalEMS@Least?, SetTotalEMS

Example:

```
:Start
        @ECHO OFF
        NOVBAT SetFreeEMS EMSAVAIL
        NOVBAT SetTotalEMS EMSTOTAL
        NOVBAT SetFreeRAM RAMAVAIL
        NOVBAT SetTotalRAM RAMTOTAL
        ECHO ----] Memory Summary [----
        ECHO EMS: %EMSTOTAL%, Avail: %EMSAVAIL%.
        ECHO RAM: %RAMTOTAL%, Avail: %RAMTOTAL%.
        ECHO ------------------------
        set EMSAVAIL=
        set EMSTOTAL=
        set RAMAVAIL=
        set RAMTOTAL=
:End
```

SetFreeRAM

Function: Sets environment variable to amount of unused RAM

Syntax: NOVBAT SetFreeRAM [VarName]

Response Type: ENVIRONMENT

Remarks: This command determines how much unused K of system RAM exists in the workstation and sets an environment variable accordingly. This command does not require NetWare and can be used in a non-network environment.

See Also: IsFreeRAM@Least?, IsTotalRAM@Least?, SetTotalRAM

Example:

```
:Start
    @ECHO OFF
    NOVBAT SetFreeEMS EMSAVAIL
    NOVBAT SetTotalEMS EMSTOTAL
    NOVBAT SetFreeRAM RAMAVAIL
    NOVBAT SetTotalRAM RAMTOTAL
    ECHO -----] Memory Summary [-----
    ECHO EMS: %EMSTOTAL%, Avail: %EMSAVAIL%.
    ECHO RAM: %RAMTOTAL%, Avail: %RAMTOTAL%.
    ECHO ----------------------------
    set EMSAVAIL=
    set EMSTOTAL=
    set RAMAVAIL=
    set RAMTOTAL=
:End
```

SetFullName

Function: Sets environment variable to full NetWare user name

Syntax: NOVBAT SetFullName [VarName]

Response Type: ENVIRONMENT

Remarks: This command sets an environment variable to the full user name. Please note that all embedded spaces are converted to the underline

"_" character. For example, the full name "Christopher M. Columbus" is converted to "CHRISTOPHER_M._COLUMBUS".

See Also: IsFullName?, SetUserName

Example:

```
:Start
     @ECHO OFF
     NOVBAT SetFullName FNAME
     IF ErrorLevel 255 GOTO Error
     ECHO ------------------------------------------------
     ECHO Your Full UserName is: %FNAME%.
     ECHO ------------------------------------------------
     set FNAME=
     GOTO End
:Error
     ECHO ------------------------------------------------
     ECHO NovBat ERROR: alert your Lan Administrator!
     ECHO ------------------------------------------------
:End
```

SetMailID

Function: Sets environment variable to your user mail ID

Syntax: NOVBAT SetMailID [VarName]

Response Type: ENVIRONMENT

Remarks: When NetWare first creates a user account, the system assigns a mail ID code. A subdirectory of the \MAIL directory is created for this user, with the same name as this mail ID. Many software packages take advantage of this unique directory provision of NetWare to make user specific temporary files. By using the SetMailID command, you can take advantage of this feature of NetWare in your batch files and login scripts. This command generates an environment variable set to the unique user mail ID of the current user.

See Also: IsMailID?

Example:

```
:Start
    @ECHO OFF
    NOVBAT SetUserName Name
    IF ErrorLevel 255 GOTO Error
    NOVBAT SetMailID Mail
    IF ErrorLevel 255 GOTO Error
map L: = \mail\%Mail% ;Drive L for temporary files.
    ECHO User %Name%'s Mail ID Code is: %Mail%.
    set Mail=
    set Name=
     GOTO End
:Error
    ECHO NovBat ERROR: please check your login status!
:End
```

SetMaxUsers

Function: Sets environment variable to maximum number of users NetWare allows

Syntax: NOVBAT SetMaxUsers [VarName]

Response Type: ENVIRONMENT

Remarks: Because Novell NetWare is sold in versions that vary in the number of concurrent users they permit, it's sometimes useful to know which size you are using. The SetMaxUsers command creates an environment variable that contains the maximum number of concurrent users which your version of NetWare permits.

See Also: IsMaxUsers?, IsUsers@Least?, SetNumberLoggedIn

Example:

```
:Start
    @ECHO OFF
    NOVBAT SetNumberLoggedIn Now
    IF ErrorLevel 255 GOTO Error
    NOVBAT SetMaxUsers Max
    IF ErrorLevel 255 GOTO Error
```

```
        ECHO ----] NetWare Usage Summary [-----
        ECHO Max Allowed Users: %Max%, Now Logged In: %Now%
        ECHO -------------------------------------------------
        GOTO End
:Error
        ECHO ------------------------------------------
        ECHO NOVBAT ERROR: please check your syntax.
        ECHO ------------------------------------------
:End
```

SetMessageMode

Function: Sets environment variable to message receive mode

Syntax: NOVBAT SetMessageMode [VarName]

Response Type: ENVIRONMENT

Remarks: The NetWare SEND command enables users to send messages to others and to block incoming messages. The SetMessageMode command sets an environment variable to the message receive mode that the user is currently in. The modes are ALL, in which all messages are displayed, SERVER, in which only messages generated by a file server are accepted, and NONE, in which all messages are blocked.

See Also: IsMessageMode?

Example:

```
:Start
     NOVBAT SetMessageMode Mode
     IF ErrorLevel 255 GOTO Error
     IF %Mode%==ALL GOTO All
     IF %Mode%==SERVER GOTO Server
     ECHO ALL MESSAGES BLOCKED AT THIS TIME!
     GOTO End
:All
     ECHO ALL MESSAGES ARE BEING RECEIVED.
     GOTO End
```

```
:Server
     ECHO ONLY SERVER MESSAGES ARE BEING RECEIVED
     GOTO End
:Error
     ECHO NovBat ERROR: alert your System Administrator.
:End
```

SetNetNum

Function: Sets environment variable to your network number

Syntax: NOVBAT SetNetNum [VarName]

Response Type: ENVIRONMENT

Remarks: The SetNetNum command creates an environment variable set to the network number to which you are connected. Many large companies have multiple networks with connections between them. In such an environment, you might want to restrict users to accessing certain functions from some networks and not others.

See Also: IsNetNum?, IsNodeNum?, IsStationAddress?, SetNodeNum, SetStationAddress

Example:

```
:Start
     @ECHO OFF
     NOVBAT SetNetNum Net
     IF ErrorLevel 255 GOTO Error
     IF %Net%=250 GOTO Sales
:NotOnSalesNet
     ECHO sorry, access to this area is restricted to
     ECHO workstations that are attached to the sales net!
     GOTO End
:Sales
     ECHO access approved.
     SALES.EXE ;Application goes here
     GOTO End
:Error
     ECHO NovBat Error: alert the system administrator!
:End
```

SetNetWareVer

Function: Sets environment variable to NetWare version number

Syntax: NOVBAT SetNetWareVer [VarName]

Response Type: ENVIRONMENT

Remarks: In a large multi-LAN environment, it's possible to be attached to several servers with multiple versions of Novell NetWare. At times, it's useful to record the version number of NetWare you are currently using. The SetNetWareVer command stores your NetWare version number in an environment variable.

> **John:** The format for the version number is expressed without periods. Therefore, if you're using NetWare 3.11, the variable is set to 311.

See Also: IsNetWareVer?

Example:

```
REM selecting a software package based on NetWare Version.
:Start
     @ECHO OFF
     NOVBAT SetNetWareVer NWVER
     IF %NWVER% = 311 GOTO Mail1
     IF %NWVER% = 215 GOTO Mail2 :Mail3
EMAIL ;Older EMAIL SYSTEM GOTO End
:Mail1
     EMAIL311 ;Email System for NW version 3.11
     GOTO End
:Mail2
     EMAIL215 ;Email System for NW version 2.15
:End
```

SetNodeNum

Function: Sets environment variable to station's node number

Syntax: NOVBAT SetNodeNum [VarName]

Response Type: ENVIRONMENT

Remarks: The SetNodeNum command creates an environment variable set to the node number to which you are connected. This is useful for many network functions. By integrating this environment variable into paths and file specs, you can develop common login and application batch files that perform uniquely for multiple users. While you do not need to be logged in to use this command, you do need to have your Net Shell loaded.

See Also: IsNetNum?, IsNodeNum?, IsStationAddress?, SetNetNum, SetStationAddress

Example:

```
:Start
     @ECHO OFF
     NOVBAT SetNodeNum Node
IF %Node% = 2B GOTO VOICEMAIL ;station-2B is voicemail
IF %Node% = A4 GOTO FAXSYSTEM ;station-A4 a Fax Server
:NormalUser
     LOGIN
     GOTO End
:VOICEMAIL
     LOGIN VOICEMAIL
     GOTO End
:FAXSYSTEM
     LOGIN FAX
:End
```

SetNumberLoggedIn

Function: Sets environment variable to number of logged-in users

Syntax: NOVBAT SetNumberLoggedIn [VarName]

Response Type: ENVIRONMENT

Remarks: In some environments, it's preferable to keep some tasks from occurring during periods of heavy network usage. The SetNumberLoggedIn command returns an environment variable set to the number of users currently logged in to a server. This enables the system administrator to delay execution of a given task until use is below a given threshold. This command could also be used to log usage on an ongoing basis.

See Also: IsUsersLoggedIn?, SetMaxUsers

Example:

```
:Start
     @ECHO OFF
     NOVBAT SetNunberLoggedIn USERS
     IF ErrorLevel 255 GOTO Error
     NOVBAT SetMaxUsers Max
     IF ErrorLevel 255 GOTO Error
     ECHO ----------------
     ECHO Currently %Users% logged in, Maximum is %Max%!
     ECHO ----------------
GOTO End
:Error
     ECHO NovBat ERROR: inform your system administrator!
:End
     SET Users=
     SET Max=
```

SetPrimaryServer

Function: Sets an environment variable to Primary Server Name

Syntax: NOVBAT SetPrimaryServer [VarName]

Response Type: ENVIRONMENT

Remarks: This command reads the name of your primary server and places it into an environment variable called NOVBAT unless you have specified the optional VarName parameter, in which case the variable name matches the parameter. Sufficient environment space must be available to avoid an error. If enough environment space is not available, NovBat displays a warning indicating so and aborts the command without attempting to write the new data into the environment. Any previous data in the environment with the same name is lost.

153

See Also: IsDefaultServer?, IsPrimaryServer?, SetDefaultServer

Example:

```
:Start
     NOVBAT SetUserName Name
     IF ErrorLevel 255 GOTO Error
     NOVBAT SetPrimaryServer
     IF ErrorLevel 255 GOTO Error
     ECHO -----------------------------------------
     ECHO User: %Name% - Primary Server: %NovBat%.
     ECHO -----------------------------------------
     set Name=
     set NovBat=
     GOTO End
:Error
     ECHO NovBat Error: alert your system supervisor!
:End
```

SetSizeOfGroup

Function: Sets environment variable to number of group members

Syntax: NOVBAT SetSizeOfGroup GroupName [VarName]

Response Type: ENVIRONMENT

Remarks: This command reads the number of members of the group GroupName and places this number into the environment variable indicated by VarName. This function can be easily used as a meter for information about department sizes, workgroup management, and so on. You don't need to be a member of the group that you are checking.

See Also: DoesGroupExist?

Example:

```
:START
     @ECHO OFF
NOVBAT SetSizeOfGroup Everyone
NOVBAT SetSizeOfGroup SALES Sales
NOVBAT SetSizeOfGroup PRODUCTION Prod
NOVBAT SetSizeOfGroup SHIPPING Ship
```

```
NOVBAT SetSizeOfGroup ENGINEERING Engin
      ECHO ------------------------
      ECHO current size of various departments:
      ECHO ------------------------
      ECHO SALES:      %Sales%
      ECHO PRODUCTION:    %Prod%
      ECHO SHIPPING:  %Ship%
      ECHO ENGINEERING:   %Engin%
      ECHO -----------------------------------------------
      ECHO TOTAL:     %NovBat%
      ECHO -----------------------------------------------
:End
```

SetStationAddress

Function: Sets environment variable to network station address

Syntax: NOVBAT SetStationAddress [VarName]

Response Type: ENVIRONMENT

Remarks: This command returns the user's station address as an environment string. The syntax for the station address is StationNum:NodeNum. The StationNum portion of the result is returned in decimal and the NodeNum portion of the address is returned in hexadecimal. For example, if the user's workstation is node number 200 (decimal) on network number 250, then the result returned by the SetStationAddress command is 250:C8.

See Also: IsNetNum?, IsNodeNum?, IsStationAddress?, SetNetNum, SetNodeNum

Example:

```
:Start
      @ECHO OFF
      NOVBAT SetStationAddress Addr
      IF ErrorLevel 255 GOTO Error
      NOVBAT SetUserName Name
      IF ErrorLevel 255 GOTO Error
      ECHO -----------------------------------------------
      ECHO you are user %Name%, currently logged into
```

```
        ECHO workstation %Addr%.
        ECHO ------------------------------------------------
        GOTO End
:Error
        ECHO NovBat Error: alert your system supervisor!
:End
```

SetTotalEMS

Function: Sets environment variable to total amount of EMS RAM

Syntax: NOVBAT SetTotalEMS [VarName]

Response Type: ENVIRONMENT

Remarks: This command determines how much K of EMS memory exists in the workstation and accordingly sets an environment variable. This does not imply that all of this EMS is available; use SetFreeEMS to determine this.

> **John:** This command does not require NetWare and can be used in a non-network environment. Use it prior to running an application that requires a certain amount of EMS. Since you are reading this, check out a game called Wolfenstein 3D from ID software. It is shareware and you can get a copy from CompuServe or by calling 1-800-GAME123. Why mention it here? Hey, all work and no play? Never.

See Also: IsFreeEMS@Least?, IsTotalEMS@Least?, SetFreeEMS

Example:

```
:Start
    @ECHO OFF
    NOVBAT SetFreeEMS EMSAVAIL
    NOVBAT SetTotalEMS EMSTOTAL
    NOVBAT SetFreeRAM RAMAVAIL
    NOVBAT SetTotalRAM RAMTOTAL
```

```
    ECHO ----] Memory Summary [----
    ECHO EMS: %EMSTOTAL%, Avail: %EMSAVAIL%.
    ECHO RAM: %RAMTOTAL%, Avail: %RAMTOTAL%.
    ECHO --------------------------------
    set EMSAVAIL=
    set EMSTOTAL=
    set RAMAVAIL=
    set RAMTOTAL=
:End
```

SetTotalRAM

Function: Sets environment variable to total amount of DOS RAM

Syntax: NOVBAT SetTotalRAM [VarName]

Response Type: ENVIRONMENT

Remarks: This command determines how much system RAM (expressed in K) exists in the workstation and accordingly sets an environment variable. This does not imply that all of this memory is unused and available; use the SetFreeRAM command to determine this.

See Also: IsFreeRAM@Least?, IsTotalRAM@Least?, SetFreeRAM

Example:

```
:Start
    @ECHO OFF
    NOVBAT SetFreeEMS EMSAVAIL
    NOVBAT SetTotalEMS EMSTOTAL
    NOVBAT SetFreeRAM RAMAVAIL
    NOVBAT SetTotalRAM RAMTOTAL
    ECHO ----] Memory Summary [----
    ECHO EMS: %EMSTOTAL%, Avail: %EMSAVAIL%.
    ECHO RAM: %RAMTOTAL%, Avail: %RAMTOTAL%.
    ECHO -----------------------
    set EMSAVAIL=
    set EMSTOTAL=
    set RAMAVAIL=
    set RAMTOTAL=
:End
```

SetUserName

Function: Sets environment variable to your NetWare user name

Syntax: NOVBAT SetUserName [VarName]

Response Type: ENVIRONMENT

Remarks: This command simply reads the user's name into an environment variable. Once in the environment, this information may be used for many purposes. By incorporating this variable into batch files, you can have applications automatically route output or temporary files into a user's home directory, where they won't conflict with other users.

See Also: IsUserName?

Example:

```
:Start  ;Assumed to be part of a login
     @ECHO OFF ;batch file.
     NOVBAT SetUserName Name
:End
     rem * HOME.BAT - takes user to home directory *
     rem this batch file assumes the user name will be found
     rem in an environment variable called "NAME".
:Start
     @ECHO OFF
     F:
     cd \home\%name%
:End
```

SetVideo

Function: Sets environment variable to graphics adapter type

Syntax: NOVBAT SetVideo [VarName]

Response Type: ENVIRONMENT

Remarks: Because workstations have different display adapters, it's useful to store information on the adapter a system has in order to select the correct software drivers for that system. This command stores the name of the adapter into the specified environment variable. The possible result strings are MGA or HERC, CGA, MCGA, EGA, VGA, and PGA. (Note that this command does not require NetWare and can be used in a non-network environment.)

See Also: IsVideo?

Example:

```
:Start ;Assumed to be part of a login
     @ECHO OFF ;batch file.
     NOVBAT SetVideo Vid
:End
     rem * SPRDSHET.BAT - uses VID var to enter a spreadsheet *
     rem batch file assumes users video adapter will be found
     rem in an environment variable named "VID".
:Start
     @ECHO OFF
     F:
     cd \PUBLIC\APPS\SPREAD\%Vid%
     SPRDSHET
:END
```

Summary

As you can see, Mr. Case did a great job in providing you with some commands to use in your everyday batch files. Good work, Phil. For more information on the commercial version of this and other slick Horizons Consulting applications:

Horizons Consulting
1432 E. Commercial Street
Springfield, Missouri 65803
(417) 839-2174
Fax: (417) 831-1329
BBS: (417) 831-9140

IdleBoot:
Knock,
Knock,
Anything
Going On?

I n the summer of 1991, while catching up with all the message traffic on the Novell Forums on CompuServe, Phil Case and the Horizons Consulting gang noticed a frequently recurring network complaint. In a nutshell, these laments focused on the great variety of problems caused by users who remained logged on to the network when they were not using their machines. The nature of these complaints varied widely, ranging from security violations to bottlenecks created by large numbers of files left open to maintenance problems experienced during backup operations.

After considering these problems for a while, Horizon developed IdleBoot, a terminate-and-stay-resident (TSR) program developed in assembly language that requires less than 2K of system RAM. Its two primary functions are to logoff and reboot network workstations that don't need to be operating, and to reset unattended machines to ensure that they are operating correctly. Once installed on a computer, IdleBoot monitors the computer to check for system inactivity. If the system is inactive, it starts a timer and after a given number of minutes sounds an inactivity alarm. If there is still no activity following the alarm, IdleBoot logs the workstation off the network and reboots the system.

Rick: Originally designed as a security tool for networks, IdleBoot's uses have grown to be far more than Horizon ever expected. Many BBS and corporate dial-up systems use it to determine when a system is locked up and needs to be reset. Voice-mail systems, fax-modem receivers, data collection systems, and even information kiosks in shopping malls use IdleBoot. A whole second niche developed from companies and individuals who use IdleBoot to ensure that their unattended systems are kept running normally. The moral of this story is that there are still programmers who start with the basics. Listen to the need and respond to it.

Getting Started

As with any software package, the first step is to make a working copy of the master disk and then store the master in a safe place. The two versions of IdleBoot are a single-user version and a network version. Although the single-user version operates on a network, only one user at a time can have it installed. After you make your working master disk, copy the IDLEBOOT.COM file onto your hard disk in a directory that is available on your search path.

John: Before going further, I strongly suggest that you take a Jolt cola break and read through this chapter before messing with this software. IdleBoot is an extremely powerful utility, but if you set it up wrong it may cause major problems.

Rick: Like everything Horizons does, if you find a special operating requirement that you need IdleBoot to help you with, or if you want technical assistance, please feel free to call Horizons Consulting. They are great folks.

How IdleBoot Works

A small, but powerful, program, IdleBoot meshes tightly with DOS and can monitor what the computers on your network are doing—such various things as keyboard, video, file, or printer activity. It can also monitor COM ports for activity or simply a carrier detect. It knows when files are left open as well as many other items central to defining system activity, and you can specify which of these activities you want IdleBoot to monitor.

You can direct IdleBoot to monitor only one aspect of your system or everything at once. By monitoring these system functions, IdleBoot also knows when activity is not occurring. You can specify just how long you are willing to let your system sit "idle." If nothing happens on the system for your time limit, IdleBoot takes over and forces your system to reboot. If on a network, you can configure IdleBoot to log off your workstation prior to reboot. This eliminates the risk of having someone walk up to your computer while you are away and access files that you consider private.

John: Before installing IdleBoot, it's necessary to define what you intend to have IdleBoot watch. This process requires a bit of careful planning. If improperly configured, you can create some unhealthy situations. For example, if you install and configure IdleBoot to watch only your COM1 port and ignore all other system activity, and then start an application that does not use the COM1 port, such as a big database sort, IdleBoot views the system as idle. A big database sort opens a lot of files and those files would be in a corruptible state. Because there would be no COM1 activity, the clock would be running. When the idle time was reached, your system would be reset. This could wreak disaster on your files.

IdleBoot is designed to do everything it can to avoid resetting your systems accidentally. Optional audible alarms and an override function are included to give you every opportunity to avoid a system reset when you do not want it. As with all new software, it's very important to thoroughly test a given IdleBoot configuration after installation to ensure that you have accomplished what you intended.

Configuring IdleBoot for Use

Because IdleBoot can monitor a wide variety of functions, you need to tell it which aspects of your system you wish it to monitor. This is done through a series of command-line parameters (or switches). Switch details are coming up, so stay tuned. These switches are specified in the following manner:

```
C:> IDLEBOOT /Switch /Switch...
```

All legal IdleBoot switches start with the "/" character and you can use as many switches as you need. Even though the above example uses spaces between the switches, spaces are not required. You can string all your switches together without any separating spaces, and IdleBoot command-line switches may be used in any order.

Command-Line Switches

The following section is a switch-by-switch description of all the legal IdleBoot switches. Please take the time to sit down at your computer and use these switches to develop a firm understanding of exactly how they function.

The switches used by IdleBoot are divided into two categories: system configuration switches and monitoring specification switches. The system configuration switches set various global operation parameters and the monitoring specification switches indicate precisely what aspects of your system you want to be monitored.

Perhaps the easiest IdleBoot switch to enter is the No Switches option. If you enter the command IDLEBOOT without specifying any switches, IdleBoot does one of two things. If IdleBoot is not installed on your computer, it returns a message indicating this. However, if IdleBoot is installed, it generates a configuration screen showing you exactly how IdleBoot is configured in memory. Typing IDLEBOOT without any switches does not affect any existing configuration. One additional feature exists with the No Switches option in that IdleBoot returns a coded error level value that batch files can read to determine which system functions are currently being monitored.

The Display Help Switch (/?)

The Display Help switch is a breeze because it simply requests a help screen. Although this switch is optional, it can also be used in conjunction with other switches. The help screen associated with this switch simply lists all the legal switches. The same help screen is automatically displayed if any of the switch parameters are not used correctly.

The Force Logoff Switch (/L)

If you are operating on either a Novell or Banyan network and you specify the optional Force Logoff switch, /L, IdleBoot forces a logoff from the network prior to rebooting your computer. Rebooting your workstation without first logging off the network leaves any open files in an open condition. This prevents other users from accessing those files until the file server realizes that you are no longer attached. Because this can take 15 minutes or so, it's preferable to use this switch if you are operating on a network. If you specify this switch and are not operating on a network, no ill effects occur.

The System Halted Switch (/S)

The System Halted switch, /S, is a simple IdleBoot switch. Some programs, if not designed properly, can cause memory related problems. This condition often prompts a "System Halted" error. When this error occurs, the only action available is to turn off the computer and start again. If your computer is running a stand-alone application such as a remote-host dialup or a fax system, you may not want your computer locked up until you return.

This switch monitors the system for a System Halted error event and forces an automatic reboot if one occurs. This switch is optional and, if it is specified, it does not require, but will work in conjunction with, any other legal switches.

> **Note:** If you are running in a network environment, an area of memory that MS-DOS reserves for various special duties, and a System Halted error occurs, your computer is rebooted without a logoff even if the /L switch is specified. This is because a System Halted error indicates that a serious condition exists and DOS can no longer reliably perform any functions. Attempting to perform a network logoff under such a questionable environment risks catastrophic results.

The Idle Time Switch (/Txx)

The /Txx or Idle Time switch is perhaps the most commonly used switch. The format for this switch is /Txx, (xx is the number of minutes a system is allowed to sit idle before IdleBoot takes action). The legal range for xx is from 1 to 99 minutes. Therefore, if you specify /T10, you are indicating that you are allowing your system to be idle for ten minutes prior to a reset. Any monitored system activity that occurs during this time resets the idle timer to zero and the ten-minute idle time starts over again. This switch is required if any monitoring functions are installed.

The /Txx switch is not required if you are monitoring for System Halted errors, or if you are installing IdleBoot only to force a boot at a specific time (the /Bhh:mm:ss option). Failure to specify this switch when you use monitoring switches generates an "INVALID PARAMETERS" message.

The Alarm Time Switch (/Axx)

The /Axx or Alarm Time switch is especially useful. By using this switch, you activate an audible alarm that notifies you when your system is idle. The xx in the /Axx switch specifies the number of minutes you wish this alarm to sound before the reboot is initiated. For example, if the parameters /T10/A02 are used, this means that you want IdleBoot to activate after ten minutes of idleness and you wish to hear the alarm tone two minutes before the reboot, which is eight minutes into the idle period. The alarm tone sounds every seven seconds until the reboot or until the idle condition no longer exists.

The legal range for xx in the /Axx switch is from 1 to the value set in the xx portion of the /Txx (Idle Time) switch. This switch is optional and can be used only in conjunction with monitoring switches. Even when specified, this switch does not activate an alarm in the event of a System Halted reboot or a boot generated from the /B switch.

> **Caution:** Some programs, mainly games, constantly reconfigure the speaker port. If you are operating such a program, it can override the alarm function of IdleBoot.

The Emergency Tone Switch

The /E or Emergency Tone switch is an optional switch that activates a solid emergency tone that starts 11 seconds before an imminent reboot. This tone continues until either the system is rebooted or the system is no longer idle. This switch is subject to the same conditions and limitations as the /Axx switch.

The Boot Time Switch (/Bhh:mm:ss)

The /Bhh:mm:ss or Boot Time switch is straightforward. By specifying a time in a 24-hour format, you can force a system reboot based upon the time of day. This optional switch is equivalent to the older TSRBOOT program. The Boot Time switch works with the /L switch, providing the network user with a logoff before reboot.

> **Note:** Because IdleBoot can be configured with only one reboot time, users who need their system reset at numerous times during the day can use the TSRBOOT program (also available from Horizons Consulting) in conjunction with IdleBoot.

The Disable Switch (/-)

The /- or Disable switch is also a simple option. It disables an IdleBoot already installed in memory. This switch generates an error if IdleBoot is not previously installed. IdleBoot is not removed from memory when this switch is used, it's merely "turned off." To reactivate IdleBoot, simply provide a new command line with the new configuration you want.

If the /- switch is used in conjunction with other switches, it first erases the old configuration, then the new configuration is specified by the other switches on the command line. This switch is optional.

The Uninstall Switch (/U)

The /U or Uninstall switch disables and removes IdleBoot from memory. For this switch to function properly, no other TSR programs can be loaded into memory after IdleBoot. This optional switch generates an error if IdleBoot is not in memory or if it is "trapped" by other TSRs. "Trapped" simply means that IdleBoot is not the last guy in the computer memory "food chain." Remember, if you intend to unload it, load it last.

> **John:** In the event that IdleBoot cannot uninstall, it suspends all operation. This may not get back the memory, but at least it gives you a way to shut down the operation.

The Halt Switch (/H)

The /H or Halt function switch enables the user to disable IdleBoot on-the-fly. This can be very important if for some reason IdleBoot is not correctly configured for the current task or if the user has made a conscious decision to let his system sit idle for a period of time.

Whenever this optional parameter is selected, the hot-key combination of <ALT>-<LEFT SHIFT>-<H> disables IdleBoot. This hot-key combination is carried out by simultaneously pressing these three keys. IdleBoot is still in memory, but no longer functions or monitors your system.

Once this key combination is pressed, IdleBoot remains inactive until it is either given a new set of configuration switches or is reactivated by pressing the <ALT>-<LEFT SHIFT>-<R> key combination. You will hear a two-tone audio response whenever the hot-key combination is pressed. This confirms that IdleBoot has registered your request to suspend system monitoring.

If the /H switch is not specified on the command line, then the Halt and Resume hot-key combinations do not affect IdleBoot's operation. Please note that if either the /S or /Bhh:mm:ss switches are selected and the user places IdleBoot into an inactive mode, IdleBoot does not reboot the system in the event of a system-halted error or at a specified time. Careful thought needs to be given as to whether users should be given the halt function option.

The Debug Mode Switch (/#)

The Debug Mode switch, /#, is used while installing and configuring IdleBoot. There are times when you may configure IdleBoot to look for specific aspects of system activity only to find that IdleBoot is not forcing a system reboot when you think it should. This happens when IdleBoot detects system activity that you don't notice. When Debug Mode is active, IdleBoot displays a series of alphanumeric codes in the upper-right corner of the display to let you know what aspects of system activity are currently being noted. For example, if IdleBoot notices printer activity, IdleBoot displays an uppercase "P" on the screen.

If further printer activity is noticed, the "P" changes to a lowercase "p" and IdleBoot continues to alternate case as long as printer activity is noticed. This feature is helpful for those times when you can't seem to figure out why IdleBoot isn't booting. It should be noted that when the Debug Mode is active, IdleBoot places an activity code on the screen—because this qualifies as video activity, a "V" code appears on the screen shortly after the activity code appears. The "V" code does not reverse case whenever it appears.

If Debug Mode is active and you enter a graphics mode, the debug display codes automatically stop until after you return to a text mode, where debug codes reappear. It's important to note that Debug Mode monitors the system in the same manner that IdleBoot does. That is, once Debug Mode sees activity during a given scan, it stops looking for further activity. This means that if at any given moment keyboard activity is noticed, no further scanning is done. If video activity occurs simultaneously, it isn't noticed until a later scan. This is not an error, it's a design feature.

This "stop looking as soon as possible" feature permits IdleBoot to take up as little processor time as possible. Also note that Debug Display codes are displayed only for the types of system activity that are selected with command switches. Refer to Appendix C for a detailed list of IdleBoot Demo Mode display codes.

The Keyboard Flag Switch (/K)

The /K or Keyboard Flag switch informs IdleBoot that one of the items you want it to monitor is keyboard activity. Whenever any keyboard activity occurs, the idle timer is reset if this flag is specified. You'll probably use this flag in almost every IdleBoot installation.

If you've configured IdleBoot with any of the alarms and you get an idle alarm, probably the easiest way to reset the idle timer is to press one of the passive keys, such as <Shift>, if the /K switch is specified. This is an optional switch.

The Video Flag Switch (/V)

The Video Flag switch /V, specifies that you want IdleBoot to monitor all video activity. When IdleBoot is monitoring video, any changes to the display resets the idle timer. This function works in all video modes (both text and graphics). If you look at the cursor of your DOS prompt you see a blinking "_". This blinking is caused by the attributes assigned to the character. The blinking itself does not constitute video activity. Using ANSI to assign blinking attributes to portions of the screen also does not constitute video activity. The /V switch is strictly optional.

The Printer Switch (/P)

The /P or Printer switch instructs IdleBoot to monitor printer activity. This optional switch watches for any BIOS printer activity that includes activity on PRN and LPT1-LPT4. This function defines printer activity as attempts to print. Therefore, even if your printer is offline and an attempt to print is made, IdleBoot interprets this as printer activity.

The File I/O Switch (/F)

The /F or File I/O Flag switch monitors all file reads and writes. File I/O is monitored at the BIOS, DOS, and network shell level. It's important to note that if you are using a software package that does its own file I/O without going through the operating system, IdleBoot fails to recognize this activity. Fortunately, this is rarely the case. This optional flag handles file I/O to any system devices, hard disks, floppy drives, printers, consoles, and so on.

The Open File Flag Switch (/O)

The Open File Flag switch, /O, is different from the /F mentioned above in that instead of monitoring file-related activity, it simply detects the presence of files left in an open state. This means that if you were in a database application with an open file and you went to lunch without closing the file, this switch notes the open file and prevents an idle boot, regardless of the inactive status of the rest of the system.

John: Because DOS does not make this information available to the user, IdleBoot identifies open files by analyzing the PSP prefix of the current task. This means that IdleBoot recognizes only files that are open for the current task. For example, if you are in a database application with an open file, then shell out to DOS with a new COMMAND.COM and start a new application that has no open files, IdleBoot won't see the file left open by the previous shell. Although this is not a serious limitation, it needs to be mentioned.

Rick: Now that John has poured the techno-stuff, I'll tell you about the practical limitation. You should carefully consider the use of this program on workstations that are starting up one application and frequently shelling out to DOS. It can get tricky. If you're depending on this tool to reboot the PC, you could get unexpected results.

The COM1 Flag Switch (/C1)

The /C1 or COM1 Flag switch is an optional flag that monitors your COM1 port for I/O. This operates independently of the system BIOS because no one really uses BIOS for serial I/O, especially when using modems. It does, of course, monitor any programs that do use BIOS for serial port activity. This optional switch can be used to monitor serial devices such as plotters, digitizers, modems, serial printers, and so on.

If this switch is specified and your machine does not contain a COM1 port, an error message is generated indicating that the port was not found and this switch is ignored. IdleBoot, however, continues to install. You can also use this switch to detect mouse activity on a serial mouse that is attached to COM1.

The COM2 Flag Switch (/C2)

The /C2 or COM2 Flag switch is identical to the COM1 flag except that it monitors COM2 instead of COM1.

The COM1 Carrier Detect Flag Switch (/D1)

The /D1 or COM1 Carrier Detect Flag switch is another IdleBoot switch that watches the COM1 port. However, rather than looking for I/O through the COM1 port, it simply monitors the port for the presence of a carrier detect. This is useful in many installations. For example, if you have a host system that you wish to be rebooted any time 30 minutes of inactivity passes, this switch starts timing whenever the carrier detect is lost. But if you dial in and sit there doing nothing for 30 minutes, IdleBoot will not reboot your computer. If this optional switch is used on a machine with no COM1 port, an error message is generated and this switch is ignored.

The COM2 Carrier Detect Flag Switch (/D2)

The /D2 or COM2 CD Flag switch is identical to the COM1 CD Flag described in the preceding section except it monitors COM2 carrier detect instead of COM1.

Configuring IdleBoot from the Environment

You can configure IdleBoot from the command line, from the environment space, or from a combination of both. As defined earlier in this chapter, an environment is defined as an area of memory that MS-DOS reserves for various special duties. One of these duties is to store character strings for use by other programs. IdleBoot takes advantage of the environment by looking for the environment string IBOOT. Any IdleBoot switches that are specified in the IBOOT variable are merged into those switches that are specified from the command line during the configuration phase of IdleBoot installation.

Although any switch may originate from the command line or the environment, if a switch is specified in both places, the command-line overrides any matching switch specified in the environment string. For example, if you set IBOOT=/T05 and the command-line switch reads /T01, the idle time is set to one minute, thus ignoring the parameter provided in IBOOT. By dynamically changing the IBOOT variable according to the needs of specific user tasks, IdleBoot is easily reconfigured according to the needs of each new task as it comes along. Please be aware that IdleBoot does not automatically monitor the IBOOT variable in real time. If you change the contents of the IBOOT string, you need to re-execute the IDLEBOOT command, either from a batch file or from the command line, before the new information contained in the IBOOT variable will be active.

Examples of IdleBoot Usage

This section contains a variety of sample IdleBoot installations and a brief discussion of how IdleBoot handles various configurations. Your installation probably requires developing your own specific configuration, and this section contains some ideas on how to proceed with your real-world applications.

Generic Network User Monitoring

Situation: Network users who leave their workstations logged on to the network while they're away for extended periods of time can create problems when files are needlessly kept open. During the workday, this creates traffic problems by preventing other users from referencing important files and locking others out of applications on a properly metered network. At the end of the day, workstations left logged in can create administrative problems by blocking file access for backup operations.

Solution: Configure IdleBoot to look for everything with a 30-minute idle time. Be sure to use all alarms. This is for users who are working late and would not appreciate having IdleBoot reset their computers.

Example: `IDLEBOOT /T30/A03/K/V/E/L/H/P/F /C1/C2/D1/D2`

Discussion: This generic configuration allows IdleBoot to watch most of the system. Please note that the second group of switches requires the COM1 and COM2 ports to be present within the system or an error occurs during installation. Also note that the /O switch is intentionally omitted. The presence of this switch would prevent an IdleBoot from occurring if the user had left open files. Depending on the installation, setting the /A03 switch to a longer alarm time might be preferable. Also, because the /H switch permits a user to defeat IdleBoot, this switch might not be desired in some installations.

BBS/Host System Monitoring

Situation: Bulletin boards and other dial-up systems usually operate for extended periods of time without any direct supervision. A software bug or modem "lock-up" during these unsupervised periods may result in extended downtime.

Solution: By configuring IdleBoot to watch for carrier detect, any extended periods without establishing a carrier causes the system to be reset, cleaning up the previous problems.

Example: `IDLEBOOT /T20/D1/S`

Discussion: Because activity on a dial-up host system requires the presence of a carrier detect, IdleBoot's monitoring is limited to this one function. This example assumes that the modem is on COM1. Also, because of the nature of being an unattended system, use the /S option (System Halted). No alarm switches are selected because no one would normally be around to hear them anyway. If this host system had offline features such as message base purging, you would want to add the necessary switches to ensure that you were correctly monitoring for these activities, too. If the failure of the unattended system was because of a hardware problem with the computer itself or such a major problem that processor execution was interrupted, IdleBoot would not be able to force a reboot. IdleBoot is, ultimately, just a program.

Switching Tasks for a Dedicated System

Situation: Sometimes, systems are dedicated to performing specific tasks 24 hours a day. A fax server, for example, might constantly receive and route faxes on a corporate network. At times, however, these dedicated systems are underutilized.

Solution: IdleBoot can be configured as a task switcher to allow a given system to take on additional job duties. By assigning multiple routine tasks to an otherwise underutilized computer, you reduce the need for additional computers and expensive human labor.

Example: `IDLEBOOT /B04:00:00/S`

Discussion: In this configuration, IdleBoot forces the computer to reboot every day at precisely 4 a.m. This allows the user to develop an AUTOEXEC.BAT file (or a login script) that checks the time, and if it is 4 a.m., executes another task, such as scanning the server for viruses, instead of its normal fax duties. Once these additional tasks are completed, the system returns to its normal duties. IdleBoot could be configured in such a way to support a great variety of tasks throughout the day.

Monitoring of a High Security User

Situation: Network users with access to either sensitive information or extended network privileges are users. It's preferable to not allow these accounts to sit idle for very long. If the payroll manager's account, for example, has been idle for five minutes, perhaps she or he has gone to the bathroom and access is now available to wandering eyes.

Solution: IdleBoot can be configured to provide tight monitoring conditions. While the possibility of nuisance resets increases as the monitoring conditions are tightened, there are instances where such tight controls are appropriate.

Example: `IDLEBOOT /L/H/P/T05/A01/K/V/E/F`

Discussion: This configuration watches the system for an inactivity period of five minutes. After four minutes, the user starts to receive audible idle alarms. At 4 minutes, 49 seconds into an idle period, the emergency alarm activates a solid tone for 11 seconds until IdleBoot forces a network logoff and then reboots the system. If the user, hearing the warning tones, decides that IdleBoot was not appropriate for this work session, she or he could disable it by pressing <ALT>-<LEFT SHIFT>-<H>, because the /H switch was provided.

Logging Underutilized Systems/Staff

Situation: In certain specific operating environments, it is often useful to know when a given workstation is not being utilized. A telemarketing operation, for example, might want to log the fact that a given operator's workstation has not logged any activity for a period of time. Sometimes, existing software does not provide automatic usage metering.

Solution: In some situations, IdleBoot can be used as a tool to log when a workstation has been idle for too long. This is accomplished by allowing IdleBoot to reset the idle workstation. Then, in the AUTOEXEC.BAT file, log an entry into a status file that contains a timestamp of when the system was reset. This file could be processed to establish how many times during working hours the system was reset. It is certainly preferable to have a better method to log information such as this, but if other options are not available, IdleBoot provides a solution.

Example: `IDLEBOOT /T03/F/O`

Discussion: With this configuration, IdleBoot watches all file activity and forces a system reboot after three minutes of system inactivity. The /O switch, however, prevents a reboot in the event any files are open. This is important, for example, if a telemarketing employee is processing a call, has started taking an order, and is placed on hold. This illustrates the need to carefully analyze any given IdleBoot application.

In this example, the keyboard or video monitoring modes are not active because it easily defeats the purpose of using IdleBoot. Also note that no alarms are activated. It might be preferable to sound an alarm after the first minute or so of inactivity just to let the employee know that his idleness has been noted.

Perhaps this type of information might be used to identify where the most underutilized systems are located for redistribution of hardware within a company. There are, of course, many uses for information of this nature.

Using IdleBoot with Other Programs

Given that IdleBoot is designed to operate as a background program, a discussion is in order about how to best utilize IdleBoot with other software packages. Because a single user often runs many different software packages that perform a variety of tasks, it's not likely that using a single IdleBoot configuration during all job tasks suffices. This is why great care was taken to make IdleBoot easily reconfigurable.

Probably the best way to customize IdleBoot to a specific task is to write a batch file that sets IdleBoot to the correct configuration for a particular software package, executes that package, and reconfigures IdleBoot, if needed, upon exit from the application. In a network environment, special consideration should be given to the question of granting access to users to reconfigure IdleBoot from their workstation. If not properly restricted, the very nature of the product makes IdleBoot a potential headache for a system administrator who happens to be blessed with undisciplined users. Please note the particular usefulness of the environment variable IBOOT when considering network usage.

IdleBoot and Microsoft Windows

The reason IdleBoot can achieve the monitoring capabilities it does is because it ties into DOS at numerous points. This is possible because DOS has been in existence for several years and is well-documented and understood. This, unfortunately, is not true of Windows. When Microsoft designed Windows, they dispensed with all the operational rules of DOS and created a new set of rules. Because Windows is a multitasking operating system (OS), the use/value of TSRs in an OS capable of true multitasking is obviously diminished. As such, the documentation for the types of OS activity that IdleBoot monitors is almost nonexistent for the Windows operating system.

Therefore, IdleBoot is not designed to be Windows compatible. It is, however, designed to be Windows "aware." If IdleBoot is loaded and you then go into Windows, IdleBoot recognizes this and automatically goes into a sleep mode. In this mode, no IdleBoot monitoring occurs. If a reboot is needed for any reason, including the /S or /Bhh:mm:ss functions, it will not occur. IdleBoot returns to normal operations after Windows is exited.

IdleBoot and Screen Blanking Programs

You need to give special consideration to the issue of using IdleBoot in conjunction with screen blanking programs. Users may have one of several types of screen blankers: some blank the screen completely, some blank the screen with a prompt box that moves around on the screen, and others rotate the color palette to prevent monitor burn-in. If IdleBoot is set to watch for video activity and a screen blanker is the type with a prompt box that moves around on the screen, IdleBoot senses this activity and therefore does not reboot what is an idle system. This situation should be considered when configuring IdleBoot into your existing system or when adding a screen blanking program to your system.

Using IdleBoot with Other TSR Programs

When using IdleBoot in conjunction with other TSR programs, you should make IdleBoot the last TSR program that you load. This is especially important if you opt to use the /S switch. If a TSR that hooks into the interrupt 21h vector is loaded after IdleBoot, IdleBoot's ability to recognize a system-halted condition is compromised. All other aspects of IdleBoot monitoring should function regardless of the TSR loading order.

Configuring IdleBoot Through a Network Login Script

As with all network products, careful consideration should be given regarding configuring IdleBoot during a users login script. Several approaches to doing global user configuration exist. Because IdleBoot supports reading command switches from the environment area, we recommend an approach where the users login scripts contains the IDLEBOOT command without any switches.

Configuring Idleboot from Your Own Programs

John: Ahh . . . my kind of tech talk! Be warned that the proceeding sections are very complex and normally appeals to programmers and those who really want to get under the hood. Follow along if you dare!

These following sections address a method by which other programs may reconfigure IdleBoot by using an advanced technique of writing directly into the IdleBoot common data area (CDA). We realize most users never need to do this, but this information is provided as technical assistance for those who would like to write functions into their software to either temporarily disable IdleBoot or change its operating characteristics.

What Is the Common Data Area?

The common data area (CDA) is a buffer in IdleBoot's segment that contains critical data necessary to reconfigure IdleBoot. IdleBoot uses the CDA when it reconfigures itself, but any program that follows proper procedure can reconfigure IdleBoot through use of the CDA. The most important factor to consider is that no error checking is done on the CDA. The parameters in the CDA must be free from errors or IdleBoot performs unpredictably.

The CDA is best viewed as a static structure of status and control variables. All the parameters entered on the command line are reflected in the values stored in the CDA. The data types are Flag (byte), Absolute Time (dword), Relative Time (dword), Far Pointer (dword), and Segment Pointer (word). All multibyte values are stored from least to greatest significance. Flags are true when 1, false when 0. No value besides true or false is authorized in a flag variable. Placing any other value in a Flag results in erratic, unpredictable, and possibly catastrophic behavior.

How Do I Find the CDA?

The first entry in the CDA, labeled FindMe, is the string "Idle-Boot^I^D^L^E^B^O^O^T". This is a mixed-case ASCII string followed by control codes that enables IdleBoot as the top-level process to find IdleBoot loaded as a TSR. Likewise, your programs can use this string to locate the CDA. This is a read-only field and is not to be modified!

What Are the Rules for Writing into the CDA?

The second entry in the CDA, a flag called GlobalEnable, activates IdleBoot when true and disables IdleBoot when false. Always turn GlobalEnable off when altering the CDA. You can turn it back on when you have made your changes. Also, again it must be emphasized that you are on your own to ensure data integrity when writing into the CDA.

> **John:** Warning! If you enter illegal values into the CDA, you can cause apparently random system reboots. In certain circumstances you could trash your system, including compromising hard drive integrity, if a reboot occurs at the wrong time. So, in a nutshell, don't screw around with the CDA unless you clearly understand what you are attempting and you are willing to risk damaging your system's data.

The proper procedure to follow when changing parameters is to find the CDA of the already loaded IdleBoot, establish the new parameters, check the parameters for logical correctness (for instance, it does not make sense to have an AlarmTime greater than IdleTime), turn off GlobalEnable, set the parameters, set Count to zero, and turn on GlobalEnable. You may also want to turn off the speaker, just in case your program alters IdleBoot while an alarm is ringing. Input a byte from port 61h, "AND" with 11111100b, and output it to port 61h. The description of the CDA is in Listing 5.1. Table 5.1 lists the legal IdleBoot switches.

Listing 5.1. IdleBoot communications buffer description CDA structure.

```
Beginning of Common Data Area (CDA)
;=======================================================
FindMe:    db "IdleBoot"        ;This is the CDA ID HEADER.
           db 9, 4, 12, 5
           db 2,15, 15, 20      ;Never Modify this header!
;=======================================================
```

continues

Listing 5.1. continued

```
; — — — — — — — — — — — — — — — — — — — — — — — — — — —
;     Variable: Index Offset from end of CDA Header
; — — — — — — — — — — — — — — — — — — — — — — — — — — —
GlobalEnable: db 1          ; +0, Type: FLAG
HotKeySw:     db 0          ; +1, Type: FLAG
DebugSw:      db 0          ; +2, Type: FLAG
NovellSw:     db 0          ; +3, Type: FLAG
HaltSw:       db 0          ; +4, Type: FLAG
VideoSw:      db 0          ; +5, Type: FLAG
KBSw:         db 0          ; +6, Type: FLAG
PrnSw:        db 0          ; +7, Type: FLAG
COM1Sw:       db 0          ; +8, Type: FLAG
COM2Sw:       db 0          ; +9, Type: FLAG
IOSw:         db 0          ; +10, Type: FLAG
FOpenSw:      db 0          ; +11, Type: FLAG
COM1CDSw:     db 0          ; +12, Type: FLAG
COM2CDSw:     db 0          ; +13, Type: FLAG
Reserved1:    db 0          ; +14, Type: FLAG
Reserved2:    db 0          ; +15, Type: FLAG
IdleSw:       db 0          ; +16, Type: FLAG
IdleTime:     dw 0, 0       ; +17, Type: Relative Time
KlaxonSw:     db 0          ; +21, Type: FLAG
AlarmSw:      db 0          ; +22, Type: FLAG
AlarmTime:    dw 0, 0       ; +23, Type: Relative Time
BootSw:       db 0          ; +27, Type: FLAG
BootTime:     dw 0,0        ; +28, Type: Absolute Time
Count:        dw 0, 0       ; +32, Type: Timer Variable
; — — — — — — — — — — — — — — —
; Interrupt Vector Address Storage
; — — — — — — — — — — — — — — —
OldInt9:      dw 0, 0       ; +36, Type: Far Pointer
OldInt13:     dw 0, 0       ; +40, Type: Far Pointer
OldInt17:     dw 0, 0       ; +44, Type: Far Pointer
OldInt1C:     dw 0, 0       ; +48, Type: Far Pointer
OldInt21:     dw 0, 0       ; +52, Type: Far Pointer
OldInt2F:     dw 0, 0       ; +56, Type: Far Pointer
pNewSegs:     dw 0          ; +60, Type: Segment Pointer
;============================================================
; End of the IdleBoot Common Data Area
;============================================================
;
```

Table 5.1 Legal IdleBoot switches.

Switch	Title	Description
/Axx	Alarm Time	Set Alarm time to xx minutes before boot
/Bhh:mm:ss	Boot Time	Boot machine at hh:mm:ss (24 Hour)
/C1	COM1 Flag	Watch COM1 for I/O activity
/C2	COM2 Flag	Watch COM2 for I/O activity
/D1	COM1 CD Flag	Watch COM1 for carrier detect
/D2	COM2 CD Flag	Watch COM2 for carrier detect
/E	Emergency Alarm	Sound solid tone 11 seconds before boot
/F	File I/O Flag	Watch for DOS/ BIOS/NET File I/O
/H	Halt Function	Activate IdleBoot Halt watching
/K	Keyboard Flag	Watch for keyboard activity
/L	Force Logoff	Perform network logoff before boot
/O	Open File Flag	Monitor for presence of open files
/P	Printer Flag	Watch for printer activity

continues

Table 5.1 continued

Switch	Title	Description
/S	System Halt Flag	Force a reboot on "System Halted Error"
/Txx	Idle Time	Set Idle Time to xx minutes until boot
/U	Uninstall	Remove IdleBoot from memory
/V	Video Flag	Watch for video activity
/-	Disable Flag	Disable IdleBoot but leave in memory
/?	Display Help	Display help screen
/#	Debug Mode	Activate IdleBoot debug mode

Detailed Description of CDA Flags/Variables

FindMe
This is the string "IdleBoot^I^D^L^E^B^O^O^T". This string enables programs to find the IdleBoot CDA when IdleBoot is loaded as a TSR.

GlobalEnable
Enables IdleBoot when true and disables IdleBoot when false.

HotKeySw
Activates the hot-key function that allows the user to turn GlobalEnable on and off from the keyboard when true (as per /H switch).

DebugSw
Enables Debug mode when true (as per /# switch).

NovellSw	When true, causes IdleBoot to perform a Novell Logoff API call immediately before rebooting (as per /L switch).
HaltSw	Causes IdleBoot to reboot on "system halted" errors when true (/S).
VideoSw	Enables video activity scanning when true (/V).
KBSw	Enables keyboard activity scanning when true (/K).
PrnSw	Enables printer activity scanning when true (/P).
COM1Sw	Enables COM1 activity scanning when true (/C1).
COM2Sw	Enables COM2 activity scanning when true (/C2).
IOSw	Enables file I/O activity scanning when true (/F).
FOpenSw	Causes IdleBoot to consider open files as activity when true (/O).
COM1CDSw	Causes IdleBoot to consider a carrier detect on COM1 as activity when true (/D1).
COM2CDSw	Causes IdleBoot to consider a carrier detect on COM2 as activity when true (/D2).
Two flags	Reserved in the CDA for future development. They are not to be altered by any external programs because incompatibilities with future IdleBoot releases will occur.
IdleSw	When true, causes IdleBoot to keep track of system idle time. If this flag is false, no reboot occurs from an idle system (/T).
IdleTime	Contains the number of clock ticks of idleness that must elapse before the system is rebooted (/Txx).
KlaxonSw	Enables the "emergency alarm" when true (/E).

> **Caution:** The alarm switch and an alarm time greater than 273 must be set for this switch to have any meaning.

AlarmSw	Enables the alarm (/A).
AlarmTime	The number of clock ticks that must elapse before IdleBoot sounds an alarm (IdleTime - /Axx).
BootSw	When true, causes a forced system reboot when the system clock equals BootTime (/B).
BootTime	Contains the time at which the system should re-boot and is expressed as clock ticks since midnight (/Bhh:mm:ss).
Count	Contains the number of clock ticks the system has been idle. Count should be set to zero when altering the CDA. OldInt9 points to the previous Int 9h handler.
OldInt13	Points to the previous Int 13h handler.
OldInt17	Points to the previous Int 17h handler.
OldInt1C	Points to the previous Int 1Ch handler.
OldInt21	Points to the previous Int 21h handler.
OldInt2F	Points to the previous Int 2Fh handler.
pNewSegs	Points to IdleBoot's segment (.COM files, of course, have only one segment).

IdleBoot Error Level Codes

IdleBoot is designed to return error level codes to your batch files. This facilitates the task of creating automated IdleBoot configuration. The two modes regarding IdleBoot's error level codes are the Configuration Mode and the Monitor Mode. If IdleBoot switches are present, either on the command line or in the environment, then IdleBoot responds in the Configuration Mode. If no command line switches are present, IdleBoot defaults to responding in the Monitor Mode. These modes respond very differently and you should pay careful attention to detail when using the error level features of IdleBoot.

Configuration Mode

In Configuration Mode, the error level values returned from IdleBoot are designed to inform your installation batch file that either IdleBoot did correctly process the requested command switches, or in the event of difficulty, the nature of the problem. The error level codes returned are arbitrary.

Configuration Mode Error Level Values

0 No Problems, requested configuration is now installed.

1 Unable to process action, required command-line switch absent.

2 Unable to process action, illegal parameter on the command line.

3 Unable to process, illegal parameter in the environment area.

4 Unable to respond to /- switch because IdleBoot is not installed.

5 Unable to respond to /U switch because IdleBoot is not installed.

6 Unable to respond to Uninstall, IdleBoot trapped by other TSRs.

7 Unable to process, an illegal combination of switches specified.

8 Unable to respond, Idleboot won't install under Microsoft Windows.

9 Security violation, maximum number of legal users would be exceeded.

10 Version mismatch, Eval & Release versions of IdleBoot cannot be mixed.

11 Compatibility, IdleBoot does not work with DOS versions prior to 3.0.

Monitor Mode

The second mode is the No Switches or Monitor Mode. In this mode, the error level returned by IdleBoot is coded to indicate which aspects of your system are being monitored. This value is bit-mapped, which means that each bit in the 8-bit binary byte has a unique meaning. This is different from the configuration mode in which the value returned is discrete (see Figure 5.1).

Batch file monitoring of a bit-mapped, error level code is more difficult than normal discrete values. However, the benefits of doing so are obvious. In the Monitoring Mode your batch files have specific knowledge regarding IdleBoot system monitoring. This can be extremely useful if you have multiple applications where it is important to reconfigure IdleBoot according to changing system needs.

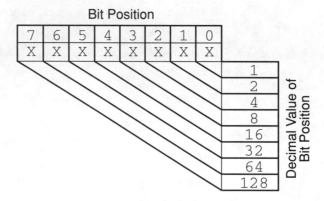

Figure 5.1. The error level decoding of Monitor Mode values can be decoded according to this figure.

This is the decimal value for each relative bit in the Errorlevel byte. "Monitor Mode" Bit Assignments:

> Bit-0 - Open files are being monitored
> Bit-1 - File I/O is being monitored
> Bit-2 - Printer activity is being monitored
> Bit-3 - Video activity is being monitored
> Bit-4 - Keyboard input is being monitored
> Bit-5 - COM1 I/O and/or carrier detect is being monitored
> Bit-6 - COM2 I/O and/or carrier detect is being monitored
> Bit-7 - This bit indicates that IdleBoot is not installed!

IdleBoot Debug Display Codes

All IdleBoot Debug Display Codes (DDCs) are displayed in the upper-right corner of the screen whenever Debug Mode is active. The appearance of a debug code means IdleBoot logged a particular type of system activity. Once a DDC has been displayed, it stays on the screen. Therefore, seeing a DDC does not necessarily mean that a particular system activity is still occurring. If a given type of activity is noticed repeatedly, the associated DDC alternates case, shifting from uppercase to lowercase, and so on. This way, you know if one-shot or continuous activity is occurring.

Table 5.2 The IdleBoot debug display codes.

Character Code	Activity Noted
V (v)	Video Activity
K (k)	Keyboard Activity
P (p)	Printer Activity
F (f)	File I/O Activity
O (o)	Open Files Detected
CA (ca)	COM1 I/O Activity
CB (cb)	COM2 I/O Activity
DA (da)	Carrier Detect on COM1
DB (db)	Carrier Detect on COM2

Use Of IdleBoot by Multiple Users on a Network

IdleBoot is designed to be used in a networking environment either by a single user or by all the workstations system-wide. To facilitate this, IdleBoot is designed with its own internal usage metering. If you're not operating on a network, this does not apply to you.

Whenever IdleBoot is installed on a workstation, it looks to see how many other users are currently using it. If you should want to see how many users currently have IdleBoot installed, type IDLEBOOT without any command-line switches. This generates a configuration screen that lists both the number of current users and the maximum number of concurrent users allowed by your purchase license. Please note that if you have 200 users on your system but only 20 are running IdleBoot at any given time, then you do not need more than a 20-user license.

If, as in the above example, you add another user (bringing the active-user count to 21) who decides to install IdleBoot, that user would receive a security violation message indicating that IdleBoot is unavailable to use until someone else releases use of the product. If another user either logs off the network, is reset by IdleBoot, or uninstalls IdleBoot with the /U switch, then the current user count is decreased by one. This brings the count down to 20, the legal limit, and IdleBoot is available to other users. If, however, a user deactivates IdleBoot with either the /- switch or through the hot-key halt function, then IdleBoot is still in memory and does not release the user count.

Determining how many users to license is often difficult. Because IdleBoot will be installed to deal with a great variety of network-oriented problems, there is no rule of thumb to follow. If you intend to use IdleBoot strictly for a few dedicated-purpose machines, then you probably know exactly how many users you have. If, however, you intend to use IdleBoot throughout a system, you probably do not need to license more than 80 percent of your total number of user workstations.

There are, of course, exceptions. If you find that users are frequently receiving security violations, it's time to purchase an additional license for more authorized users. For more information regarding IdleBoot usage metering or questions regarding any aspect of IdleBoot, please contact Horizons Consulting at (417) 839-2174. If your questions are technical in nature, ask for technical support.

Summary

When used properly, IdleBoot is great for backup devices, shared stations, and lots of other ideas. Phil Case and his team did a great job with this and all the Horizon Consulting utilities. Contact Horizon for details on commercial versions of this and other great products.

Horizons Consulting
1432 E. Commercial Street
Springfield, Missouri 65803
Phone: (417) 839-2174
Fax: (417) 831-1329
BBS: (417) 831-9140

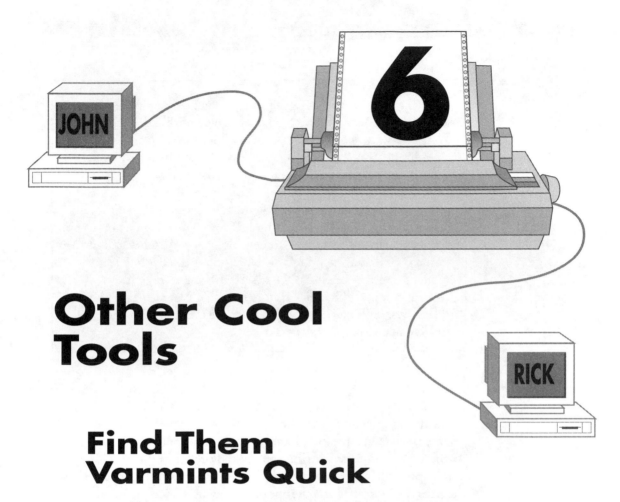

Other Cool Tools

Find Them Varmints Quick

NetWare has many limitations on the length and content of user names. Many networks use naming conventions that are somewhat cryptic, especially as new users are added. In an environment where the whole network is spread out among buildings or even countries, the built-in tools are not really that helpful.

Rick: The lesson for this section is to use names that make sense and are easy to remember. Many network administrators still use FS1, FS2, and so on as server names. This can create problems in a couple of areas. First, users are confused when they have to log on or look for a server. Secondly, when you are reporting status, making charts, and so on, it's more professional to use "real" names (for example, Accounts, Testing, and Markets). This lesson also applies to user names. I'll never forget that sunny day in Cleveland when I was trying to help a guy over the phone. I asked him to "do a userlist and tell me who is on the network." He replied, "Let me see, User1, User2, User3, and so on." It seems that his company bought a 100-user copy of NetWare and had Users 1 to 98, Guest, and Supervisor. Use meaningful names, folks, it makes life a lot easier.

NetWare has a command-line utility called USERLIST that can be used to obtain a list of users. However, this list reports only those users currently logged in to the invoking user's file server and does not list users of other servers. As shown in Figure 6.1, the information is pretty sparse. As the LAN administrator, you can take advantage of the details or full-name option that is part of a user's "file" on the server. Figure 6.2 shows the SYSCON screen where the option is. Having something in this spot is a good idea, and WHOIS (see the following section, "What Is WHOIS?") shows it to you without the hassle of going through SYSCON. In addition, getting this information in real time from all servers on the network is a lengthy chore.

What is WHOIS?

With a single command, WHOIS provides you with a complete list of all users on all file servers. WHOIS searches all file servers that are connected or bridged to the invoking workstation and reports every user's user name, full name, and home file server. This list is alphabetized by user name for ease of reference. Unlike USERLIST, WHOIS reports users whether they are currently logged in or not.

```
User Information for Server LANLORD
Connection  User Name      Login Time
-------------------------------------------------
    1       JOHNLU         7-23-1992  5:12 pm
    2       JOHNRI         7-23-1992  3:14 pm
    3       DOUGTR         7-23-1992  4:12 pm
    5       GERARDOB       7-23-1992  2:34 pm
    6       GERARDOB       7-23-1992  4:55 pm
    8     * RSEGAL         7-23-1992  4:41 pm
    9       GERARDOB       7-23-1992  3:42 pm
   13       GERARDOB       7-23-1992  3:50 pm
   14       GERARDOB       7-23-1992  4:15 pm
   15       GERARDOB       7-23-1992  3:54 pm
   16       GERARDOB       7-23-1992  3:59 pm
   17       GERARDOB       7-23-1992  4:03 pm
   19       GERARDOB       7-23-1992  4:08 pm
   20       GERARDOB       7-23-1992  4:04 pm
   21       GERARDOB       7-23-1992  4:07 pm
   22       GERARDOR       7-23-1992  4:11 pm
   23       KEVINY         7-23-1992  5:21 pm
   24       GERARDOB       7-23-1992  3:41 pm
   25       GERARDOB       7-23-1992  4:01 pm
   27       GERARDOB       7-23-1992  3:28 pm
Press any key to continue ... ('C' for continuous)
```

Figure 6.1. A USERLIST.

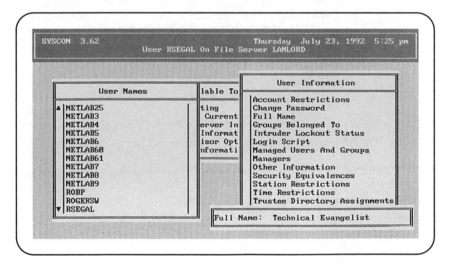

Figure 6.2. SYSCON user information.

197

Using WHOIS

WHOIS is very simple to use and requires no command-line parameters. Simply type WHOIS and press Enter, to generate a list of all network users on all file servers that you can attach and log into. Figure 6.3 shows a sample of the output generated by WHOIS. Notice in the example output that the only thing the program looked for was Rsegal. I also asked for information from only one server, LANLORD.

```
Alternate username (none = skip this server):

Server CHARLOTTE disallowed login as GUEST
Alternate username (none = skip this server):

Server MICROSOFT disallowed login as GUEST
Alternate username (none = skip this server):

Server NOV311 disallowed login as GUEST
Alternate username (none = skip this server):

Server SNAFU disallowed login as GUEST
Alternate username (none = skip this server):

Server NOV22 disallowed login as GUEST
Alternate username (none = skip this server):


Username        Full Name                       File Server

RSEGAL          Technical Evangelist            LANLORD

1 registered network users found

C:\FORBOOK\TEMP\FINAL>
```

Figure 6.3. A WHOIS sample output.

Specifying Users

Although not required, WHOIS accepts an optional network user name as a command-line argument. This enables you to obtain information about a specific user without having to view the entire list. For example, to obtain the full name and home server of user CHARLIE, type:

```
WHOIS CHARLIE <Enter>
```

Wildcards in User Names

WHOIS also supports the use of wildcards in user names. The standard DOS wildcards "*" and "?" may be used to obtain information about users whose names share common characteristics.

For example, to obtain a list of all users whose names begin with C, type:

```
WHOIS C* <Enter>
```

WHOIS finds all matching users on all servers. Interpretation of wildcards is performed in exactly the same manner as for DOS filenames: question marks indicate a single unknown character, and an asterisk indicates zero or more unknown characters. It should be repeated that WHOIS finds all matching users on all servers. This means that like-named users on different servers are listed individually and like-named accounts for the same individual on multiple servers are each listed separately. WHOIS is not case-sensitive. All input is automatically capitalized prior to use.

Redirecting WHOIS Output

WHOIS uses standard DOS functions to display characters on the screen. This was specifically done so that its output could be redirected to a printer or file using the standard output redirection character ">". For example,

```
WHOIS C* >userlist.txt <Enter>
```

creates a file containing a list of all users whose user name begins with the letter C.

John: Some notes on how this crunches and gets this stuff. WHOIS interacts with the NETx, EMSNETx, and XMSNETx shells to obtain network services. It initially confirms that the invoking workstation is attached and logged in to a NetWare file server. WHOIS then finds a file server on the network and checks if the user is logged in to it. If not, WHOIS attempts to log in as GUEST, a default account on all NetWare servers that generally does not require a password. If the login is successful, WHOIS

continues

continued

execution continues. If WHOIS is unsuccessful in its attempt to log in as GUEST, it reports the name of the problem file server and prompts you for an alternate user name with a password. (Some network supervisors delete the GUEST account or assign a password to it.) Simply type an acceptable user name for that server, follow it with the appropriate password, and WHOIS proceeds. The information gathered is stored internally for later display. WHOIS then decides whether to stay attached to the server. If you were already attached to server when WHOIS was started, nothing happens. If you were not attached, WHOIS detaches from the server. This means you won't end up with more or less server attachments than you had before the program runs. Nice piece of work.

Summary Comments

WHOIS is brought to you by Richard L. Hartman, a 12-year electronics industry veteran. Rich started in analog circuitry and progressed through the disciplines of discrete digital, integrated digital, microprocessor, software, and management. He has done some cool things in his glorious past, including designing the Key Tronic KB5151 Enhanced PC Keyboard, the first to have separate cursor and numeric keypads. More than 250,000 KB5151s have been sold and its standard continues to influence keyboard design to this day. Rich is now a consultant concentrating in the area of local area networks, specifically the development of software that runs with and takes advantage of Novell's NetWare Operating System.

WHOIS and other AdWare programs like it, are his answer to the extremely high cost of advertising in magazines and trade journals. Write good stuff, and that will become your calling card. Rich is a great programmer, a good guy, and someone you should keep in mind for those LAN consulting jobs. He can be reached at:

5205 North Mulvaney Court
Spokane, Washington 99212
(509) 924-6576
CompuServe: 76350,2275
GEenie R.HARTMAN9

At the Sound of the Tone: Answering Machine for Windows

Answering Machine for Windows (ANSMACH.EXE) is one of those "send 'em the money" type shareware items. At first, it's nice to have, and all of a sudden, it's indispensable. First, take a look at what this software tool is all about.

ANSMACH.EXE is a replacement (not an enhancement) for NWPOPUP.EXE. The program enables you to do a number of things that NWPOPUP.EXE cannot accomplish, thus making it far superior to NWPOPUP.EXE.

John: NWPOPUP.EXE is a piece of code that Novell/Microsoft provides to deal with broadcast messages flying into a workstation running Windows. When you send a message to a workstation, it normally pops up on the bottom of the screen—the 25th-line thing. If you don't have NWPOPUP.EXE loaded, messages can lock up your PC because of the way the workstation tries to deal with the incoming message. NWPOPUP prevents problems. If you don't use ANSMACH, make sure your users have NWPOPUP loading on their machines.

ANSMACH.EXE Features

Answering Machine for Windows is completely configurable, thus giving you more flexibility to handle your incoming messages. Listed below are the features and options that are available when you run the program.

- The Intercept Message from DOS Windows option forces Answering Machine for Windows to intercept all of those stupid messages that appear on line 25 asking you to press Ctrl-Enter to continue. Answering Machine for Windows intercepts all messages in that mode.

> **John**: Because a message sent to your machine causes your machine to stop processing until you press Ctrl-Enter, this feature is wonderful for letting you drop out to a DOS box with no worries about a process being interrupted. In addition, if you set up the program to intercept all messages, you can work in either Windows or the DOS box with no problems.

- The Record Incoming Messages and Send Busy Signal option forces Answering Machine for Windows to record all incoming messages and sends a busy signal message (if present) out to the sender of the incoming message without your intervention. The dialog box is shown in Figure 6.4.

- The Busy Signal Message field specifies the message that you want Answering Machine for Windows to send if you tell it to record all incoming messages. If this field is empty, Answering Machine for Windows does not send anything to the sender. This message is sent without your intervention. Figure 6.4 shows a sample message that goes out when a message hits the workstation.

- The Send Message option brings up a dialog box with a selector and an edit field. Choose the recipient of your message in the selector and type your message into the edit field. When you're ready to send your message, select OK. If you want to abort your message, select Cancel. If you send a message to another person and get a busy signal, Answering Machine for Windows clears your busy signal indicator to avoid endless loops of busy signals going back and forth. Figure 6.5 shows the dialog box and a sample message that would go out to the highlighted user.

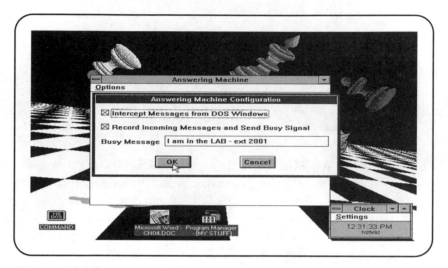

Figure 6.4. The options dialog box.

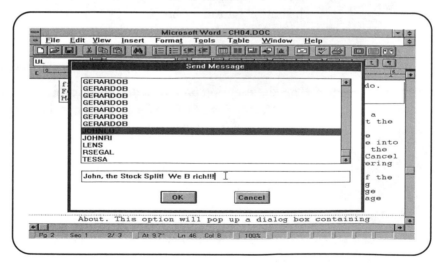

Figure 6.5. A Send Message dialog box.

Rick: This is where you can get some particularly good value out of this tool. Create a batch file called WhereU. Inside WhereU.bat you can put:

```
@echo off
  Send "Help!" to Rsegal
```

Then when your users type WhereU, they receive a message from your machine telling them where you are or what to do. For example, you could say "page me" or "out to lunch."

- The Check Messages option brings up a dialog box with a list of all waiting messages. Select the message that you wish to respond to and press the OK button. Another dialog box pops up with the entire received message and an edit field. Type your response into the edit field and press OK to send your reply out to the sender. If you wish to abort your message, select Cancel. Once you choose to respond to a message, Answering Machine for Windows removes the message from your waiting message list. Clicking on the Cancel button of the Check Messages dialog box returns you to Answering Machine for Windows main window. Clicking on Purge removes all messages from your waiting message list. Figure 6.6 shows the dialog box with a sample message.

- The About option pops up a dialog box containing information about Answering Machine for Windows, including the current release number and information about the authors of the program.

- The Exit option closes down Answering Machine for Windows. If you choose this option and you have messages waiting, Answering Machine for Windows asks if you want to save the messages to disk. If you choose Yes, the program saves the messages, and the messages are loaded back in the next time that you load Answering Machine for Windows.

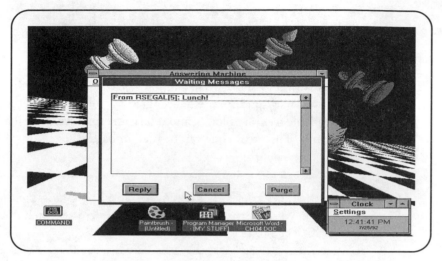

Figure 6.6. The Waiting Messages dialog box.

Note: If you have messages waiting and the program is iconized, a red light flashes at the top of the icon to indicate that you have messages waiting.

Summary

A cool utility brought to you by Michael Ball, resident tax programmer. Michael can be reached at the following address:

Michael Ball
500 Maryland Street NE
Warren, Ohio 44483
CompuServe: 70410,3043

205

RAMMAP: Your PC Memory Roadmap

RAMMAP is another Marc Perkel special that accomplishes three tasks. RAMMAP can display what programs are loaded in memory, free up any available memory blocks, and return an error level code if a TSR is loaded or not. This error code can be used in batch files.

Rick: Error levels being returned from programs like this are a really neat way to build power batch files. John, tell them what they've won.

Operations

RAMMAP is very easy to use, and it has four options. First, you can use it by typing:

`RAMMAP`

After pressing Enter, you get something like the screen shown in Figure 6.7.

As you can see, RAMMAP gives you a list of what is loaded in memory. You'll see the program name, and also pay particular attention to the command-line parameters. Notice in the example that you can see the preferred server. This was a result of using the PS= command-line option when NETX was loaded. From a troubleshooting perspective, this is handy, as in the case of a user calling up and saying that their server connection is not happening. In the autoexec file, you have the PS option set for the NETX.

You normally check the autoexec.bat to see if perhaps the user trashed the file. Looks good, eh? Hmmm . . . Well, if you run RAMMAP, you can quickly see if the PC thinks that is the preferred server. In some cases, your user could be loading a TSR that is messing up or writing to certain areas of memory. In this case, if the PS= line didn't have the server name or garbage was in that spot, you would check to see what is being loaded after NETX and also what the user is starting up before trying to get onto the LAN.

```
C:\COLLAGE>rammap

Blk   Own    Size Program Name Type  Parent Program    Command Line Parameters
_____
0254  0008  11152
050E  0008    64
0513         2368 command.com  Prog  0513 command.com
05A8          64  -- free --
05AD  0513   256  - Master -   MEnv
05BE          64  -- free --
05C3        28304 SMARTDRV     Prog  0513 command.com
0CAD  1B9E   112  SAVE.EXE     Env
0CB5        17312 IPX          Prog  0513 command.com
10F0        43728 NETX         Prog  0513 command.com   ps=lanlord
1B9E        72352 SAVE.EXE     Prog  0513 command.com
2D49  2D52   128  RAMMAP.EXE   Env
2D52       469728 RAMMAP.EXE   Prog  0513 command.com

C:\COLLAGE>
```

Figure 6.7. A sample RAMMAP output.

The two other options are easy to use as well. Inside a batch file, you can have RAMMAP test for TSRs or running batch files. For example, the TSR check is handy to use to determine if IPX loaded properly. RAMMAP returns an error level of 0 if it's not loaded and 1 if it's detected.

The following is an example listing from a sample batch file that tests for TSR Fred being loaded. The error-level line shows that if it was not loaded, the batch file skips to the label NOPE.

```
@Echo Off
SK
RAMMAP InMem SK.COM
IF ERRORLEVEL 1 GOTO LOADED
IF ERRORLEVEL 0 GOTO NOT_LOADED
:LOADED
@Echo Sidekick is loaded...
```

```
GOTO END
:NOT_LOADED
@Echo Sidekick is not loaded...
:END
```

Finally, you can use RAMMAP to free environment space that is taken by TSRs when they load. In many cases, this is very little space, but hey, a byte's a byte! To do this, simply run RAMMAP as shown in Figure 6.8. This could be put in a batch file as well.

```
C:\COLLAGE>rammap free

Freeing Environment of SAVE.EXE      144 bytes

144 bytes recovered in 1 memory blocks.

C:\COLLAGE>
```

Figure 6.8. The free memory RAMMAP option.

Summary

Yet another Perkel pick. Marc Perkel and his wife, Vicki, are the last of a dying breed—call in a feature request by noon, get it back by 4 p.m. They are an amazing pair. To get details on all the Perkel offerings. Write or call Marc at:

Computer Tyme
411 North Sherman, Suite 300
Springfield, Missouri 65802
(417) 866-1222
Compuserve: 76505,1120

Break.sys: Keep Those Fingers Off Ctrl-C!

Overview

Break.sys is a little goodie that you can stick into the config.sys file of your workstations to prevent people from breaking out of batch files. This device driver is smart enough to prevent Ctrl-C stuff only if you are in command.com and not in an application program. In other words, when you want a user to run something to completion, it will. When they are in an application that uses Ctrl-C, the Ctrl-C is passed to it.

Operation

Nothing to it: inside the workstation config.sys file, insert the following line:

```
DEVICE=BREAK.SYS
```

Rick: In the interest of keeping your systems clean, here is a suggestion. On your workstations, have a subdirectory for DOS and stuff your system files (*.SYS) in this directory, or create a directory called DEVICES and put them in there. Then, in the config.sys file, use the full path with the device command. For example, let's say that you put this break.sys in your DOS directory. The line in the config.sys would be:

DEVICE=C:\DOS\BREAK.SYS

If you had a separate directory for device drivers, you would put in your config.sys:

DEVICE=C:\DEVICES\BREAK.SYS

continues

continues

The reason for all of this is to keep the root directory clean. The only files you should have in your root are autoexec.bat, command.com, and config.sys. The rest of the entries are directories. In my opinion, folks, it's a cleaner way to manage the PC.

The two basic commands you can use with this driver are:

```
BREAK ON
BREAK OFF
```

BREAK ON turns on Ctrl-C and BREAK OFF turns it off. A sample batch file could look like:

```
@echo off
Break off
Test
Break on
```

This disables the Ctrl-C key and allows the program test to run. After the test is done, the BREAK ON command turns Ctrl-C back on.

One advanced feature is to include:

```
DEVICE=BREAK.SYS /C
```

The /C completely disables Ctrl-C. Nothing will see the Ctrl-C; break.sys catches and kills all of them.

Another feature is the /B command switch:

```
DEVICE=BREAK.SYS /B
```

This enables you to break out of programs by pressing Ctrl-\. This is really handy when you are debugging a problem that is causing the user's station to lock up in a loop within an application.

Summary

This is another great Perkel pick. Contact Marc and Vicki Perkel at:

> Computer Tyme
> 411 North Sherman, Suite 300
> Springfield, Missouri 65802
> (417) 866-1222
> CompuServe: 76505,1120

NOVSYNC.SYS: Keep On Ticking (In Sync!)

This is a very small (300 bytes) device driver that keeps the workstation clock synchronized with the server clock. Every two minutes, the workstation reads the server time and adjusts the workstation clock as required. The polling among workstations is staggered by connection number so all the stations don't slam the server at once.

Operation

This is a piece o' cake: add the following line to the config.sys:

```
DEVICE=NOVSYNC.SYS
```

> **Rick:** I gave a long speech on device drivers and how they should be stored on the PC. Check out Chapter 5, "IdleBoot: Knock, Knock, Anything Going On," for the inside scoop.

This is handy for getting all PCs in sync if you change the time on the server. This prevents time from sliding on the workstation.

John: A sneaky management trick. If you use this, you can prevent people from changing the time on the PC, doing something, and trying to prove it with a timestamp.

Summary

Once again, hats off to the Perkels at:

> Computer Tyme
> 411 North Sherman, Suite 300
> Springfield, Missouri 65802
> (417) 866-1222
> Compuserve: 76505,1120

KILL.EXE: Everybody Outta the Pool Now!

Sometimes during a troubleshooting session you may need to clear a workstation from the server. Normally, you have a couple of ways to do it. The first is to use Fconsole as shown in Figure 6.9. The other way is at the server console, where you can clear the station.

Kill is a program that is a command-line way to clear a workstation. It enables you to clear a station without going to the server and without going through the hassle of bringing up Fconsole for this one feature.

 Caution: This thing is dangerous if you are not careful. Use extreme caution and be sure you know what you are doing. The grief you save may be your own.

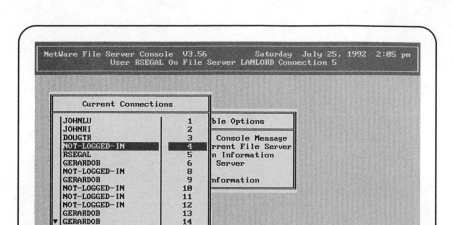

Figure 6.9. The Fconsole screen.

Usage

It's simple—type Kill and the connection number. Bang, bang, they're dead. The station is cleared. To use this utility:

1. Run a userlist (see Figure 6.10) to confirm that you know which connection you are clearing.

2. Type:

```
Kill <number>
```

(The <number> is the connection number.)

Summary

That one was short and sweet, folks. A handy little goody brought to you by Kurt Kellner, who can be reached on CompuServe at 70754,3112.

```
C:\TOOLBOOK\CH08>userlist

User Information for Server LANLORD
Connection   User Name        Login Time
                             ------------------
       1      JOHNLU          7-23-1992   5:12 pm
       3      DOUGTR          7-24-1992   3:24 pm
       5    * RSEGAL          7-25-1992   2:08 pm
       6      GERARDOB        7-23-1992   4:55 pm
       9      GERARDOB        7-23-1992   6:59 pm
      13      GERARDOB        7-23-1992   3:50 pm
      14      GERARDOB        7-23-1992   4:15 pm
      15      GERARDOB        7-23-1992   3:54 pm
      16      GERARDOB        7-23-1992   3:59 pm
      17      GERARDOB        7-23-1992   4:03 pm
      18      LENS            7-24-1992   6:37 pm
      19      GERARDOB        7-23-1992   4:08 pm
      20      GERARDOB        7-23-1992   4:04 pm
      21      GERARDOB        7-23-1992   4:07 pm
      22      GERARDOB        7-23-1992   4:11 pm
      25      GERARDOB        7-23-1992   4:01 pm
      27      TESSA           7-24-1992   3:22 pm
      28      GERARDOB        7-23-1992   3:56 pm

C:\TOOLBOOK\CH08>
```

Figure 6.10. A sample userlist.

WINBUG: Reporting Those "Features" to Microsoft

We are pretty sure you have never encountered a problem with Windows or any Windows program. But just in case, we ran across an excellent program that provides some order for your bug reporting procedures.

Winbug is a Visual Basic application that Steven Stern wrote during the Windows 3.1 beta so he could report bugs in the "official" format without leaving Windows to run the "official" bug reporting tool. Because this is a Visual Basic application, you need the Visual Basic runtime VBRUN100.DLL somewhere in your path.

This program creates a file that has all the required information you need to send to Microsoft for reporting a software problem. This format is probably great for other software vendors as well.

214

Set Up and Usage

The first time you run Winbug, it takes you through the setup procedure. There are three areas that you need to set up:

1. Directory information: This is where you tell Winbug where it can find autoexec.bat and config.sys and where you want it to store the finished reports.

2. Personal information: Who you are, where can you be reached, etc.

3. System information: What type of machine you have, video card, processor type, and so on. Also be sure to include anything special about your machine (for example, CD-ROM, two SCSI adapters, and so on).

The personal information and system information are recorded in the directory specified in Directory Information. The other information is recorded in WINBUG.INI, in your Windows directory.

Record information about your problem on the main screen of Winbug. State the problem as clearly as possible. You can use File.Insert to import all or part of an existing text file to support your description.

Bug Reporting Procedures

The information below is what Microsoft passes to beta testers. This is helpful for you to read and heed when you are dealing with software vendors. It can also help you guide your users as well.

> **Rick:** Having a standard procedure for reporting problems is vital if you are to maintain some consistency in your operations. Read this carefully to see if this can help you develop internal reporting procedures.

Reproducible

Whenever you submit a bug report, in the bug description file (explained below), you should indicate somewhere whether the bug is reproducible:

A. Always
B. Sometimes
C. Never

When reporting a bug, try to reproduce the bug with the simplest system configuration. That is, when you come across a bug, remove all unnecessary drivers and TSRs from your config.sys/autoexec.bat files. This means every driver/TSR except the driver himem.sys, which is in your config.sys. This also means removing subst, smartdrv, ramdrive, append, share (if you're using DOS 5), and so on. If you're using any type of stacks= statement in config.sys, try it without this as well.

Although taking most everything out of your config.sys and autoexec.bat isn't the answer you seek, you need to do this as a way to possibly track down the cause of your bug.

Here are the ideal autoexec.bat/config.sys files to use when testing against a bug:

config.sys:

```
files=30
buffers=20
device=c:\win\himem.sys
```

autoexec.bat:

```
prompt $P$G
path <your path>
```

Of course, there are exceptions to this. You may have a printing bug on a network printer where you must have your network drivers loaded; or you may have a drive controller that requires you to load a special driver in your config.sys in order for your computer to interface with one or more of your disk drives.

Using this method, you might be able to come across the source of your bug. Bugs are often caused by drivers and/or TSRs that you might be using. Removing such programs may get rid of your bug, and it at least helps add to the information about your bug.

Put Things Back

If you do strip practically everything out of your config.sys and autoexec.bat and the problem goes away, start adding the deleted items back, one at a time, until you (hopefully) find the source(s) of your problem.

Mention The Cause

Please be sure to mention in your report if altering your config.sys and/or autoexec.bat did anything to change the behavior of your bug.

Experiment with win.ini and system.ini

Advanced users may also experiment with their win.ini and system.ini files in trying to isolate and/or fix bugs.

Multiple Bugs Under the Same Configuration

Note that if you have several bugs to report on an identical configuration (config.sys, autoexec.bat, hardware, and so on, all matching), you could put all of them into a single bug file. This facilitates the job of trying to track down the source of a bug. Please keep in mind, however, that this does not free you from having to detail your bugs. If your report contains multiple bugs, each should be detailed as if it were the only bug in the report.

Use Complete Sentences

Please use complete sentences when describing a problem, giving as much detail as possible. More than one or two short phrases are required in order for development people to do their job. Also, be sure to give the exact steps (in detail) necessary to reproduce a bug.

Send Messages About It

Feel free to send messages about your problems to others. These users may be able to help you work through your problems and offer valuable advice.

217

Include Third-Party Information

If the bug is found in an application such as WinWord, Ami Pro, or Adobe Type Manager, be sure to include the version number of the product that is conflicting with Windows. If the product is from a smaller company, be sure to include the company's phone number in your report so developers can contact the company directly.

Shareware Programs

If the product is shareware, be sure to include a copy of the file with your bug report. Note that in the case of shareware, it cannot be reported to development without a copy of the program, so it's your responsibility to provide a copy of each shareware program containing a bug.

> **Note:** Check with the Microsoft Sysops first. They may already have the program available.

Checking Mail

Please check your CompuServe mail at least once a week after you've reported a bug or set of bugs. You may receive messages requesting you to provide more information about your problem(s).

Dr. Watson and Your Report

> **Note:** If your problem is causing General Protection Faults, run Drwatson.exe and reproduce the problem. Drwatson captures important information about the state of Windows at the time of the fault. Winbug adds the Drwatson.log file to your report.

If you have a certain bug that you can readily reproduce and it's producing Dr. Watson output, follow these steps:

1. Delete the Drwatson.log file from your Windows directory.

2. Run through the steps necessary to duplicate the bug. You should now have a small (2 to 10K) Dr. Watson file, and it pertains only to the bug you are about to report.

3. Detail the problem in a text file.

4. Run the Winbug program and answer "y" to the prompt where it asks you if you'd like to add your Dr. Watson file.

Bug Reporting Instructions

Include the following information in your System Information (Setup.SystemInformation):

1. Your DOS version.

2. Your machine name/type (for example, Genesis 386/40).

3. Your BIOS brand/version/date (for example, Phoenix BIOS v 1.1.2 dated 3/6/88).

> **Note:** The BIOS brand, version, and date often comes up when you first boot up your computer. You may also be able to glean this information by running MSD and poring through the MSD output file. In any case, your BIOS description usually fits on the same line as your computer brand/model and should never take up more than one line. Also note that of brand, version, and date, brand and date are the most important.

4. The amount of RAM on the machine.

5. The type of hard drive and controller (for example, 124M Maxtor HD with WD 1007 controller).

6. The type of video card/monitor and the mode you're running under (for example, Trident 8900 card with Emerson VGA in 640x480 mode).

7. The kind(s) of floppy drive(s) (for example, 1.44 A: and 1.2 B:).

8. The brand/type of mouse and the mouse driver version, if any (for example, Microsoft Bus Mouse using 8.00 driver). Be sure to mention which COM port it's on if it's a serial mouse.

9. Please mention any other peripherals (net cards, etc.) that are on your machine.

Note: Floppy information is usually not important, but if your problem is specifically with your floppies, it helps to have as much information on your floppy drive(s) as possible.

Here is a sample system configuration file:

```
DOS 5.0
Genesis 386/40 with AMI BIOS dated 3/91
4 MB of RAM
Maxtor 124 MB HD with IDE controller
Trident 8900 card with 1 MB & Emerson VGA 640x480 mode
1.2 mb A: 1.44mb B:
Microsoft Serial Mouse on COM2 with 8.00 driver
```

Note: You can sum up your machine information in a few lines. If the tech support or development people need to contact you for further details, you can be sure they'll do so.

John: As a reporter of bugs, I can tell you that most software companies running large beta programs do a great job of getting information from you, do well at getting software out, and just stink at talking to you about bug status.

Sample Bug Report

A bug report file should include the following:

1. A description of your bug (please use complete sentences).

2. The steps needed to reproduce the bug. Please be sure to give the exact steps necessary to reproduce the bug. Provide complete information in your initial report so that the software company doesn't need to contact you for additional information.

3. A description of all third-party applications involved. Please include the product names and version numbers. If you are running on a network, provide the network brand and version numbers for the drivers you're using. Give enough information here so that the debugger can obtain a copy.

Summary

As you can see, the Microsoft folks have it down to a science of sorts. Our thanks to Steven Stern for creating this program and giving it away to one and all. Nice guy, eh? You can send Steven thank you mail on CompuServe at 70327,135.

DoRun/DontRun: Automated Making Up Your Mind

These two programs are used inside a batch file to determine whether you want to run programs by default. In addition, these programs enable you to set the time that the system waits for you to press a key to change the default action. The format for these programs is simple:

```
DoRun <delay> <program>
```

```
DontRun <delay> <program>
```

where <delay> is the time delay that you want the system to wait (this can be a number of seconds that you want to delay), and <program> is the command or program that is acted upon.

Examples

```
DoRun 5 DIR
```

This example means that after five seconds, the DIRectory command is executed unless the user presses N.

```
DontRun 5 DIR
```

This example means that after five seconds, the DIRectory command is not executed unless the user presses Y.

Rick: There is practical use for this stuff and it is worth a few bucks. Consider your own autoexec batch file. You should run chkdsk every so often just to clean up those "lost clusters," so you could use the DontRun command and run it every so often by pressing Y. In your batch file, you could put:

```
Dontrun 5 chkdsk
```

If you press Y, it runs. For a program that you run all the time, but might want to avoid for a test or something, put:

```
DoRun 5 whatever
```

This runs it all the time unless you press N.

Summary

These handy, little utilities cost five dollars each (with server/site licensing available). Try them out and send that money today! Contact:

> Paradigm
> 805 South Filbert Court
> Sterling, Virginia 22170-4712
> (703) 450-0829
> Fax: (703) 450-2683

Space, the Final Frontier (or Where Did the Disk Space Go?)

Space Map(SM) is a program that addresses the following scenarios:

- You're installing a new application that takes 15M of disk. You have only 6M. Quick, which directory can you zap to free up enough space?

- You're about to do a backup and want a list of every file on your disk to compare to your backup copy should the worst happen. Quick, how do you get it?

Space Map to the rescue. This little program zips around and gives you space, both used and allocated, for a single directory and the subdirectories, or "children," contained within. It comes in handy when you need very selective information about what directory trees are sucking up disk space. Almost all utilities offer you a directory of files or the whole drive. This utility is giving you information in yet another way.

> **Rick:** Practically, this utility is great on the network when you want a fast look at different directories on the LAN to determine what is eating up space.

How to Use SM

Copy the SM.COM file to some directory on your path. On my computer, I have a UTIL directory that includes all of my one-program utilities (like LIST and PKZIP). The syntax of the command to invoke SM is:

```
SM [pathname] [options]
```

All parameters to the SM command are optional. When the program is invoked, it always descends through every subdirectory under [pathname]. As it goes, it adds up the sizes of all the files it finds. As it backs out of each directory, it displays the total of the sizes of all files in the directories it found along the way.

Option Details

The /Dnn switch displays nn levels of directory depth. Use this option to limit the amount of information displayed by SM. SM can generate a tremendous amount of information, most of it inconsequential. By using this option only those directories (and files, if specified) no more than nn levels above the base directory path specified are displayed (although all directories are still scanned). /D1 means only those files and directories immediately below the specified path are displayed; /D0 means to print only one summary line and no detail lines.

Use the /I option [s ¦ l ¦ a ¦ t ¦ d ¦ f ¦ n] to tell SM what information you want displayed about each file or directory that is displayed. The parameter characters have the following meaning:

- s: displays the DOS size of the file or of the total files in each directory.

- l: displays the amount of storage allocated to the file or to all of the files in a directory.

- a: shows the attributes (hidden, system, read-only, and archive) associated with a file or a directory.

- t: displays the last modification time of the file or directory.

- d: displays the last modification date of the file or directory.

- f: displays the number of files contained in the directory.

- n: displays the number of subdirectories contained in the directory.

The opposite of the /I option, /X[s ¦ l ¦ a ¦ t ¦ d ¦ f ¦ n], causes SM to exclude the specified information column from the display.

/F displays files as well as subdirectories. SM normally just summarizes the totals in each subdirectory it encounters. /F causes SM to display every file it encounters.

/S[+ ¦ -] [s ¦ a ¦ d ¦ n] sorts the display in ascending or descending order on the specified key. Note that each subdirectory level is separately sorted; no sort option can override the basic order imposed by the DOS tree structure. You can sort on any of the following keys:

- s: the DOS file size or the total DOS size of all files in all subdirectories.

- a: the allocated file size or the total allocated space given to all files in all subdirectories.

- d: the creation/last modification of the time and date.

- n: the file or subdirectory name.

- You can control the sort order by specifying "+" to sort in ascending order (the default), or "–" to sort in descending order.

Normally, SM displays its information in a monochrome format, suitable for redirection to a disk file or printer. Enabling the /C[+|-] (control ANSI color display) switch (using /C+) causes SM to change the background color of each group of three lines, causing a "green-bar paper" effect on the screen. ANSI.SYS must be loaded for this function to operate properly, and if the output is redirected, the ANSI escape functions are sent to the redirected device.

When displaying a directory entry with time and date fields enabled, SM by default shows the time and date of the directory itself. The /L (display latest file dates) flag causes SM to find the most recent file (or subdirectory) within the subdirectory being searched and to list that date instead.

SM uses IBM line drawing characters to create the lines and boxes you see. Many printers (earlier Epson models, particularly) do not properly print these characters. Use the /G (format display for generic printer) switch to force SM to use more generic characters (like "–", "+", "=", and " ¦ ") to form the lines and boxes.

The same information can be obtained by typing SM/H or SM/?. You then see the summary screen as shown in Figure 6.11.

```
Space Map              Version 2.1
Copyright (c) 1991,1992 Ben Smith

Usage:  SM [directory-spec] [options]
        Valid options:
        /F - display (F)iles in each directory
        /I[s¦l¦a¦t¦d¦f¦n] - (I)nclude file information:
            s - file (S)ize
            l - a(L)located size
            a - (A)ttributes
            t - creation/modification (T)ime
            d - creation/modification (D)ate
            f - count of (F)iles
            n - cou(N)t of directories
        /X[s¦l¦a¦t¦d¦f¦n] - e(X)clude file information
        /S[s¦a¦d¦n[+¦-] - Sort report:
            s - sort on accumulated file (S)ize
            a - sort on accumulated (A)llocation
            d - sort on creation/modification (D)ate/time
            n - sort on file (N)ame
            + - Perform ascending sort
            - - Perform descending sort
        /C[+¦-] - Enable/disable ANSI color display
-- More --
```

Figure 6.11. The Space Map summary screen.

```
C:\FORBOOK\TEMP>sm c:\forbook
Space Map 2.1   Copyright (c) 1991,1992 Ben Smith

 Tree              |    Size    |   Alloc
-------------------|------------|-----------
 C:\FORBOOK        | 1,676,906  | 1,851,392
 |-DOC             |    10,882  |    16,384
 |-TEMP            |    75,109  |    98,304
 | |-TEST          |       240  |    49,152
 |-TEMP            |    75,349  |   147,456
 C:\FORBOOK        | 1,763,137  | 2,015,232

106,004,480 bytes free of 324,444,160 bytes available on drive.

C:\FORBOOK\TEMP>
```

Figure 6.12. A sample Space Map ouput.

As shown in Figure 6.12, the top line of the tree display gives the complete pathname of the subdirectory being mapped. The columns "Size" and "Alloc" show the actual DOS-reported size and the space that DOS allocates, respectively, to the files.

The next row (pertaining to the DOC subdirectory) shows the storage belonging to the files immediately within the DOC directory. Note that after the TEMP directory, a subdirectory, TEST appear, and then TEMP appears again—this time, reporting the cumulative total of the sizes of all files in all child directories. The idea here is to give you subtotals along the way to help you figure out what is really eating up the space.

You can, if you wish, include additional information about the directories you display. For instance, you could include directory creation time and date in the above display by typing (the results are shown in Figure 6.13):

```
SM/IDT
```

```
C:\FORBOOK\TEMP>sm c:\forbook /IDT
Space Map 2.1   Copyright (c) 1991,1992 Ben Smith
┌─────────────────┬───────────┬───────────┬──────────┬──────────┐
│ Tree            │ Size      │ Alloc     │ Date     │ Time     │
├─────────────────┼───────────┼───────────┼──────────┼──────────┤
│ C:\FORBOOK      │ 1,676,906 │ 1,851,392 │ 92/07/22 │ 22:03:48 │
│ ├─DOC           │    10,882 │    16,384 │ 92/07/23 │ 18:11:26 │
│ ├─TEMP          │    75,109 │    98,304 │ 92/07/22 │ 23:17:06 │
│ │ └─TEST        │       240 │    49,152 │ 92/07/27 │ 23:36:02 │
│ ├─TEMP          │    75,349 │   147,456 │ 92/07/22 │ 23:17:06 │
│ C:\FORBOOK      │ 1,763,137 │ 2,015,232 │ 92/07/22 │ 22:03:48 │
└─────────────────┴───────────┴───────────┴──────────┴──────────┘
105,979,904 bytes free of 324,444,160 bytes available on drive.

C:\FORBOOK\TEMP>
```

Figure 6.13. A sample Space Map with extended information.

Figure 6.14 shows the restricted output if you type:

SM / XL

```
C:\FORBOOK\TEMP>sm c:\forbook /XL
Space Map 2.1   Copyright (c) 1991,1992 Ben Smith
┌─────────────────┬───────────┐
│ Tree            │ Size      │
├─────────────────┼───────────┤
│ C:\FORBOOK      │ 1,676,906 │
│ ├─DOC           │    10,882 │
│ ├─TEMP          │    75,109 │
│ │ └─TEST        │       240 │
│ ├─TEMP          │    75,349 │
│ C:\FORBOOK      │ 1,763,137 │
└─────────────────┴───────────┘
105,955,328 bytes free of 324,444,160 bytes available on drive.

C:\FORBOOK\TEMP>
```

Figure 6.14. A sample Space Map with restricted output.

You can show information on individual files by including the /F option. To see information on the files in the TEST subdirectory, you'd type SM C:\FORBOOK\TEMP /F, and see the display shown in Figure 6.15.

```
C:\FORBOOK\TEMP>sm c:\forbook\temp /f
Space Map 2.1   Copyright (c) 1991,1992 Ben Smith

 Tree                    Size      Alloc

 C:\FORBOOK\TEMP       75,109     98,304
 ├─~$sm.doc                51      8,192
 ├─sm.com              7,893      8,192
 ├─sm.doc             31,282     32,768
 ├─read.me             1,061      8,192
 ├─~doc0e30.tmp       34,822     40,960
 ├─TEST                  240     49,152
 │  ├─dsn                 40      8,192
 │  ├─dxs                 40      8,192
 │  ├─ddd                 40      8,192
 │  ├─dddd                40      8,192
 │  ├─ddddww              40      8,192
 │  ├─dddw                40      8,192
 ├─TEST                  240     49,152
 C:\FORBOOK\TEMP       75,349    147,456

105,906,176 bytes free of 324,444,160 bytes available on drive.

C:\FORBOOK\TEMP>
```

Figure 6.15. A sample Space Map with file information.

Notice that file names are displayed in lowercase letters, and the directories are displayed in uppercase letters.

Finally, you can restrict the depth to which SM "digs" into directories. Of course, SM always keeps track of every file and subdirectory, but you may not want to actually see all that information. You can restrict the depth that SM displays by using the /D option. For instance, typing SM C:\FORBOOK\TEMP /FD1 should produce what is shown in Figure 6.16.

```
C:\FORBOOK\TEMP>sm c:\forbook\temp /f/d1
Space Map 2.1   Copyright (c) 1991,1992 Ben Smith

 Tree                     Size        Alloc

 C:\FORBOOK\TEMP         75,109       98,304
  ├─~$sm.doc                 51        8,192
  ├─sm.com               7,893        8,192
  ├─sm.doc              31,282       32,768
  ├─read.me             1,061         8,192
  ├─~doc0e30.tmp        34,822       40,960
  ├─TEST                   240       49,152
 C:\FORBOOK\TEMP         75,349      147,456

105,906,176 bytes free of 324,444,160 bytes available on drive.

C:\FORBOOK\TEMP>
```

Figure 6.16. A sample Space Map output with D1 option.

You can sort on size (S), allocated size (A), time and date (D), or file name (N). Only one sort option can be used at a time. Figure 6.17 shows the test case sorted by name.

```
C:\FORBOOK\TEMP>sm c:\forbook\temp /f/d1N
Space Map 2.1   Copyright (c) 1991,1992 Ben Smith

 Tree                     Size        Alloc

 C:\FORBOOK\TEMP         75,109       98,304
  ├─~$sm.doc                 51        8,192
  ├─sm.com               7,893        8,192
  ├─sm.doc              31,282       32,768
  ├─read.me             1,061         8,192
  ├─~doc0e30.tmp        34,822       40,960
  ├─TEST                   240       49,152
 C:\FORBOOK\TEMP         75,349      147,456

105,857,024 bytes free of 324,444,160 bytes available on drive.

C:\FORBOOK\TEMP>
```

Figure 6.17. A sorted Space Map example.

John: Take note, folks. The sort in Figure 6.17 is done alphabetically and the ASCII weights are used. Notice how it comes out. Pretty slick, eh? The following section is a review of some technical information about reported versus allocated disk space. It's great reading with a lite sandwich and decaff. Enjoy.

When DOS reports the size of a file, it reports only those bytes that are actually in use. But when a program asks for a block of storage, DOS may actually give the program more storage than it asked for because a disk generally consists of one or more platters, which are round aluminum disks on which ferric oxide has been coated. Each platter is generally served by two heads—one on the top and one on the bottom. Each surface is divided into circular tracks, and each track is divided into arc-shaped sectors which generally contain 512 bytes each. The tracks have to be divided into sectors because the write signal to the head can't actually instantly turn on and off. If you tried to change, say, byte 2,345 on a track, you'd probably wipe out a few hundred bytes on each side of the one you were trying to change. To prevent this, the disk manufacturers make you read an entire sector, make the change to the sector in memory, and then write back the entire sector. Each sector is surrounded by an "inter-record gap" which is a safe place to turn on and off the current to the write head. The space taken up by these gaps is not inconsequential. In fact, it may consume ten to fifteen percent of the disk. Consequently, it's advisable to make the sectors as large as possible (that way, less good disk surface is taken up by the inter-record gaps).

The problem here is that the sector becomes the smallest unit of storage that you can address. A typical disk has 512 bytes per sector, and this means that if you have a 1-byte file, it's stored on a 512-byte sector, with the other 511 bytes unused. Worse, DOS usually treats 8 physical disk sectors as the smallest allocatable unit of storage (called a cluster), which means that one-byte file actually wastes 4,095 bytes! Some disk compression programs encourage even larger clusters.

The "Allocated" number tells you how much DOS has allocated for your files. The difference between that number and the "Size" tells you how much disk space the file system is "wasting" because of the granularity of the file system itself. Unfortunately, there's not much you can do about this—it's a problem built into the file system. But if you want to see the problem in all its glory, look at a directory full of Windows icons. Each 766-byte icon is allocated 4,096 bytes.

The SM program now reports the total number of bytes available on the disk to store programs and data, and the number of free (unused) bytes. You may note that the number of free bytes and the number of bytes in use (which SM has always told you) don't add up to the total number of bytes on the disk. Why? The "Total Bytes on Disk" number is the number of available clusters multiplied by the number of clusters on the disk. But the "Used" number does not include two types of clusters: Clusters marked as bad, and clusters that are used as subdirectories. Take a look at Figure 6.18, which shows a chkdsk run.

```
C:\>chkdsk

Volume RSEGAL      created 11-05-1991 11:07a
Volume Serial Number is 18FB-90D9

 324444160 bytes total disk space
  10616832 bytes in 11 hidden files
   1892352 bytes in 229 directories
 205996032 bytes in 3772 user files
 105938944 bytes available on disk

      8192 bytes in each allocation unit
     39605 total allocation units on disk
     12932 available allocation units on disk

    655360 total bytes memory
    436208 bytes free

C:\>
```

Figure 6.18. A chkdsk output.

Note: Look at the number of clusters allocated to the directory entries!

Summary

Ben Smith, we salute you. You've got a great utility. Ben is a programmer out in the Lone Star state, and for those who wish to thank Ben directly, he can be contacted at:

Ben Smith
110 S. Gardenia
Celeste, Texas 75423
CompuServe: 70143,2023

Rick: This utility was offered as freeware, but I think you should send something to Ben. Rumor has it he is collecting postcards from weird places. Send him one (or cash, stamps, etc.) He's a Texan, so don't send him recipes for barbecue sauce or tacos, or hints on how to properly say "y'all."

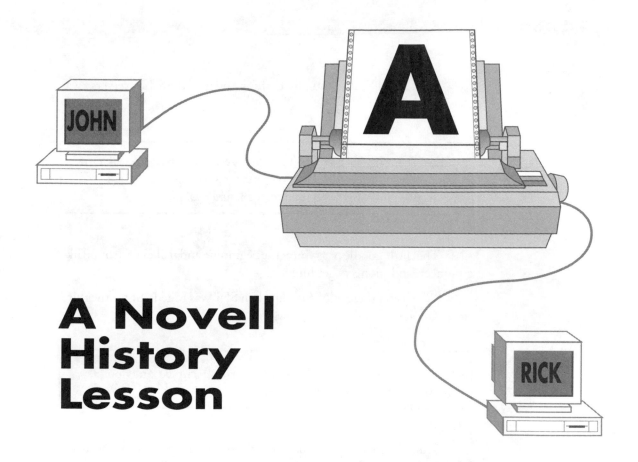

A Novell History Lesson

Why You Should Know This Stuff

You've probably read the history of Novell a thousand times, and frankly couldn't care less about Ray, Superset, and all of that. Well, not so fast; there are some reasons to know this stuff. The first and probably most important reason is career impact. If you are looking for a job and you put "25 years of Novell experience" on your resume, then this book just paid for itself because Novell and NetWare have only been around since 1983— you can thank me now for stopping you from saying something embarrassing. Also, think of all the subtle things you can slip into the interview:

"[Chuckle] Yeah, I shudder to think about all the S-Net servers I was chasing wire on."

 John: The term "S-Net" isn't too hip. In the business we call 'em "star" servers. That'll really show them you've been around! The terms 68A and 68B were used in the later days.

That little goodie pegs you at the beginning and makes you sound like a pioneer, and pioneers get hired.

"Were you there at Networld when SFT was rolled out for the third time? Cool, me too."

 John: How 'bout when Networld partially occupied one floor at the Infomart in Dallas!

Stuff like that makes you sound like one of the gang from way back. Most interviewers these days already own this book (shameless plug) and they might slip something in on you—like the year Ray Noorda showed up. Heck, you paid for this book, so relax and soak up some history.

In the Beginning . . . Sneakernet

Real networking began with Sneakernet. Sneakernet had a couple of fundamental protocols and some error checking. For example, a request for a lost resource:

"All right! Who stole my box of new eight-inch floppies?"

A broadcast message:

"Close the blinds, the glare is blinding me!"

John: Rick, snap out of it, you've regressed to the '70s!

File transfers were handled on a point-to-point basis—Joe walked a disk to Julie. Sneakernet was a great way to meet people and that was about it.

Corvus Constellation

If you were like me and owned an Apple II+, you had the makings of a network long before these hotshot PC people. Corvus produced an environment that, to the user, was a big disk drive that a bunch of Apples could tie into. There were lots of limitations, but when the PC cowboys start with the "I remember when" stuff, nail them with things like Corvus, and see how many remember it.

John: Another inside trivia tip: Corvus' Constellation network did not actually share files. It was a disk that was partitioned out for each node. Wacky!

Printer Sharing

While Corvus was helping people share disk drives, the vast majority of the business world was trying to share printers. Most people were running word processing machines that we hacks of the CP/M (control program for microprocessors) operating system and printers thought unbelievable from two perspectives: price (unbelievably high) and speed (unbelievably slow). Many companies came out with ways to run parallel or serial cables from these machines and early PCs to shared printers. This technology has matured and you can still find a healthy market for this stuff. BlackBox Corporation, Digital Products, and INMAC are all companies that sell products in what is called the "sub-LAN" market.

Novell Data Systems

In the late '70s, a computer equipment vendor was founded called Novell Data Systems (NDS). The company was doing Z-80-based computers. Zilog's Z-80 computer chip series was the leading computer chip in the late '70s, aside from the Motorola 6502, which was the heart of the Apple II computer family.

The operating system of choice about that time was a control program for microprocessors found on everything from S100-based systems to a version for the Apple. This was during the days when a multiuser system was either a big hunk of mainframe with some terminals, a minicomputer with terminals, or a variety of business systems based on the then-popular S100 bus. S100 was a term used to describe hardware systems that were based on a motherboard that contained 100 parallel lines across it. This board sat in a cabinet or cage and other boards were placed into the cage and plugged into the S100 board. The 100 lines were defined by a specification that told hardware vendors what lines should be used for what. For example, line 100 was defined as a ground, line 1 was power, lines 10-50 were data lines, and so on. This allowed a system integrator to really do a job of integration. An integrator could buy, for example, a hard-drive controller board from one company (Konan being the best), a processor board from another (COMPUPRO, being the leader), shove all this stuff into a cabinet, get some software (CP/M), a few applications (WordStar and dBASE II), and have a system.

Rick: At this point, please feel free to insert your favorite, witty "and Bill Gates was still in high school" type remark. I, on the other hand, refrain from Bill jokes. It's got something to do with working at Microsoft.

This was what NDS was into. They made up a bunch of this stuff and privately labeled it. (For fun, ask a Novell employee if they've seen any NDS printers around the Novell campus.)

NDS decided to differentiate themselves by developing some networking products. The main claim to fame was the 68000-based file server. The server had direct attachments to stations and could support 24 users. The speed wasn't bad for the time and the connections were simply serial interfaces. The cool part was how the machine handled the 24 users. Inside the server was a 6-port multiplexed (MUX) board. This board could manage serial input from 6 stations. The server was able to handle up to 4 of these MUX boards—hence 24 connections.

Superset

All great hardware requires great software, and a group of Brigham Young graduates was called upon to supply it. Called Superset, these folks acted as consultants to NDS and wrote a disk-sharing operating system that supported CP/M stations. As the original short-term contract was extended numerous times, Superset added features, improved the directory services, added security, and formed the basis of what grew to become NetWare.

Naturally, this life was not a bed of roses. NDS went down the tubes into bankruptcy in the early '80s. The venture capital folks who had coughed up most of the start-up funds took over the company to oversee the reorganization and attempted to salvage the company. While NDS was on life support and being reorganized into Novell, Inc., Superset had acquired an IBM PC. They created software programs that allowed the PC to interact with the NDS file server. These "shell" programs let the PC run either CP/M-86 (all five copies sold) or PC DOS plus the shell program. This combination allowed the user to gain access to files on the local drives or the NDS file server.

Rick: Given that the first PCs didn't have hard drives, most of this local access was to floppies. The available hard-drive technology involved large amounts of money, hardware, and patience.

Uncle Ray Comes Calling

In 1983, Novell came out of the court system with Ray Noorda at the helm. Stories get fuzzy at this point about Ray and his first days at Novell. The unauthorized biography, whenever it's written, is your best bet for the real dirt. As CEO and president, Ray kept just two items from the old NDS days: the 68000-based file server as the hardware line and the Superset software, which had been continually upgraded and, at that time, renamed ShareNet. ShareNet is also the name of the package that Novell sold for the IBM PC world. Powerful at this point in high-tech history meant 256K of RAM, a 68000 processor, and a stomping 5M removable hard drive. PCs contained network interface cards (NICs) that talked to the server (more on this technical stuff later).

XT Arrives Along with NetWare

IBM launched the IBM XT and Novell renamed ShareNet to NetWare/. The first flavors were called NetWare/S-Net. This positioning act was designed to let Novell release an operating system that allowed these new fancy "hot" XTs to be file servers in smaller networks. S-Net continued to be the topology. The "S" loosely stood for "star" because all the stations had a wire that led back to the server in a star arrangement. (Sit tight, more techno-stuff coming up.) At this point you had a couple of choices: you could buy an IBM XT and turn it into a file server, or buy a Novell file server along with a hard-disk drive system to create a shared file system. Both systems would have versions of NetWare available.

John: That is, "NetWare/S", "NetWare/X" (later renamed "NetWare/G"), "NetWare/O", "NetWare/E", "NetWare/P", "NetWare/PC", "NetWare/SM", "NetWare/D" and "NetWare/N" just to name a few.

Trouble in Paradise

At this point, the computer industry lost some of its innocence. No longer a hobby market aimed at the Heathkit crowd, big business stuck its nose into the game.

> **Rick:** Remember Heathkits? Keep in mind that in 1992, I attended an auction where an unopened Heathkit 20-inch color TV project went for $2,800. Think about that as you go snooping in your garage tonight!

Two operating systems were competing for control of the desktop: PC DOS and CP/M-86. CP/M-86 was a remake of the CP/M program for the IBM PC line. For a while, IBM actually offered both operating systems. The story about CP/M, DOS, Digital Research, Microsoft, and so on, is filled with fascinating tidbits about this weird business. Check out *Accidental Empires* (Addison Wesley, 1992) by Robert Cringely. It goes more deeply into this than I do.

> **Rick:** Because I'm a Microsoft trooper, you might guess that I'm slightly biased in how I tell the story of Digital Research being crushed beyond recognition. Not!

> **John:** Trust me on this, people. This dude wears Microsoft pocket protectors and sleeps with a Bill Gates Teddy Bear.

The best part of this early and first "war" was that Ray knew how to hedge the ol' bet and keep the ship sailing right down the middle. Almost from the beginning, Novell was set up to support almost every machine and every operating system that popped up. Folks, we are talking anything and everything. Quick show of hands, how many of you remember the TI Professional or the Victor 9000? Novell had versions for both.

John: How about the IBM 3270PC or the DEC Rainbow, and how about the fact that the IBM 3270PC used all available interrupts so only the Novell I-NIC could initially be used?

Novell supplied software for CP/M-86 and PC DOS. In fact Novell hung in there with CP/M-86 even after there was no question PC DOS would be the primary OS on the desktop. Today, with vendor support, vaporware, and all the things we love and hate, Novell has done a pretty good job of trying to support everyone and to keep everyone happy. The CP/M-86 support died around 1986 or 1987.

The NetWare Steamroller

At this point, Novell took off and pretty much owned the PC network operating system (NOS) market. After several attempts at revival, Corvus died, IBM was fooling around with Microsoft on silly things like MS-NET (don't ask), Digital Research was waffling around with MP/M (the multiuser version of CP/M), and 3Com was trying to put its software on the market. In short, there were no real alternatives.

Rick: MP/M was kept alive by system integrators who were still selling "systems" based on the S100 bus. MP/M and a few other multiuser systems were sold primarily to scientific and government interests.

For the most part, Novell fine-tuned the business model, as well as NetWare's design. Known by many names, the key to the power of NetWare is the remote file system model. This model, simply put, allows

NetWare and its file system to be independent of the client or workstation operating system. This means that DOS, SUN, MAC, and DEC stations can all access NetWare by means of writing shell programs. This design flexibility was extended to the core of NetWare and resulted in a product called Portable NetWare. Portable NetWare is available on a wide variety of computer platforms such as minicomputers from DEC and IBM.

John: Another name for Portable NetWare is NetWare for UNIX.

Rick: This is where you hard-core PC bigots jump up and scream "Mini? Ha! My laptop's got more power than them things. Why, I could run a densely populated third-world nation from my floppy drive." Careful, folks. The people running the management information systems (MIS) shops these days take a more balanced view of computing and which technology is appropriate to reach a business solution. Never come off as a technology bigot. Trust me, it's a career killer.

NetWare Flavors

NetWare has evolved over the years with several versions and flavors. Today, there is the 2.x and 3.x versions. The 2.x is an updated and consolidated NOS for the 286-based servers. The latest version in the 2.x series is Version 2.2. The latest version of the 3.x series is Version 3.11. In addition, there is a low-end version of NetWare called NetWare Lite, which I'll discuss later.

In addition to releasing new versions of NetWare, Novell concentrated their efforts in the area of software support. In 1984, Novell worked hard to get software developers to write applications that would take advantage of NetWare. Within two years, thousands of multiuser applications for NetWare were on the market. Novell also did (and continues to do) terrific work in the area of application programming interfaces (APIs). By exposing API calls to software developers, Novell was able to simplify the software development process. This also created momentum for more software development.

Currently, three "versions" of NetWare are available. The 386 version (NetWare 3.x), the NetWare 2.2 stuff, and the NetWare Lite offering. The following section describes the old and new versions from the perspective of power. Note that Advanced NetWare formed the basis for the entry level system (ELS) flavors that are mentioned.

Rick: Actually, most books and articles about Novell pass these three versions off as the total product line. Job interview tip: impress the interviewer by pointing out that there are more versions if you include the Portable NetWare versions on various hardware platforms. However, try to avoid rolling your eyes and making the interviewer feel like a washed-up COBOL programmer!

Your Menu of NetWare

- NetWare Entry Level System I (ELS I) was the cheapest way to get into a Novell LAN. The Volkswagen of NetWare, it ran on limited hardware, was limited to four users, didn't support OS/2 or MAC workstations, and didn't allow DOS workstations to use earlier than version 3.0 or later than version 3.3 DOS.

John: Just for the record, with the correct "shells," you can actually attach other versions of DOS and OS/2. The limitations were there at the time the product shipped.

> **Rick:** See gang, they don't call him the Wizard for nothing.

ELS allowed you to set up a station to function as a workstation and a file server. In this nondedicated mode, with one workstation acting as both server and client, the user count went to five. This free user was "free" in the sense of dollars only. The tradeoff was a large performance hit and potential conflicts with many different software packages. Like NetWare with training wheels, it served many small businesses well.

- NetWare Entry Level System II (ELS II) was the next entry level system, and it contained some good enhancements. The first was an increase in the number of users to eight. Like ELS I, ELS II could run in nondedicated mode as well, meaning it could have an additional user. Although this degraded performance, as it did in Level I, the effect was not as great. Novell has always recommended that Netware should run in a machine that is a dedicated server. This is good advice and should be followed unless pennies are being pinched to the screaming point. Performance was improved and the number of supported adapter boards increased. Also, the Novell message handling system (MHS) was included so that Level II could talk with the outside world. MHS was, as the name implies, a messaging system upon which many electronic mail systems are based. It was no screamer, but ELS II was a reasonable product for what it was designed to do.

- Advanced NetWare 286 (ANW) was the mainstream NetWare flavor for years, and the ELS versions were based upon it. The ANW software was the next move up from the entry level stuff. As the ELS versions were all based upon the mainstream ANW, most of the limits were raised and other important items were addressed. Support for up to 100 users, more than 25 different types of network cards, multiple external and internal disk drive devices, internetwork support, and significant performance over both ELS versions made ANW a powerful network operating system. ANW could run in nondedicated mode, but Novell discouraged it because of the overhead it required. The performance hit from running ANW in nondedicated mode was often worse than it was for ELS running the same application. If you have the feeling that network operating systems should have machines of their own and not run in nondedicated mode, you are quite correct.

- With system fault tolerance (SFT) NetWare 286, all of a sudden, the MIS people dropped into the back rooms where the PC folks were playing with all this Tinkertoy stuff.

 Rick: This is the last one for you legal freaks out there. Tinkertoys is a trademark of some toy manufacturer. I owned a set when I was a kid. That and Tonka Trucks were my life until computers. At this point, I'll note there's a ton of trademarks in this book. Be nice, pay attention, and don't steal any of them for your own stuff.

Having come from a mainframe background, these MIS people started looking for little things like backup systems, audit logs, mirrored drive systems, and other "normal" things one would associate with mainframes, minis, and any other mission-critical system. Large NetWare users were demanding system fault tolerance (SFT) and Novell responded with this version of NetWare. SFT provided the same features as ANW, with some new items to address SFT requirements. You should be familiar with the features described in the rest of this section.

- The transaction tracking system (TTS) was added to ensure that data written to the file server is completely written and verified before the system considers the write or transaction complete. In the event of a power loss during a transaction, when the server comes back up it sees the uncompleted transaction and backs out of it so that the original, "before-the-change" data is in place. This feature is invaluable as a safety net for databases on your LAN.

Novell offers programmers an application programmer interface (API) so third-party developers can include TTS within their own programs.

Rick: Most database vendors write their software to take advantage of TTS. If this comes up, be darn sure you understand to what level they have done this. You can ask questions about what set/version of the APIs were used to do the code, and so on. As the person managing this system, you should know this stuff. Besides, you'll shake up the sales/marketing people and they'll know that you do know your stuff.

John: Novell, however, did design NetWare to work with programs that were not TTS-aware by the simple use of record locking. See the SETTTS command in your manuals.

- Disk mirroring was the next feature added and it allowed the server to keep running in the event of a disk failure. Disk mirroring involved keeping identical copies of data on two different disk drives. If one drive failed, NetWare automatically cut over to the other drive. Some server overhead is associated with this feature, but it has never been shown to be excessive.

- Disk duplexing enabled the entire disk system to be duplicated. The server contained both a pair of drives and two drive-controller boards. This covered the situation of drive and controller failure.

John: An additional drive protection against power problems is to have the drive access power from a separate power supply.

- SFT NetWare could run only in dedicated mode because of the overhead SFT added to the server. This was a good thing because at the same time, terminate-and-stay resident (TSR) programs exploded all over the PC software market. Borland Sidekick was the first of these babies. TSR programs would climb up into memory and hang out until you pressed the secret keystroke. The problem was that TSR programs were not clean programming efforts. At best, they were hacks into MS-DOS and PC DOS that allowed DOS to accomplish things it really was not intended to do. TSR programs were, by design, watching everything coming from the keyboard or whatever points the programmer had coded to watch. Sometimes (actually, quite often), these programs didn't work right and would lock up PCs. It was bad enough if this happened to a workstation, but if it happened to a file server, it was a disaster because it killed everyone running off of the server.

NetWare 2.2

The latest in the 286 family of NetWare is Version 2.2. It is in effect a new release of SFT software. Most of the improvements focus on the installation process, performance, and an elimination of the different low-end versions of NetWare. NetWare 2.2 adds other items such as improved file attributes (to match NetWare 3.11). The pricing makes it easier to go from 5 to 100 users without switching to different NetWare flavors. NetWare 2.2 is a good seller and brings in a lot of upgrade revenue from customers who outgrew the old ANW and ELS versions.

Rick: News reports say that Novell got (and still gets) a major portion of its revenue from 2.2 upgrades and sales over 3.x upgrades and sales. It beats me, but they are making a lot of money and still dominate the network operating system market.

NetWare 3.x

The original title of this product was NetWare 386. Some older versions are still floating around, and if you own it, you should replace it with an upgrade. Most upgrades are free, and you may have the upgrade sitting around somewhere.

John: Most notably, any ".0" version should be killed and upgraded.

Rick: The upgrade on this was a class act. When Novell finally got its 386 act together, they kept to their word and upgraded everybody. In addition, Novell provided customers with components, such as connectivity for Macintoshes, that they had promised. It was a textbook, great upgrade process and Novell scored lots of credibility points.

John: Novell's headquarters are located in Provo, Utah, south of Salt Lake City. Utah gets to claim the Mormon church, WordPerfect Corporation, BYU, great skiing, and Novell as the five biggest things in the state. Travel note: Salt Lake City is one of the nicest, cleanest places I've ever visited.

Rick: Yo, John, for a really clean city, fine times, and wonderful people, try Redmond, Washington. Tour both places, gang, you can't lose.

NetWare 3.11 is a high-performance, robust, expandable, and powerful NOS. It remains compatible with older versions of NetWare while adding significant new features in the areas of security, performance, number of users, and a totally new method of adding functionality to the NOS. NetWare loadable modules (NLMs) are program components that can be loaded and unloaded at the file server as system requirements demand.

John: Unlike the kludge, value-added process (VAP) technology of 286 NetWare, NLMs are easier to write, install, and manage.

NetWare Lite

As you may recall, I discussed the "sub-LAN" marketplace. This low-end section of the market typically includes small/medium businesses that have printer sharing and minimal file sharing requirements. A company called Artisoft is the leader in this field. Artisoft has a product called LANtastic and it does a great job of providing print and file services. There are other, similar products but none has the market presence of LANtastic. LANtastic is usually purchased with hardware and cable all as one bundle. The product has been very successful. Novell, still managed by Ray "Business" Noorda, figured out that this is a good way to get people into NetWare. LANtastic has software to allow LANtastic stations to talk with NetWare servers. Novell, in effect, said buy it all from us, and NetWare Lite was born. Lite is a simple file/print share (peer-to-peer) operating system designed to get little workgroups and small businesses into the Novell fold. The problem is that NetWare Lite is not as good as LANtastic in the areas of performance and features, and it also has problems with some software. As of this writing, it's still a version 1.x product, so you can expect it to improve. This is a big market, and I would guess that others will be getting into the game as well.

Novell of the Future

As NetWare continues to evolve, it remains a robust, high-performance, secure platform for mission-critical software operations. NetWare 2.2 is already discussed in terms of improved performance, new security features, file features, naming services, and so on. Several Novell corporate customer sites have 1,000-user versions of NetWare, and there's no sign that Ray and the Provo gang intend to slow down or fade away.

Good for Me?

Yes, this is good for you because you have lots of company. You can be sure that an entire software and hardware industry segment is tracking right along with NetWare. Superservers, large-scale storage devices, improved desktop operating systems, and so on, all are combining to keep NetWare a strategic and an important part of the corporate MIS mission.

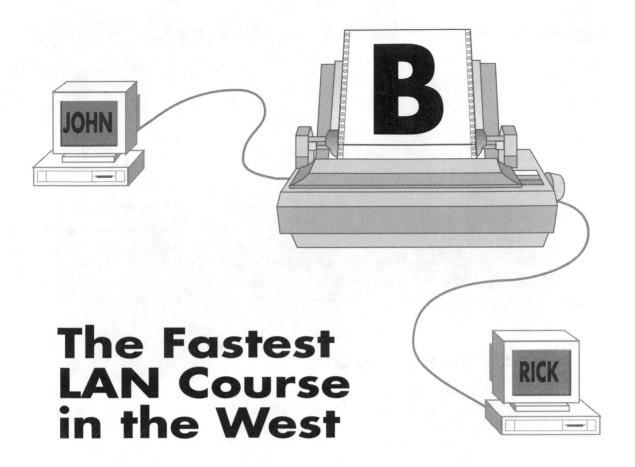

The Fastest
LAN Course
in the West

Nuts and Bolts

It probably comes as no surprise that you need hardware to make all this NetWare magic happen. The purpose of this appendix is to bring you up to speed on the major hardware components of a LAN. Armed with this knowledge, you should be able to identify all major hardware points of a LAN, have a feel for where trouble can occur, and be able to understand and avoid vendor hype.

Cables

It's true that 90 percent of network administrators never have to deal with the cables in their buildings. You won't be ordering cabling or negotiating a cable plan with a builder. That's okay, but cable issues do come up and you'll have an easier time understanding them if you have the basics down.

Rick: To use a corny analogy, LAN cabling is the highway on which your data travels. It's the one area that can cause problems without being an obvious cabling issue. An overview of the types of cabling you can build your LAN with follows.

Cable Flavors

Commonly referred to as "phone wire," twisted-pair cabling is simple to handle, easy to run, cheap, and relatively reliable. Thin cable is most popular with EtherNet configurations. The two variations on this cable are unshielded and shielded. Unshielded cable is the thin cable that connects telephones. Although in most cases this is adequate, there are some cautions regarding the use of unshielded twisted pair (UTP), particularly in the areas of building wiring codes and noise.

Shielded cable has protection around the basic wires to reduce noise—the electrical signals in the air that interfere with LAN traffic. If you're interested in explaining "electrical noise" to your kids, grab an AM radio and tune in your favorite golden-oldies station. Take the radio to your kitchen, fill up the blender with water, and kick it into high gear. That crackling on the radio is "noise."

John: You could also crush some ice so that after this intense science section, you'll have the ice ready for some cold drinks. Note also that shielding absorbs the signal it's protecting. However, when used over long distances it becomes less effective.

254

The cabling of choice for mainframe and time-sharing systems is coaxial cable, which is still widely used in hostile environments such as a shop floor or a manufacturing plant. When purchased by the foot, coaxial cable is more expensive than UTP, but coaxial cable is more resistant to external signals (noise) that can interfere with clean network transmissions. However, coaxial cable made with a Teflon jacket can be difficult to handle because it's stiff and not much fun to twist and turn around corners, on desks, and so on. Laying the stuff along the floor in a steel mill, for example, is no problem. You should use coaxial cable any time you are concerned about environmental issues, such as the wire being exposed to harsh weather.

The latest cabling medium, fiber optics, presents some opportunities in the area of performance and noise resistance. The cost of fiber-optic cabling is now considered as higher only if you get into fancy network interface cards (NICs), hubs, and other parts. Fiber optic performance is about the same as high-quality, shielded, twisted-pair or coaxial cable. The ease of installation for fiber-optic cable is about the same as other types of cable.

John: Isn't it amazing? Fiber has been around for at least ten years. Some things take longer to catch on than others.

John: PVC versus Teflon: Teflon is quite stiff, but it's required by most municipal fire codes because PVC releases a poisonous gas when it burns.

The big advantage with fiber optics is its tremendous resistance to noise and its capacity for high-speed exchange. Fiber makes an excellent backbone for your servers with workstations cabled in a more conventional mode. If you get wind of a cable plan going into a multiple-floor building, suggest fiber as the backbone of choice between the floors and different wiring closets. The reason for this is speed. With good, clean, high-speed connections between floors, you can concentrate on breaking up your plan into logical units while being sure the backbone for the file servers is a solid, high-speed highway. Figure B.1 shows an example of what a backbone is.

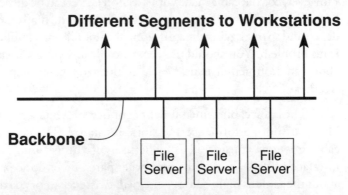

Figure B.1. An example of a backbone.

Cable Fact List

The following paragraphs serve as a checklist of cable facts and figures you should know.

Label Everything

In the air force, we were told to paint it if it didn't move and to salute it if it did. So, as the network administrator, if it's a cable, label it. Believe me, when you are in the office on a weekend trying to move a workstation from one cubicle to another and you can't figure out what wire goes back to the smart closet (the place where the wiring comes together), you're going to remember this advice. Label all the cables and do it at both ends.

Cable Plan

The most important part of your cable plan request is to be triple-sure you ask for and receive an "as cabled" plan. This means you don't want the original plan that doesn't consider such things as a brick firewall. You want the cable plan that shows exactly how all the cables were laid out. Why? Well, there's lots of reasons. For example, you can buy printers that can be directly connected to the cable so that people can share them without going through a print server.

Rick: The best printer for this kind of sharing is the HP IIIsi. This is a hot printer. Hewlett Packard, in my opinion, still makes the best laser printers in the world.

The cable plan helps you understand what your possibilities are, as well as where you can tap in and run new cable. You can use it to mark cubicles and offices in relation to the wiring. You'll also become a particularly valuable asset when people start having wiring problems because somebody took out a wall to make a new office.

Follow the Codes

You should be careful to follow code regulations in terms of colors, types, and restrictions. For example, in many places, you can't just flip cable in the ceiling without cable jackets because of fire regulations. Be good, follow code. If you find your inherited system is not up to code, report it.

Rick: I was working late on a Friday night trying to finish an important report for my boss. She was one of those folks who had no problem dropping in on Sunday afternoon to review the report and chat. I was working on 60 pages of the best technical data you've ever seen, and I was good about backing it up on a regular basis. The time came to print this baby and head to the beach for a late-night fish fry, so I sent the job to the printer and then saved it—lock up. Huh? Error reading from the server? What? I'm the only guy in here! I jumped up and headed for the server room. Locked. I punched in the magic code, opened the door, and there he was—a man and his vacuum cleaner. He was sitting on the floor trying to unravel the cable from the brushes in his Hoover.

continues

continued

The cables had been dropped on the floor and the Hoover tried to eat them. Someone thought that nobody came in here to clean. Wrong. A new cleaning contract required the workers to "clean it all." I had to deal with a crashed server, a toasted print job, and a destroyed file. Needless to say, I missed the fish fry. I'm sure you get the point. Find a quiet time and walk through your setup. Think back to those carefree days of your youth. Any cables loose that could be used as a jungle gym? Any connections just barely hanging on? Get this stuff fixed and save yourself some grief.

Ground

The ground is a frequently overlooked item in many installations. I'll spare you all the gory and boring technical details and give you one suggestion. If you experience any random or weird network errors that are just not fitting the troubleshooting patterns, be sure your system is properly grounded. In fact, it would be a good idea to check your system anyway (most systems are not grounded). I suggest having an electrician come in and do it, or get out your ohmmeter and do it yourself if you know how.

Disaster Plan

Do you have a disaster plan? What should you do if a cable segment is cut? Who is affected? Do you have alternate plans? How many stations can be kept up if a couple of segments go down? You should be able to answer all of these questions. Simply put, you need to know how to get to the servers from at least a couple of stations or understand what to do if a construction crew hacks a cable. For example, in Figure B.2 if segment A is cut off, the rest of the network can still function. Review this figure and try to imagine what happens if a problem occurs on the backbone or elsewhere. If you know this stuff and have plans, you can keep your company network running even during a problem.

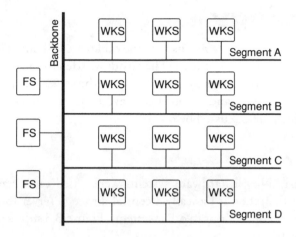

Figure B.2. A sample system layout.

Don't be a Cowboy

This is one of my favorite and most important rules when it comes to cables. If the documentation says 20 feet, use 20 feet—don't cheat. While it's true you can squeeze a bit more out of almost anything, it's just not a good idea. If you stay within the manufacturer's recommendations you will eliminate one possible trouble spot. Don't let those other people cheat either—those "other people" being vendors, and others who might work on your network. Remember, the problem you avoid might be your own!

Rick: The only occasion when I break the manufacturers recommendation is with regard to laser printer toner cartridges. I am here to tell you that when the "Toner Low" indication comes on your laser printer, you are not low on toner. Open up the printer, take out the cartridge, and carefully shake it a bit. This loosens up the clumps and you can print quite a few more pages with that cartridge. In fact, I usually do this shake bit three times before replacing the cartridge. Remember, however, to use care!

Topology

Topology simply means how the cables are laid out. There are a variety of layouts that can be used. The layout will determine how the cabling is run from workstations to the server, how the server is connected to the rest of the network, and so on. Each layout has advantages and disadvantages which are discussed below.

Star

Early Novell hardware systems were based on a star topology. A star configuration is basically a central device (a server for example) that has direct connections to other systems. Figure B.3 shows an example of a star layout.

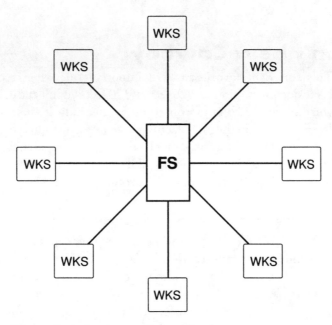

Figure B.3. A star topology example.

Although the star arrangement has some pros and cons, its greatest advantage is dedicated lines to each station. This means that network traffic loads don't affect each station. For example, if one station were to start an enormous copy operation that flooded the line between the server and the station with traffic, it would not affect the other stations in terms of network load. Keep in mind, however, that this affects the server's ability to respond to other stations. That's a different issue. Cable failures are easy to trace provided that you have labeled everything.

The biggest disadvantage to this arrangement can be limitations in the wiring scheme. Remember that the star's runs are limited to the number of lines that can be accommodated by the server. In the case of the older 68B servers from Novell, you could get 24 connections. In addition, if the server goes, that's the ball game—everything connected is dead.

 John: Distributed star is a twist to the star layout. ARCnet (attached resource computer network) and some EtherNet setups allow the cable plant to be arranged in this manner, which is a series of "stars" that are connected back to a central location. There can be no loops in a distributed star network and each star does not need to be fully populated. Merely observing the cable arrangement does not reveal where the server has to be; indeed, it can be anywhere in the arrangement.

Bus

Another popular topology is the bus scheme. As shown in Figure B.4, it usually is the layout that prompts the highway analogies.

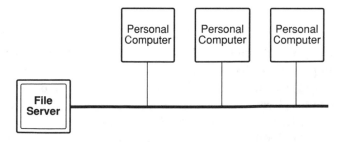

Figure B.4. The bus topology.

261

The main advantage to this scheme is its simplicity. Run the cable, slide in the connectors for the stations, and you are all set. The corresponding disadvantages are the distance issues and the inherent security problems. Security is a problem in that, unlike the star, the network traffic goes to everyone along the bus, and with some clever programming and minimal hardware you can have an unauthorized station grabbing data off your network. In addition, it's difficult to run a diagnostic on the network as a whole because the network is hard to isolate from the stations themselves. Bus systems are usually great for small networks, trade show setups, and other quick-and-dirty configurations.

Ring Around the Network

The third major topology is the ring. It is so named because of the logical way it is laid out (see Figure B.5).

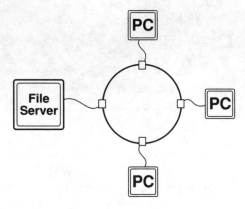

Figure B.5. An example of a ring topology.

In a ring layout, a data packet called a "token" goes from station to station to determine if the station contains data and to drop off any data or packets for that station. This prevents one station from taking down the entire network. Figure B.5 shows the logical layout of a ring, not the physical layout. The actual layout is more like a star when you look at the parts. Remember that an actual ring implementation is composed of the cable and multistation access unit (MAU). An MAU is the box in which the cables from the server and the workstations are linked together. Stations are connected with cable to the MAU. The file server also is equipped with a cable that goes to the MAU. Figure B.6 shows a ring arrangement in the physical sense.

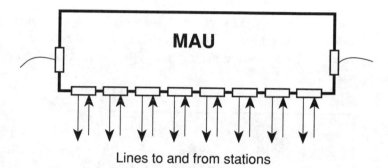

MAU

Lines to and from stations

Figure B.6. The line arrangements for the stations and MAU.

The stations all come together in the MAU but the token still goes in a logical circle. It's weird, but remember this next time you try to put some smart guy in his place when he draws a ring on the board. Ask the know-it-all to draw the physical layout of the equipment—gets 'em every time.

Network Types with Protocols

You have some cable and you know how to lay it out, and now it's time to figure out the protocol to use for your network. Protocol is the method the data packets will use to move around on the physical cable. The four basic configurations are EtherNet, ARCnet, token ring, and fiber distribution data interface (FDDI).

ARCNet

Clearly the oldie, but goodie, ARCnet was once the exclusive domain of Datapoint. These days, Thomas-Conrad and SMC are the best places to go for ARCnet parts and information. The up-front costs with ARCnet are low, and it's easy to install and troubleshoot.

263

> **John:** ARCnet is a natural for retrofitting those 3270 terminal-type systems.

ARCnet is also the slowest "rated" system. By that I mean that all the tech books rate FDDI, EtherNet, token ring, and ARCnet, in that order, when it comes to speed. As they say in the car business, your mileage may vary.

> **John:** Here's where network protocol arbitration comes into play. Note that ARCnet has an efficient protocol. For instance, Thomas-Conrad has taken its theory and applied the appropriate time derivatives to make it run at 100Mbps (this product is called TCNS—Thomas-Conrad Network Services).

I can assure you that for some network operations, such as large-scale copies and massive database operations, an ARCnet configuration outperforms a token ring setup. It all depends on station loads, cabling, applications, network hardware, and a host of other little things. The point is that you should avoid speed wars and concentrate on other issues. If cost is a major factor, most ARCnet configurations are cheaper than other types of networks. ARCnet runs on coaxial, twisted-pair, and fiber-optic cable, and it can be set up in bus or star configurations.

In an ARCnet system, each device on the network must have a unique station or node address. This address is set by the DIP switches on the ARCnet NIC. The network itself can have only 255 different station addresses on the network. Remember, this is per network and total connections. If you have more than 255, you can have different segments containing the stations. Each of those segments are different networks, each with an NIC card in the server. The server acts as the bridge for all the stations, and each leg has a different network number.

EtherNet

A personal favorite, EtherNet is cheap, simple, and a snap to deal with. EtherNet runs on thick or thin cable, and shielded or unshielded twisted-pair cable can also be used.

John: When you use twisted-pair cable, use the 10BASET standard.

EtherNet uses a scheme called carrier-sense multiple access with collision detection (CSMA/CD) to move the data around. This method boils down to the following steps that a station uses to get data on the network.

1. The station listens for other traffic on the network. How this listening takes place is a bunch of techno-babble that you don't really need to know. Suffice it to say that the station "looks" on the wire and "listens" for traffic or other packets zipping around the wire.

2. When the station finds an opening, it blasts its packets onto the network.

3. Should another station also send packets at the exact same time, a collision occurs. However, a mechanism is in place to provide for retransmission and spacing between packet transmissions.

John: Two stations could have a collision even if they start sending at a different time because the distance in the wire causes a delay. This means that the stations are sending at the "exact" time.

Later, I'll give you some basic rules regarding the setup of an EtherNet network.

Token Ring Networks

We've already discussed the ring architecture. The token passing protocol is what happens on a ring. This scheme involves stations passing a packet, or token, around along with data attached in a "pass the baton" fashion. The token and attached data goes from station to station where data is added and removed from the data train as the baton is passed from station to station. This method is great for ensuring that all stations get equal access to the network. Collisions are not a problem, and network management is a snap. Stations can be taken out of the ring from a logical perspective without interfering with the other stations.

John: Due to the excessive retransmissions of a single packet while it makes its way around the network, there is an inherent delay to this protocol which lessens its efficiency.

Rick: You can manage which stations are effectively handling the token, which stations are "out of sync" with the network, and a host of other management issues. Other types of networks are faster but not many are easier to manage.

Fiber Distribution Data Interface (FDDI)

Speed is the name of the game with FDDI, and FDDI has this speed advantage, in part, through the method it uses to get data around the network. Like the ring, FDDI uses the methodology of a token with a twist. Each station, after receiving and passing on a token immediately transmits another one without waiting for a reply to the first. In this way, multiple tokens are passed at once, which improves the speed. In addition, the physical media of fiber-optic cabling resists noise and other environmental considerations.

Rules of the Data Network Road

The next several pages contain the general rules and tips you should keep in mind regarding the different types of networks.

ARCnet Comments

Again, ARCnet is the easiest network to set up, and it has the fewest "parts." Remember that the ARCnet material in your Novell documentation set is referenced as RX-NET—Novell used to be in the hardware business, and they made an ARCnet board called RX-NET.

> **John:** Novell called their ARCnet board "Novell ARCnet" until Datapoint requested licensing fees from them to use the ARCnet name. Novell paid Datapoint and changed the name to RX-NET.

The SMC boards are functionally the same and most of the information is the same between RX-NET and ARCnet. To set up an ARCnet network, each workstation must contain a network interface card cabled to a hub. The hub acts as a signal splitter or relay, sending signals from one station to another. A passive hub just passes the signals without doing anything else. An active hub passes and amplifies signals.

General ARCnet Pointers:

Please make note of the following points about ARCnet. These notes are general instructions and guidepoints that will aid you in setting up a stable network. Again, don't cheat. Weird server errors, slow networks, and unexplained server crashes can often be traced back to poor cable design and installation.

1. The cable of choice is RG62/U.

2. Passive hub ports that don't have a cable installed must be terminated. These ports are terminated with a 93Ω resistor, which is in the form of a BNC connector. Don't cheat—terminate the connections that are not being used, or weird network errors will occur. In some cases the hub will fail and some stations will not be able to "see" beyond the hub. Do a walkthrough of any ARCnet system you inherit and check for terminations.

John: Personally, I hate passive hubs. I don't use them because they are not worth the irritation!

3. Active hub ports not being used don't have to be terminated.

Rick: I think that you should terminate active hub ports that are not being used to be consistent across the network and because almost everything else you work with requires some type of termination. Get in the habit now and avoid trouble later.

John: Rick is nuts. I think it's a waste of money. You won't have any terminators if you don't use passive hubs.

4. The standard connections between cables, hubs, and so on, are BNC and RJ45. This is handy to remember when you need the wiring folks to build a cable for you. When they ask about the connections you'll be ready.

5. You can connect active hubs to other active hubs, or workstations to passive/active hubs.

6. Don't connect passive hubs to each other. This does not boost the signal, and by the time the packets get through two connected, passive hubs, they are in rough shape and you'll encounter network errors.

7. For planning purposes, you need the following to create a simple three-station network:

   - Three workstations
   - One file server
   - Four network interface cards
   - No more than 2,000 feet of coaxial cable between any two points
   - One passive hub (the maximum distance between passive hub and node/active hub is 100 feet)
   - A bag of BNC connectors for cable connections
   - A small set of tools

> **John:** Use a crimp-on type connector, not the twist-on type, and be sure you have the proper crimping tool.

Table B.1 lists the general distance limitations you should know. Keep in mind that new stuff comes along all the time and each piece of equipment has the limits for it. Use this as a general planning guideline.

Table B.1. Network general distance limitations.

From	To	How Far
Network End	Network End	20,000 feet
Workstation	Workstation	2,000 feet
Workstation	Hub (passive)	100 feet

continues

Table B.1. continued

From	To	How Far
Workstation	Hub (active)	2,000 feet
Hub (passive)	Hub (active)	100 feet
Hub (active)	Hub (active)	2,000 feet
Hub (passive)	Hub (passive)	Don't!

EtherNet

Remember that EtherNet cable comes in four varieties: thick, thin, twisted-pair, and fiber optic. Workstations should be connected in a bus fashion along one piece of cable with terminations on each end.

- Thin: RG-58A 50 Ω coaxial cable.

- Thick: Standard .4-inch 50 Ω coaxial cable.

- Twisted-pair: 22 or 24 AWG (common phone wire). Note that twisted-pair connections are RJ45, not RJ11.

Thin EtherNet cable is restricted in the following ways:

- The maximum trunk segment length is 602 feet.

- The maximum network trunk length is 3,035 feet.

- The maximum number of trunk segments is 5.

- The maximum number of stations on one trunk cannot exceed 100.

- Both ends of each trunk segment must be terminated.

- The terminating resistor is 50Ω.

- The minimum distance between T-connectors is approximately 1.5 feet.

- One end of the network must be grounded with a real "earth ground," not a wall outlet type. Be sure you have a true ground source.

Thick EtherNet is restricted in the following ways:

- The maximum trunk cable length is 8,200 feet.

- The maximum trunk segment length is 1,640 feet.

- The maximum number of stations on one trunk cannot exceed 100.

- The maximum number of trunk segments is 5.

- The maximum distance between transceivers is 8 feet.

- The maximum transceiver cable length is 165 feet.

- Both ends of the trunk segment must be terminated.

- Thick EtherNet uses "N" series terminators, which are different from those used for thin EtherNet.

- One end of each trunk must be grounded. Again, remember to make it a true ground.

Twisted-pair cable is restricted in the following ways:

- The maximum number of repeaters is 4.

- The maximum number of trunk segments is 1,024.

- The maximum segment length is 328 feet.

Token Ring

Token ring networks have many benefits, mostly in the area of management. IBM has always supported token ring and continues to recommend it to most of its customers. Although token rings can be expensive to put together if you are buying IBM equipment, many other vendors also offer token ring equipment. Note the following token ring restrictions:

- The maximum number of stations on one ring is 96.

- The cable between the MAU and the workstation should not exceed 158 feet. (The number is odd because of the way in which you might end up cabling the workstation. Distance from an

MAU to a wall connection may not exceed 150 feet and the cable from the wall connection to the PC's NIC may not exceed 8 feet.)

- You can run cables between two MAUs, but the distance may not exceed 150 feet. Don't ignore this recommendation—you may lose data packets. Use special line boosters or repeaters if you need more distance.

- Use caution when you install cabling, and don't forget to take into consideration the twists and turns you'll encounter as you go around things and not through them. Pad the numbers a bit so you stay within the limits set by the vendor.

- You can have a maximum distance of 400 feet between MAUs.

- A station that is eight feet or less from an MAU must use the eight-foot adapter cable. Don't shorten the cable—it must be at least eight feet long.

- A station that is farther away than eight feet can use either a longer, single cable or two eight-foot cables connected with extension connectors. If you inherit a token ring network, this is a hot item to check as you walkthrough the network.

Boards

Now that I've covered the connections, you should know that all of this stuff should be connected to network interface cards (NICs), the boards that are inside the workstations, and the file server. The NIC is the station's link with the rest of the network. It connects the station to the network, and it is the traffic cop for information flowing in and out of the station. Be warned, however, that it can be a source of problems and a choke point within the workstation or the server. The NIC depends on a couple of items for its performance, and you should keep the following factors in mind when you're evaluating boards or considering upgrades.

The NIC can have its own on-board memory and intelligence. This means that the boards can cache or queue up requests for data and receive information and provide intelligent diagnostic information if required.

The NIC's memory and processing power is a big advantage, especially in the server. By having the board handle much of its own work without the need for server computing power, two things happen: the server is free to handle other things, and the resulting traffic in and out of the server is faster because of the lower server overhead. In general, it makes sense to have a high-performance, intelligent NIC inside the file server.

NIC data buses are available in 8-bit, 16-bit, and 32-bit versions. In most cases, you should use a card that can keep up with your PC and the speed of your physical network. This means that for XT-type workstations, 8-bit boards are about it. However, newer 486 PCs probably take at least the 16-bit and maybe even a 32-bit board. In the case of a fiber backbone, for example, it would be silly to use a first generation 8-bit board to connect a server, assuming you could find one. The board would be a bottleneck for data coming in and out of the server because it would be the slowest part in the arrangement of file server, network, and NIC.

Which version you select also affects workstation performance. Assuming the workstation frequently accesses the network, performance is probably affected by NIC choice. To reiterate, buy the best board you can afford. Everything passes both in and out of the server through the NIC.

PCs: They're Not Just for Flight Simulators Anymore

This section first looks at PCs in general and then reviews the key points as they apply to workstations and file servers. This discussion covers only PCs and not other stations that could connect to the network, such as Sun workstations or Macintoshes. PCs are typically set up with a main box that contains the motherboard, memory, video card, disk controller board, parallel/serial/mouse ports, and a power supply. Hundreds of variations on this theme are possible, but you get the basic idea.

Video

Video, of course, is how users see all this cool software and computer gee-whiz stuff. The video portion of the system is the monitor and the video interface board within the PC.

> **John:** An issue you should be aware of regarding the video board is that it can potentially conflict with the I/O address of a particular NIC. For example, 3b0h is a popular address for many monochrome boards, and using this as an I/O address for your NIC board simply won't work.

If users are taking advantage of the graphical user interfaces such as Microsoft Windows, think carefully about the video you offer. Forget using CGA or EGA monitors. Besides being incredibly ugly, much of the perceived speed of the system is determined by the refresh rate of the monitor. A monitor and video board that are slow in handling the input from the computer software makes the system seem slower. This can also cause eye strain and general fatigue when sitting at the station for prolonged periods of time.

Be cautious when you swap video components and remember to reconfigure the PC when you are finished. Some monitors are not compatible with particular video boards. In addition, there's the issue of internal settings that tell the PC what kind of monitor is in the system. In the case of Micro Channel Architecture (MCA) or Extended Industry Standard Architecture (EISA) machines, have the configuration or reference disk handy before you change anything. You would be amazed at how many of those diskettes go into hiding after the cover is popped off the machines. The old XT or AT and PC-1-type machines usually have charts showing jumpers and DIP switches that need to be reconfigured on the boards to get the required settings.

Ports

Most recent-model PCs are equipped with parallel and serial connections. Some even contain a second communications port. However, you need to be aware of several snags. Each port in your machine has an interrupt request (IRQ) line assigned to it. In almost all PCs, COM2 is set at IRQ3. This conflicts with many NIC boards. The point here is to advise you that when you are checking out an installation, be sure you document the IRQs used by the particular machine components so you can reference them against your network boards for possible conflicts. Table B.2 lists popular settings that you should know about. Remember to check interrupt settings and port addresses before you pop the top and drop in a board. In some cases, conflicts lock up the PC a couple of seconds after you turn it on.

Table B.2. Selected devices with interrupts and I/O addresses.

Device	INT	I/O Address
COM1	4	3F8h-3FFh
COM2	3	2F8h-2FFh
LPT1	7	378h-37Fh
LPT2	5	278h-27Fh
Floppy Controller	6	3F0h-3F7h
Hard Drive Control	14	1F0h-1F8h
VGA Cards	9 (or 2)	3C0h-3BAh (mono)
		3C0h-3DAh (color)

Memory

The PC would be pretty worthless after it went through its internal startup sequence if it weren't for the basic ability of the device to load some programs into its memory chips.

275

As DOS loads into a machine, it looks at the different settings in your config.sys and autoexec.bat file, and configures itself based on what these files tell it. For file servers, there are equivalents to the config.sys and autoexec.bat files.

I can tell you, though, when it comes to memory, every software program wants a piece of the action and NetWare is no exception. For a workstation, the two components required to effectively work on a Novell Network are IPX.COM and NETx.COM. IPX is the transport protocol software. This terminate-and-stay resident (TSR) program transports data packets from a sender to receiver based on a particular communications methodology. It's interesting to note that by running only IPX on two stations, you create a transport "highway" that programs on both stations can use to "talk" with one another.

I bring up this issue because there are third-party devices on the market that allow workstations on a Novell network to share resources between them without a "network shell" by simply communicating between themselves using IPX as the way to deliver messages back and forth. In situations where you're trying to limit the memory overhead on small or simple devices, you could code just software that requires only IPX. It's rare, but you should be aware that it can be done because when you are troubleshooting the workstation and there is now NETx, you won't just blindly think that's the problem. It might be, but remember that it may not be there on purpose. The NETx program is more specific in that it is controlling what is happening with the file server requests. NETx.Com is the program that actually does the work of getting messages ready for IPX to send and acting upon those messages that are returned from IPX. In addition, this TSR sets up some space in memory to keep track of drive mappings, server connections, and so on.

Disk Controller

The disk controller is the board that allows data to be written and read from your hard drive. You should be aware of controller interrupt and memory settings. Be especially cautious when a new user gets a tape backup or an external drive unit. These folks almost always set two items to the same interrupt and the machine either hangs or something that used to work doesn't any more. In most cases, take out the tape controller, bring the machine back up, and then read about the interrupt settings of the fancy new equipment.

File Server Hardware Notes

This section focuses on what makes up the server and where server bottlenecks occur. Unless you use a superserver, a mini, or a mainframe for your file server, most of this information applies regardless of what type of PC you elect to turn into a server. Each of the items discussed below have specific characteristics with which you should be familiar. This is important with regard to workstations as well, but it's more important with the file server because the server affects the work of everyone on the network.

Machine Bus Speed

Inside your server (or any computer), you usually find a board that has a ton of wiring, computer chips, and other boards sticking out of it. The common name for this is the "motherboard" because the main board houses all the required chips and is home to the other specialized boards as well.

If you look at the space between each slot, you'll notice a number of parallel lines running between the slots. These lines make up the physical connections that your boards need to interact with the basic machine. The board gets power, ground, and a data path from these lines along with other signals. Bus speed refers to the speed at which data can come off one board and get to another destination (for example, another board or memory location).

The bottom line to all of this is that a new million-dollar NIC board talking to the fastest memory on the planet, controlled by the fastest CPU around, needs a bus to support all this nifty stuff. Don't shove a new, high-performance NIC into a first-generation PC and expect the NIC to perform at its peak. The reverse is a bigger problem and one which causes many problems. A new, fast 486 may not support an old first-generation board. Remember that the faster the bus speed, the more likely old cards will not work in the machine. Keep this in mind when you are upgrading the server. You might have to budget for new boards such as the NIC or the disk controller.

One other thing you should remember is that there are three main bus types: Industry Standard Architecture (ISA), Extended Industry Standard Architecture (EISA), and IBM's Micro Channel Architecture (MCA). ISA refers to the AT type of stuff that exists in most clones and the IBM AT machines. MCA is the next generation of IBM bus architecture. It ran into a few problems, however—all of them political. The first problem was that many clone makers worried that IBM was going to try to kill off clones by creating a new architecture and then sucking royalty money out of everyone. The second problem was that lots of people had a ton of ISA type machines and tons of ISA cards that would not work in an MCA. A bunch of PC makers got together and formed a committee to create an extension to the ISA bus. This was called EISA and was designed to protect investments, resources, and so on. It was a classic business move that appealed to the soft issue of investment protection and ignored the technological debate.

EISA got lucky, because in IBM's haste to proclaim MCA as the way to go they failed to have lots of boards ready and lots of board vendors lined up with third-party boards. If you are getting an EISA machine, however, be sure that you have boards that exploit the EISA bus, not just old-fashioned boards. If you find the boards and the system you are creating is not taking advantage of EISA, consider the extra expense and be sure you have sound reasons for the choice.

Brains

The central processing unit (CPU) is the heart of the machine. It is a common misconception that the faster the CPU, the faster the machine. Beware of advertisements screaming at you about 50MHz, 100MHz, or super 1,000,000MHz. You need to understand that CPU speed is just one part of the overall performance equation. When you jump from a 386 to a 486, you get a certain improvement in the number crunching. After that, it gets cloudy (a high-speed 286 CPU, for example, compared to a first-generation, low-speed 386 may prove faster in some cases). Besides the actual speed of the CPU, you should consider several other factors regarding speed or quality.

Clock speed is one of these factors. Each instruction that a CPU chip executes takes a fixed amount of time or machine cycles. The length of each time bit or machine cycle depends on the clock speed of the chip. In the pure sense, an instruction that takes three cycles to execute is going to be faster on a chip with a faster clock speed. In most cases, however, the PC is not going to just be talking to itself. For example, our speedy new 486 box has a clunky old hard drive with a slow disk drive controller board. If the chip makes a blindingly fast data request to this old pile of drive garbage, it has to wait for the data. If it wants to write data to the hard drive, it has to twiddle its CPU thumbs while the old clunker writes out the data and then finally tells the CPU it's finished. If you get a reasonable 286 chip and the hottest, fastest, hard drive/controller on the planet, start an experiment in which two PCs just do a mountain of reads and writes to the drives, and it's a good bet that the 286 and its kickin' hard drive will win the time trials over time.

The important point to all of this is to do yourself and your users a favor by avoiding the trap of jumping on faster servers that come along touting fast CPU chips. A ton of factors determine if all of that zippy chip can be used.

Fixed Media

John: A long time ago IBM coined the phrase direct access storage device (DASD). In today's technological world, however, this term has lost its meaning. Originally, it referred to disk drives because they could access data directly. For instance, to read the 500th record of a file, all you have to read is the 500th record of the file, instead of reading records 1 through 499 first. Now this term can refer to magnetic hard-disk drives, CD-ROMs,

continues

> *continued*
>
> WORMs (write once, read many), magneto-optical disk drives, RAM/ROM, and so on. There are solid-state disk drives for instance, and IASD (indirect) equipment, namely tape drives, and punch cards. Generally DASD refers to magnetic hard-disk drives.

PC disk storage consists of two parts: the disk controller board and the disk drive. As discussed, the drive and its controller board can be a source of performance problems, with two possible choke points. One of these points is the transfer rate of the controller board. This is defined as the rate at which the board can process data in one direction or the other. In other words, how fast the board can take data off the machine bus and route it to the physical drive and how fast the board can take data from the drive and put it onto the bus. This "rating" is completely independent of the speed of the disk drive or the machine bus speed. Here too, be careful. Buying a hot disk controller board and attaching a first generation old drive can potentially waste the resources of the controller. The overall disk system would be only as fast as the slowest part. Some controllers have intelligence that dramatically increases overall system performance. This acts in somewhat the same way as the intelligence of an NIC. The board handles much of its own processing and frees the main system CPU to do other things. In most high-performance file servers, the disk controller and the NIC have intelligence on board. For the disk controller, this intelligence might also include caching.

Caching is a process whereby previously accessed data is kept in memory on the assumption that it will be needed again (accessing a bunch of database records, for example). If they are cached in memory, the next time you or another person goes after the data, it is returned from the quick cache versus an access to the disk drive. Caching also works in the reverse, where writes to the server are cached or stored up and then the intelligent board writes a bunch of things at once. Your applications see a write complete faster because the write is to the fast memory chips. Novell has both read and write cache as part of the operating system.

You may hear vendors promoting boards that are sometimes called intelligent caching controllers. This means that the board has been designed to optimize the reads and writes from your disk drive in order to give you the fastest possible response time. In a NetWare environment, there are debates as to the value of the hardware caching because the operating system is designed with caching. I did some unscientific tests with a board from a company called Konnan. They make a controller board that claimed to improve response times over a traditional controller board. In my limited testing it did help a little. Your results, however, may vary.

After you've optimized the controller board, you still have to consider the drive itself. Every drive is rated as to its read/write speed, as well as a variety of other performance data. Avoid getting caught up in this technical marketing mumbo-jumbo and concentrate on what gives you a good, high-performance system. For example, if you have the latest and greatest disk drive with an old, tired 8-bit controller, the drive will spin around waiting for the controller board and it will give data to the board faster than the system can handle it. Normally, the reverse is the common problem— a great controller board and clunky hard drive. One final word on cache: sometimes an old hard drive with that tired controller board works just fine; for example, if you have a 2M sales file that is the primary thing a bunch of users look at all day. After that first read, the file is accessed out of cache memory that has the drive and board sitting idle.

So remember that you, the LAN guru, have many things to be aware of when it comes to the overall server and your system. One vendor you should be aware of is Adaptec. I don't think any company builds a better disk controller. There are a couple of reasons for this. The most important reason is the packaging. Adaptec packs their controller board in a box with everything you need to set up a disk system within a NetWare system, stand-alone, OS/2, and so on. All the driver software is included on disks for the appropriate system. The packaging is outstanding, the cost is reasonable, and the technical support is probably the best around. For disk subsystems there's no contest: Storage Dimensions, Inc. (SDI). SDI is my favorite. Most of the drives SDI uses come from their parent company, Maxtor.

John: Pay attention to these company names. They will come in handy when you are searching for information on a particular component or item for your network. In all cases, we'll tell you about lots of companies, but we only recommend those with which we have personally worked.

Maxtor makes good, rugged hard drives. They have some of the best engineers around, excellent documentation, plug-and-play systems, and, overall, the company is an excellent source of drive systems and should be considered any time you need additional storage for your systems. SDI's subsystem combined with an Adaptec controller board is an incredible combination of storage and access power.

John: While SDI makes a nice subsystem cabinet, I prefer CDC/Imprimis/Seagate "Wren" disk drives (originally sold by CDC, then by their spinoff, Imprimis, and then finally Seagate).

NICs

Although I have discussed network interface cards, I want to go over a few items again as they relate to the server. As I mentioned before, the NIC board is your server's link with the outside world. If at all possible, get the best you can afford so this does not become a bottleneck. Remember that everything is coming to the server, and that all the data passes through the NIC. For the server, it's advisable to look at "smart boards," boards that have both on-board CPUs and their own RAM. They can buffer requests, offload some work from the main CPU, and generally give your system a performance boost. My favorite EtherNet NIC vendor is 3Com. I've always liked their boards, documentation, diagnostic disks, and technical support. IBM is without question the choice for token ring boards. Because

IBM and Novell get along reasonably well, you can bet that the boards and the drivers work well together. Thomas-Conrad and SMC make good ARCnet boards.

Server Memory

Novell has documented several minimum specifications for the amount of memory each version of NetWare needs in order to run effectively. Table B.3 shows those amounts.

Table B.3. The minimum memory specifications for each version of NetWare.

Version	Minimum (in megabytes)
NetWare 2.15	2
NetWare 2.2	2.5
NetWare 3.1	2.5

Server Memory Minimums

Here's a friendly tip on server memory: put in more than the minimum, because you're going to need it. The minimums are barely enough to get the system up and running. For running almost anything at all, you need more memory. My recommended minimum is that no server be running with less than 6M of memory.

Power

I put this section here for two reasons. The first reason is to tell you that you need to have a power supply that has enough juice to supply plenty of power to the server even with the NIC boards, memory boards, and so on. Don't skimp on the power supply. If you're the new kid on the block, open up the server and check out the power supply. You need 300 watts or more.

If the server doesn't have a solid power supply, make replacing it a priority. This can be a sneaky problem. Consider the following scenario: you are running out of disk space and you decide to add an additional 600M hard drive to the server. If the server is already packed with drives, interface boards, backup interface board, printer connections, modems, and so on, you might just put the server over the edge when you fire it back up.

> **John:** Don't skimp here, folks. The larger the better.

The second point about power is that a server needs to have a steady flow with no surprises. Poorly grounded power, brownouts, surges, and losses are sure to cause major problems. Again, as a checkpoint, verify your power supply. If there is damage due to power loss, it is related to what the server was doing at the time of the interruption. For example, if the server was writing something to the hard drive and the power shuts down, the interrupt can cause the hard drive to function improperly and corrupt data. Also, in cases of brownouts or surges, you may not know why the server hangs all of a sudden or why the disk has corrupted data. The best thing you can do to eliminate power as a source of potential problems is to be sure that you have an uninterruptable power supply (UPS) with line conditioning and surge protection, features that are found on most good UPS devices. Every server should have this protection.

Hardware Walkthroughs

The following pages detail some items you should consider making part of your routine. You may want to create your own weekly, monthly, and occasional lists of things to do. Feel free to tear out the pages of this book for your checklists.

I have come up with some things that belong on checklists for preventive maintenance, ownership transfers, shift changes, and so on. You should make up your own mind as to the frequency and depth of each item. These lists are not inclusive of everything you can do, but they should serve as starting points that you can enhance as your situation dictates.

UPS Cutover Check

Frequency: Weekly.

Comments: Most UPS devices have a test switch. This is a critical item. The UPS is of limited value when it fails. Be sure it is always ready to go. Check the plug connections and be sure the devices that are supposed to be protected are properly plugged in. You'd be surprised what effect moving, cleaning crews, and equipment swap-outs have on things being properly plugged into the UPS.

John: Don't plug a printer into a UPS. It is wasteful and useless. If the power goes and the printer is plugged into the same UPS as, say, the server, you will drain the UPS faster and force the server into a premature death. Don't do it.

Cable Labeling

Frequency: On assumption of responsibility and then monthly.

Comments: When you assume responsibility of a network, get a cable plan (as wired) and make sure the cables are labeled. Check the smart closets to ensure they have a plan. Each closet or place where the cables come together should have a plan. Patch panels and the wires coming in and out should be labeled. Beware of the label trap that happens with small groups thinking that they'll be one happy family forever. Don't accept "Fred's other machine" as a label. Insist on a plan that can be applied to the whole network and that makes sense to future players. A monthly walkthrough should be used to catch cables that were added and not labeled. After you get the place in shape, you'll develop a sixth sense about this. You'll smell unlabeled cables, and the first time you have a major troubleshooting issue, you'll appreciate the labels.

In addition, don't forget the labels at the desktop end. Many companies put a label that contains a variety of information on the PC itself (see Figure B.7).

Port Number:	3BC
Serial Number:	3403044-e1d-243
NIC Settings:	IRQ2 300H, NO DMA
Help Desk:	555-HELP 8-5:00 (M-F)

Official CIS Label: mm/dd/yy

Figure B.7. A sample system label.

Connection Integrity

Frequency: On assumption of responsibility and as deemed appropriate.

Comments: This involves checking the connections on the patch panels and on the server. You should be looking for frayed cables, loose connections, broken connectors, loose grounds, and loose terminations.

Dirt Check

Frequency: Monthly.

Comments: Unless your equipment is in a *very* clean room, dirt and dust will accumulate inside the server and other places. You should check and clean all filters (including UPS filters, cabinet filters, air conditioning filters, and so on) and keyboards and open the servers to remove any accumulated dust and dirt.

Server Preventive Maintenance Check

Frequency: Quarterly.

Comments: The server should be checked on a regular basis. Create a schedule and stick to it. You should regularly remove the server cover and check for dust/dirt within the machine.

- Check the internal cables from the controller board to the floppy or internal hard drive and be sure they are secure. Check the cables from the power supply to the drives.

- Visually review the motherboard and note any cracks, burnt chips, foul smells, or chips not properly seated in their sockets. The burnt-chip, foul-smell stuff is in reference to power spikes that may have fried a capacitor or resistor. This may happen after lightning hits a building. Should you sense any problems, get your PC maintenance guru on the case at once.

- Before closing the cover, check those pesky screws on the interface boards. Replace missing screws and tighten them. This keeps boards from working their way out of the motherboard slot. The half-in, half-out boards are a troubleshooting nightmare because they are not very obvious. Make sure boards are properly seated in the motherboard and screwed down.

- Replace the cover with all the screws. A sudden shift or slide while moving can strip a screw and cause the unit to pop out from the cover.

- Check the cables coming into the server. Look for frayed wire, loose connections, and worn-out connectors on both the board and the cable itself. Tighten, repair, and replace as required.

- Clean off the monitor with a screen wipe.

- Boot the server with a MS-DOS disk and use a diagnostic tool to check the memory. I recommend a tool called Checkit.

- After checking the memory, check the ports using the diagnostic tool to see if the PC sees them and if they are being correctly identified by the diagnostic software.

- Check the monitor, keyboard, interrupts, and any other items that the diagnostic software is capable of checking.

- If you have an internal hard drive and want to check it, two products on the market, Norton Disk Doctor, which comes with Norton Utilities, and SpinRite (in my opinion, the better of the two) from Steve Gibson will do the trick. SpinRite executes a low-level check of your drive. Use caution, however, as this is only for DOS partitions, not NetWare. This product is great for checking a drive before going into a server, provided the drive has not been pre-formatted for NetWare.

 John: Remember to turn off the power if you are going to take off the server cover.

Shared Laser Printer PM Checklist

Frequency: Monthly (or at each toner cartridge change).

Comments: Laser printers are the most popular shared printers. You can prolong the life of these gems by following a few simple rules:

- Always blow out the inside of the printer when you open it to change the toner cartridge.

- Follow the manufacturer's cleaning advice. Most people don't use all the little tools (cotton swabs, brushes, etc.) that come with the toner cartridge. The wires and dirt catch must be cleaned, or the overall quality of the output decreases. In some cases, globs of dirt are caught up on the rollers or the drum. This causes a permanent spot on every printed page and makes the printer worthless for anything other than drafts.

- Use caution when buying recharged toner cartridges because they may not come with the tools you need to clean the wires or rollers. Be sure you have at least one set on hand.

- Check the connection on the back of the printer. Because people are constantly adding paper and the tray is being removed and put back in all the time, you can expect that the printer will be moved around. Check the cable to be sure the connection is solid. Parallel cables often lose their covers and slowly come apart. Pay close attention to the cable because it's one of those places that can cause random errors.

- Most printers run their own diagnostics when powered up. You should run a test page after every toner cartridge change, ideally a two- or three-page test job that has a graphic and some fonts in it just to make sure things still look good.

- Check the paper tray for cracks or other damage. If the tray is messed up, it may cause paper jams that stress the printer.

- When using a large or extended paper bin, be sure it's properly installed and seated. Many people let these things hang over the edge, and this eventually fails. Checking for proper installation and seating helps avoid paper jams and formation of cracks on the paper bin.

Backup System PM

Frequency: Monthly.

Comments: It would be easy to tell you to follow whatever the vendor says, but that probably will cause trouble for you. Running the simple check program that comes with the unit is not going to be a real-life check. Follow this list instead:

- Run the diagnostics that come with the unit. This should catch any gross problems with the unit and the interface board.

- Create a backup tape that has a reasonable amount of data on it.

- Attempt to restore the tape both on that machine and a different machine. If the tape fails from one backup unit to another, you have a problem with head alignment or something internal. This is an unacceptable situation. For example, if a fire destroys your equipment but not the tapes, you are in a world of hurt if the only tape device that can read your tapes is in ashes.

- Attempt to restore a backup tape that you made some time ago. If this restore fails, it might mean that all the tapes you have in the firesafe are unreadable.

- Tighten any connections from the cables to the unit and the interface board within the PC.

- Check the fuse, if any, for signs of wear or corrosion.

Caution: Use care when fooling around with the fuses. Turn off the power and unplug the unit.

Oldies but Goodies

Wrapping up this hardware chapter, I want to mention uses for all of that old equipment that is floating around. Besides creating good tax write-offs if you donate it to a school, you can use it for a variety of things. Listed below are some of the hardware components you might have on your network and how you can use that older hardware.

Print Server

This one should be obvious, but it is often overlooked because of a couple of myths.

Myth number one is that you need a hard drive to create a print server. That's not true. Spooling print jobs takes place on the file server, not the print server.

Myth number two is that a slow PC results in slow printing. That's not true either. Even the slowest PC and its parallel port is fast enough to drive most printers. Keep in mind the data flow. After your print job is queued up on the server, it is passed to the print server over your speedy LAN. This data goes from your LAN to the PC NIC and ends up going to the printer. There is no question that a 486 is faster than an 8088 clone, but the difference probably amounts to one or two printed sheets a month, over time. In other words, the slower, old 640K machine can be an excellent print server.

Modem Server

The same is true with the modem server as it is with the print server except in cases where you need speeds that are not supported by the serial port or UART chip within the PC. In most cases, 2400 or 9600 baud modems can be attached and used without any problem.

Host Gateways

Older PCs can be used as effective gateways primarily because the interface card that gets you the host connections has its own CPU and memory. It is getting power and ground from the PC. The only potential bottleneck is the data transfer from the host board to the PC NIC.

Bridges

Here too the PC acts more as a host, with the interface boards doing almost all of the work. Except in cases of really fast data transfers, you can use a 286 PC to bridge LANs together. Keep in mind that you can also do the bridging inside the server as well, thus saving a PC all together.

Summary

It's been a wild ride through the world of hardware, and I hope you picked up some useful information. A couple of key points are worth repeating:

- Connections—tighten everything and don't cheat on the screws. Cables were designed to fit tightly and securely.

- Label everything.

- Performance—consider the performance of any piece of hardware as a balancing act. Don't use just a vendor's data sheet. Be sure you know all the factors and then come up with a balanced view.

- Keep it clean, and you'll impress your boss.

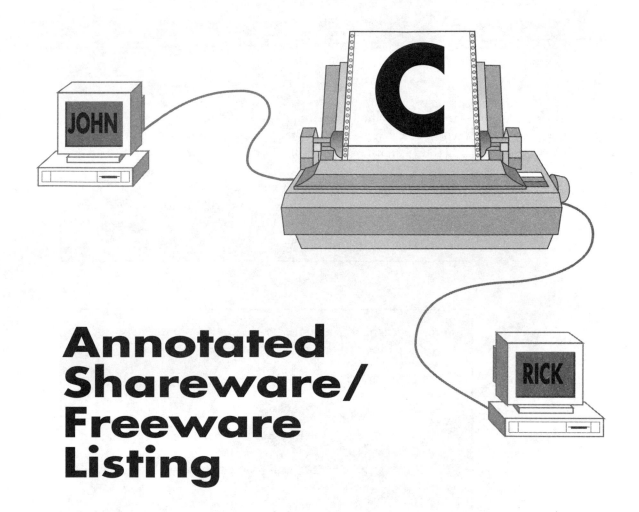

Annotated Shareware/ Freeware Listing

File Reference Guide

Rick: One of the largest electronic information systems in the world, CompuServe is a manager's tool that you must have. On CompuServe, almost every major software and hardware vendor maintains a forum for you to post questions, get patches, and "talk" with colleagues who probably either have been or are going

continues

continued

through the same problems you face. For Novell, you should type
GO NOVELL when you are on the system. The files are found in the
Library section. As a point of reference, you can find most major
vendors by company name: Go Micrsoft, Go IBM, Go Borland,
etc. You can also do a "Find" to look for a company or product.
For example, at the CompuServe command prompt you can type
FIND Modem. This will give you a list of all the possible places that
modems come up on the system.

John: Hey, gang, if you find a file that you would like to obtain,
log on to CompuServe and follow these steps:

>   At the ! prompt, type GO NOVLIB and press Enter.

>   When "Join" is returned, follow the instructions
>   to join the forum if you are not already a member.

>   At a Forum prompt, type DL17 and press Enter.

>   At the Library prompt, type:

>   BRO File=<filename>;LIB=ALL and press Enter.

Replace the <filename> with the name of the file you want to see.
This command causes CompuServe to find the file regardless of
the library section. It displays the summary information, and then
you can download the file and use it!

Note: In most cases you will need to have PKZIP or the PKXARC program. Both can be found in Library 1 of the NOVLIB section, and both come in what is called self-extracting format. This means you just download and run what you downloaded. It uncompresses, and you then have what you need to uncompress the files listed below.

XOR.ZIP: Parity Generation Speed Test for NetWare (XOR.NLM)

The Parity Generation Speed Test for NetWare (XOR.NLM) contains the source code and the make files for an NLM called XOR.NLM. The purpose of XOR.NLM is to measure the parity generation speed of a given processor. To run it, unzip it, then LOAD XOR from the console. This produces parity for ten seconds, then reports results and exits.

John: You need the Novell NLM Developer Kit to build XOR.NLM. Personally, I'll pass on this one. The last time I needed to generate parity, a tooth fell out.

CODES.ZIP: Xerox/IEEE Assigned Vendor Codes for Network Cards

This list of Xerox/IEEE Assigned Vendor Codes for Network Cards also provides multicast and broadcast addresses.

John: Sign me up. This list is interesting, especially if you have EtherNet or token ring networks—you'll never again wonder about the first part of your network address.

SNLVI.ZIP: SoftStone Network Library Volume I

The SoftStone Network Library Volume I is four powerful network management programs for NetWare: Configuration Manager is a full SYSCON replacement with built-in reporting; Monitor provides graphic representations of vital FCONSOLE information and features built-in reporting; Backup&Restore copies configuration data (bindery, trustee rights, and others) to any device, enabling you to restore a network if this data is lost or corrupted; and QuikStat is a comprehensive testing program with user-defined thresholds.

Rick: This is a good set of utilities that gives you a Swiss Army knife approach to creating a decent toolbox.

DUMPQ.ZIP: Kill All Jobs in a Queue

DUMPQ.EXE is a simple utility that can be used from the DOS command line to delete all the jobs in a particular queue, such as a print queue. C source code for Microsoft C and NetWare C Interface for DOS is provided, as well as executable program. For help, type DUMPQ with no parameters. This comes with no warranties. It's provided as is and uploaded by the author, Glenn Scott.

CPU-UT.ZIP: Fileserver CPU-Utilization NLM

The fileserver CPU-utilization histogram NLM running on the FSCONSOLE is based on Novell's SS.NLM. This needs SS.NLM, and source CPU-UTIL.C is included.

John: This is nice, and it's worth the download effort.

BENCH.ZIP: Benchmark and Timing Utilities for Networks

The benchmark and timing utilities for networks generate a known/fixed amount of traffic on the network and a utility to measure the execution time of network commands. Although designed for the network environment, these utilities can also be used for stand-alone workstations.

John: This utility requires a little bit of effort to set up to get usable results, but it might be worth it to you. As an alternative, you could set up your own test consisting of copy statements.

TAKEOV.ZIP: The Reassign File Ownership Utility

TAKEOVER enables supervisors to reassign ownership of files to other users, or by default, to the supervisor, and it accepts filename wildcards. This is a useful tool if you have disk space limits on your server. C source code is enclosed.

John: Talk about giving away the store. Get this one before time runs out. It's quite useful.

Rick: What my partner means is that if you get into DASD management like you should (that is, knowing who owns what, and so on), this kind of thing helps.

NETUTL.ZIP: Dave's Network Utilities Version 1.1

NetDrive Version 1.1 is a program that locates the first network drive, changes to it, and sets an environment variable to that drive letter. This eliminates the need to hard-code the network drive into any login batch files that you might be using. NetTest Version 1.0 checks to see if the network shells have been loaded and sets the DOS ERRORLEVEL to indicate the result. This is freeware, and the source code is included.

SOSS Version 3.2: Son of Stan's Server

This source code for SOSS Version 3.2 turns a PC into an NFS server. When attached to any Novell server, it provides many of the same services that are provided by the NetWare 3.11 NFS NLM. Unpack with the command `pkunzip -d soss_src` (create and unpack subdirectories).

GLPRNT.ZIP: Creating Global PRINTCON.DAT Files

This is a description of a simple method to provide global, conditional, and group PRINTCON.DAT files.

John: Yet another in a long list of methods to achieve a global PRINTCON.DAT. I would add this one to my collection.

UPLOAD.DAT: Upload Script for Hard Disk Install of Version 2.2

This is an edited script file for use with the UPLOAD program that shipped with NetWare Version 2.2. This file, when used with UPLOAD.EXE, uploads only the five diskettes necessary for a true hard disk installation. The original UPLOAD.DAT file was used to upload all diskettes to a network drive generation area. To use this, rename your old UPLOAD.DAT (on the SYSTEM-1 diskette) to UPLOAD.NET, and copy this to your SYSTEM-1 diskette.

John: Nice little shortcut. If you find yourself multiply loading Version 2.2, you might just like it!

299

SHOLOC.ZIP: All Filelocks on a Server!

This utility (with C source) displays all the filelocks on the default file server. It includes the LOGIN and CONNECTION numbers, and it saves you from banging through FCONSOLE connections for the information. Unfortunately, this does not work on a NetWare 386 server.

John: It's too bad that it doesn't work with NW386, but for now it works okay with NW286 and it's useful when you need to see who has locked up the database files.

PKTDR9.ZIP: Clarkson University Packet Drivers 9.x With Source

Clarkson University packet drivers 9.x with source code is used to run Novell and TCP/IP simultaneously on the same NIC.

John: This one requires an investment in time, but it might be just what you need. Being able to run TCP/IP and NetWare allows for a much better way to access UNIX (and NetWare) stuff.

Rick: The other point here, John, is a possible cost savings in the one-card approach. The downside is that this can require more support than you may want to deal with.

TN3270.ZIP: Public Domain TN3270 for LAN WorkPlace for DOS

This file contains an implementation of TN3270 that requires LAN WorkPlace for DOS Version 4.0. The emulator is essentially the same as the 3278 Model II Telnet that was included with LWP for DOS Version 3.5. A PostScript image of the documentation is included, and Novell has released this emulator to the public domain. No support is available for this application. The sources are available in the file T3270S.ZIP.

T3270S.ZIP: Sources to the TN3270 Executables in TN3270.ZIP

To work with these sources, the C programmer needs a copy of the LAN WorkPlace Toolkit for DOS and a Microsoft C Compiler. This implementation of TN3270 requires Version 4.0 of LAN WorkPlace for DOS. Novell offers these sources "as is." No support is provided or is available for this TN3270 implementation.

John: Don't forget TN3270.ZIP!

FILEOW.ZIP: File Repair Utility for NetWare

The FILEOWN Version 1.00 program replaces invalid owners of files in the current directory with the ID of the person running the FILEOWN program. The program cures a problem that causes NetWare to incorrectly report "disk full" to applications. Turbo C source code is included with API calls.

BENCHM.ZIP: Benchmark of Compaq and IBM

This file is a benchmark of the Compaq Systempro, IBM PS/2 Model 95, and IBM Model 80.

BOOTST.ZIP: BOOTCONF.SYS Editor

BOOTSET.EXE is a compiled BASIC program that adds workstations to BOOTCONF.SYS. It is public domain and unsupported. It's handy when you're installing a number of diskless workstations. Source code and limited documentation are included in this ZIP file.

> **John:** This one is a time saver if "bootless" is your handle!

CHECKS.ZIP: Free Utility for Sitelock

This little utility enables you to see if Sitelock is loaded on a user's machine. When used in the system login script, it beefs up file server security. A complete application note is included. This file is of value to Sitelock owners/users only, and it is uploaded by Rick Segal.

TAUDIT.ZIP: Trustee Audit Report Version 1.0

This program outputs the access rights and owner of NetWare directories, subdirectories, or entire drives.

John: This is another tool for that box of yours that can be quite revealing.

SRINFO.ZIP: Bridging, Routing, Source Routing, and NetWare

This file contains a discussion on bridges, routers, and source routing bridges as they apply to NetWare. It also includes considerable background information on how these various internetworking devices work. It places particular emphasis on source routing and token ring, but much of this document is useful to anyone planning or maintaining an internet that contains nodes other than NetWare.

John: Don't wait for your network to give out. Be sure you know the scoop. This is recommended reading.

POPCAP.ZIP: TSR Print Capture

PopCapt contains a TSR print capture utility for NetWare 286/386.

John: This might be just the thing for nondedicated NW286.

IPXEDT.TXT: Edit IPX for Custom IRQ, I/O, DMA, Etc.

This file details how you can edit IPX.OBJ or IPX.COM so that you can have your own "brew" of IRQ (interrupt), I/O, DMA, and so on. This one is by the Wizard, John T. McCann.

> **John:** This one gives you details on how you can customize an object.

> **Rick:** Warning: Kids, don't try this at home. This is heavy technical hacking—be careful.

HPLJ3.ZIP: HP LaserJet III Device Definition for NetWare

HPLJ3.ZIP is an HP LaserJet III "device" definition for NetWare PRINTDEF. A supervisor-equivalent user can import this definition to PRINTDEF. (Novell does not support this file.)

SETSER.ZIP: Set File Server Time from Workstation

This file contains a program that sets the time on all attached file servers to workstation time. It also includes a program to set workstation time to the National Institute of Standards time through a modem. It includes a Turbo C source code program. For this to work you must be a file server console operator on the file server. This is in the public domain.

> **John:** SYSTIME in reverse. I love it!

> **Rick:** Actually, this has value in getting the server to sync with the workstation.

KEYLOK.ZIP: Locks the Keyboard and Waits for NetWare Password

KEYLOCK locks up the computer and waits for the user's NetWare password to be typed in. KEYLOCK works only if a user is logged in. If DESQview is active, KEYLOCK also locks the DESQview menu. Uncompress this with PKUNZIP (uploaded by the author, Francois Bergeon).

> **John:** This gives your users some added security, but be sure they don't tape a copy of their password to the screen!

> **Rick:** Hey, McCann, don't be giving out any of that managerial advice—that's my thing. Make sure your users protect their passwords.

DVCAST.ZIP: Manager for NetWare Broadcast under DESQview

DVCAST displays NetWare broadcast messages in a DESQview window without interrupting the operation of the active task. DVCAST is equivalent to the NWPOPUP utility that comes with Windows 3. Uncompress this with PKUNZIP (uploaded by the author, Francois Bergeon).

TRACK.ZIP: Display Service Advertising on PCs

After entering "TRACK ON" on any workstation with IPX loaded, TRACK.EXE displays routing information on the network similar to the information that can be displayed with the console command "TRACK ON" on a file server or bridge. Output can be redirected to files or printers. This is uploaded by the author, Wolfgang Schreiber.

John: The Wolfman has done it again. A fine utility—watch this stuff without RCONSOLE!

Rick: Download everything Wolfy has done. He's one of the best. In my book, *LAN Desktop Guide to Troubleshooting: NetWare Edition* (Sams, 1992), you'll find some of Wolfgang's stuff.

MONITO.ZIP: Display Service Advertising on PCs

MONITOR.EXE displays compact file server usage information on the workstation screen of a console operator or supervisor. It displays user names, addresses, activities, and open and locked files for all file servers to which one is attached. Short help is available in MONITOR.DOC (uploaded by the author, Wolfgang Schreiber).

UNLOCK.ZIP: Releases Print Server Lockouts

If intruder detection is active, a print server can be locked out after entering invalid passwords. There is no chance to release the print server (like SYSCON does with users) until the lockout time has passed. This file releases print servers (and users) accounts. Help is available by entering UNLOCK without options.

> **John:** Sounds like an escape for a poor manager, but, hey, that's not you, is it? You should get this anyway!

ULIST.COM: Self-Extracting ARC Enhanced USERLIST

Like USERLIST, this file provides information on active users. It also provides connection number, login name, and Full Name. It is useful at sites where the employee number is used as the user ID.

> **Rick:** I should mention again that using full names and login IDs helps you in your quest for decent managerial control over your environment.

QSTAT.COM: Self-Extracting ARC Queue Status Utility

This file contains a command-line utility to display print queue status information. This gives the same information as PCONSOLE (print queue information, <pick a queue>, current job entries) without the menus and uses much less memory. It displays information for one queue specified on the command-line or all queues to which the PC is currently capturing. It's small enough to be run from almost all programs' DOS shells.

UTILS.ZIP: Some More Utilities for NetWare Users and Managers

Similar to USERLIST, this file contains utilities such as ARCHIVE.C, DSERCH.C file list WHO.C, and lists files that have been on a drive for a given number of days.

NETPRI.EXE: Print Job Configuration Copy Utility

This utility copies a print job configuration from the supervisor's MAIL directory to all the other users on the file server. If the user already has a configuration, then it's renamed with a .BAK extension. This is self-extracting with a READ.ME file.

John: Another method for that all-important "Global PRINTCON.DAT" simulation.

RECV.ZIP: A TSR to Make the Novell SEND Command Nice

This file contains a TSR called RECEIVE that handles reception of Novell SEND messages in a nice way. It pops up and flashes the message while the foreground task continues to run.

Rick: This is not required for Windows or OS/2 machines. Also, check out the answering machine software (ANSMACH.EXE) included on the disk that comes with this book.

LOGOFF.ZIP: LogOff Version 1.1 Logout Utility

LogOff Version 1.1 is the new LogOff program discussed in the December 1991 issue of *LAN Times*. LogOff logs you off the network and fixes your path and removes references to directories that you can no longer access. It also hunts up a new COMMAND.COM if COMMAND.COM is not accessible. This is a free program. A product of Computer Tyme, it's uploaded by the author, Marc Perkel.

John: Yes, Marc has done it again—a simple but useful tool for those in need.

LOGDIS.ARC: Login Display

This file displays an ASCII text file if a certain amount of time has passed since the user last logged in. Use this to display system messages once a day, or remind users to log in more often to check their E-mail. This was developed for the U.S. government. It is public domain, includes source in C, and requires Novell C Library to compile. This is uploaded by the author with 170 previous downloads.

HSECLE.ZIP: File Management Aid

HSCLEAN contains a file lister that shows the last access dates and has some filtering. It's intended as a file management aid for system administrators.

> **John:** This one is definitely of use to those who are archiving their networks.

KILL.ZIP: Terminate User's Connection from Command Line

This program uses the NetWare Clear Station API to disconnect the specified user from the current file server. The program requires the user have console operator or supervisor privileges to run and uses the following syntax: KILL <username> <password>.

> **Rick:** The reason why you want this kind of a utility is for those times when you have a critical job, like backup, that must go forward. Also, because you are actually reading this stuff, here's a little secret: this one is on the disk that came with this book (KILL.EXE). Are we good or what?

WHO386.ZIP: WHO_USES
a File for NetWare 386

WHO386.EXE and WHO_NLM.NLM are client server applications that bring back some of the functionality of FCONSOLE to the NetWare 386 user. This is a command-line program that enables any user to know who has a certain file in use on the network. It contains two files: an NLM to load on the file server and a DOS program as an interface. These applications include documentation, are in the public domain, and are made by Bart Mellink.

John: An old favorite, our friend from the Netherlands brings this winner to a LAN near you!

Rick: I agree with Big J. Bart Mellink has done some outstanding software and is an excellent coder. He's one of the best.

TCCHEL.ZIP: Thomas-Conrad's
ARCnet Utilities

This file contains a utility that shows the board layout and switch settings on Thomas-Conrad's ARCnet and TCNS boards. This also contains TCONFIG.EXE and EXEFIX.EXE utilities, as well as a README that explains when to use the EXEFIX.EXE.

WHERES.ZIP: Where's the Beef?

This file contains WHERES, a short utility that accepts, as a command-line argument, the name of the user you wish to search for in NetWare. For more information, refer to the July 1990 *NetWare Technical Journal* article "WHERES the Beef?" by Charles Rose.

John: This is a fine utility that shows what connections a specified user is logged into. Unfortunately, it's not necessary because the Novell-supplied "USERLIST" command can do the same thing for no download time. However, an error level is set by WHERES if more than one user is logged in with the specified name, so you may find it worthwhile after all.

NEWUSE.ZIP: A Utility for NetWare to Add New Users

This file contains NEWUSER, an add-user utility for NetWare (Version 0.01 beta). It enables you to configure and add new users to your NetWare LAN. You can configure and create users, home directories, subdirectories under home, group membership, and rights to other directories. Add multiple users simultaneously. This is a wonderful tool for network supervisors (produced by R&S Data Systems, Inc.).

MOVE.ZIP: A File Moving Program from Computer Tyme

Computer Tyme's MOVE is a program that moves files from one directory to another. It moves files between drives and file servers, supports wildcards, and has many nice features.

AUTO47.EXE: Magee Enterprises Menuing System

Automenu is a sophisticated menu facility that enables you to organize and control the use of your computer system by creating menus to access all of the following features: multiple passwords, parameter passing, unlimited menus, timed execution of any menu selection, network support, customization of colors and screen formats, mouse support, auto blackout, and complete documentation. This is produced by Magee Enterprises, Inc., and it is a shareware-ASP member product.

Rick: Marshall Magee is another expert who has done some excellent work. His company is into network management, and his team is a good group of people to know.

BINDSU.ZIP: NetWare Bindery Service Utility

BIND.EXE is a NetWare bindery service utility that enables the user to view the organization and relationships of the bindery.

NETWOR.ZIP: A Utility for NetWare's MENU Program

This file contains a program to help work around the deficiencies in NetWare's MENU utility. This appeared in the September 1991 issue of *LAN Times*.

313

OPENED.ZIP: Lists Users Who Have a File Open

This file contains OPENED, a utility that enables you to list the users who have a particular file open on a file server. It is easier than the NetWare utilities and is useful when you need to get exclusive access to a file but you don't know who is using it.

> **John:** This one is a must if you are experiencing file lockout problems.

DXREAD.ME: READ.ME File for Directory eXtended Version 2.60

This file contains an ASCII description file for the DX directory/file management utility. Its features include extremely powerful file matching (multiple inclusion and exclusion extended patterns, date/time/size ranges); batch file generation; move/copy/compare, delete/rename/append/ checksum/CRC any tree of files; sort and search entire disks including ARCs, ZIPs, LZHs, ZOOs; file transfer test; and much more.

DX-D20.ZIP: Documentation for Directory eXtended Version 2.00

This file contains documentation for DX Version 2.60, a powerful directory/file management utility. It hasn't changed since the 2.00 version. See DXREAD.ME for more information (available separately). DX-260.ZIP contains DX Version 2.60 and DXREAD.ME. Unpack it with PKUNZIP. See *PC Magazine* review (June 13, 1989) for more details.

DX-260.ZIP: Directory eXtended Version 2.60

This file contains DX, a powerful directory/file management utility. New in Version 2.60: LZH, ZIP, and ZOO processing; compare files in LZHs to DOS files or ARCs, and so on; copy/move entire disk structures, prune and graft subtrees; logical drives; wipe sensitive file data; set/clear/report Network Share attribute; and much more. See DXREAD.ME for more information (available separately or in this ZIP). Unpack with PKUNZIP. See *PC Magazine* (June 13, 1989) for more details.

LOGRUN.ZIP: Run Menu from Login Without Memory Penalty

LOGRUN Version 1.1 contains a utility for use in login scripts that allows you to run up to two programs when LOGIN.EXE is about to terminate without sandwiching LOGIN.EXE's memory. It provides a surefire way to invoke menus without relying on stuffing the keyboard queue. It can also ensure that users log out.

VU.ZIP: Reports Space Use on Mounted Volume

VU volume utility is a network-aware utility that reports space use on all mounted volumes. A bar graph gives quick visual status for each volume. VU includes a PIF and ICO file for use with Windows 3.0 (this is shareware from ErgoSoft).

PRINTZ.EXE: PRINTCON Definition Extended Copy

PRINTZIP.EXE is a self-extracting utility called PRINTCON.EXE, which enables a user to copy PRINTCON definitions from any user to any

315

other user, or to any group of users. This utility uses menu functions that are very similar to Novell's MENU.

NFAU.ZIP: Network File Attribute Utility

This file contains a network file attribute utility that enables the user to alter the file attributes and extended file attributes for files on a NetWare network. It is similar to Novell's FLAG.EXE program.

John: Similar to FLAG, but better, that is. It allows for manipulation of all those flags!

GMCOPY.ZIP: Global Copying of the PRINTCON.DAT/LOGIN

This file contains an update to GMCPY.ZIP, with added tagging features for the user list. It's a simple utility that enables a network supervisor to copy either a login script or print job configuration to specified users' mail directories on the default server. This file changes all existing user files. LOGIN or PRINTCOM.DAT can be renamed to ".OLD" extensions if specified. Written by Bart Reese of Novell.

COMMAN.ZIP: Problem with COMMAND.COM

This file deals with the problem of loading COMMAND.COM if COMSPEC is set from the login script.

BINDLO.ZIP: Bindery Scanner

This file contains a menu utility (uses C-Worthy) to read the contents of binderies. It displays properties in dump or full format. Uploaded by the author, Pierre Baco, in ZIP format, Novell France. BINDLOOK is a shareware utility to check and read the bindery of NetWare file servers. It uses C OSUSES/EXIT.

QLIST.EXE: Queue List

With this program you can quickly see what jobs you have in your various print queues. It is like the console "Q" command, but with a little more detail. You don't have to get up and wander off to the console.

GETUSR.ZIP: Get Login Name, Group Membership, Supervisor Equivalency

This file contains three programs: GETUSER.EXE, which returns the user's login name; ISMEMBER.EXE, which determines whether the user is a member of a specified group; and IS_ASUPER.EXE, which determines whether the user is a supervisor or an equivalent. It also contains partial Turbo Pascal source code with information on where to obtain all additional source code needed to compile. The author is Rob Roberts, and it is in the public domain.

ENVUTI.ZIP: Utilities for Manipulating Master Environment Variable

This file contains utilities to manipulate the master environment table. SETDRV creates two variables with current drive and directory. Use SETENV to create your own master environment variable with a passed

317

value. CLEARENV clears all or unneeded master environment variables. This one is uploaded by the author, Scott Hansen, of DBNet Software Solutions, Renton, Washington.

> **John:** This may be a good solution for those of you who have complex setups.

BINDIN.EXE: NetWare Bindery Information Displayer

This file contains a utility that lists all available information in the bindery. It accesses most properties from almost any type of object and is useful for getting complete reports of what the server knows. BindInfo is donated to the public domain, provided it is distributed in unmodified form and with a proper copyright notice. Future updates will be made available. (Accounting data is not yet listed.)

WOGIN.COM: A NetWare/ MS Windows LOGIN/ LOGOUT Utility

WOGIN is a multiserver LOGIN/LOGOUT utility for Microsoft Windows Version 2.x/Version 3.x and supports Novell NetWare Version 2.x/ Version 3.x. WOGIN can log a user into and out of multiple servers simultaneously while creating drive mappings on a per server basis. It also offers variable substitution (for example, %LOGIN_NAME) for drive path specifications, logo display, and support for all the different modes of Microsoft Windows Version 3.0.

> **John**: This one overlaps with some functionality already available, but it may be worth a look.

GETND2.ZIP: Gets ARCnet Node Address

This file contains GETNODE Version 2.00, a program that displays the node (station) address of an ARCnet card. GETNODE does not rely on the I/O address of the ARCnet card or on what interrupt number is used for the ARCnet card. This program does not require network software to be loaded onto the workstation. This version enables the user to supply the memory address segment for the ARCnet card.

NETUTI.ZIP: Net Drive Utilities, Version 1.00

This file contains batch file utilities to locate the first Novell network drive or to test if the NetWare shell has been loaded. The source code is included.

IDE.TXT: IDE Drive Explanation and Compatibility

This file contains the truth about IDE hard-disk drives and their compatibility with Novell NetWare.

IPRINT.ZIP: An NPRINT Utility

IPRINT is a replacement subset for Novell's NPRINT, with a few additions. The ZIP Version 1.02 file contains the .EXE file and the Turbo

C source code. Novell's NetWare C Interface libraries are needed for relink. The EXE file and documentation file are in English, but the source file is in French. This is freeware with no restrictions.

SLEEP.ZIP: Delays Start of Batch File or Login Script

SLEEP is a program that suspends the operation of a batch file or login script until a predetermined date and time. This program includes a utility called KBFLUSH that flushes the keyboard buffer and is designed to be used with the programs KBOFF/KBON in KBD.ZIP.

John: This is a great utility for those late-night backups.

PS.ZIP: QMS PostScript Printer Utility

This file contains PS.COM, a utility that adds the necessary header and footer code to an ASCII file so it can be printed on a QMS PostScript printer without changing the switch setting. It is a simple file, handling only one file at a time and using DOS redirection. This is uploaded by the author, Dennis Steinert.

BS301.COM: BSEARCH Version 3.01

This file contains BSEARCH Version 3.01, a simple utility that can track 16-bit and 32-bit checksums of files. It can also be used as a file finder and a global file deleter. It passively watches for virus infections by comparing file sizes and checksums stored in a database. This is the latest version (as of February 14, 1990) and was previously uploaded as BS200.COM. It uses a new syntax, but it's easy to use and self-extracting.

> **John:** Be warned that newer viruses can avoid this type of detection program!

GBIND.COM: NetWare 386 Version 3.0 BACKUP Utility

This file contains GBIND, a simple utility that enables you to close or open the NetWare 386 bindery. The file includes two sample batch files that show how to use it to back up and restore the bindery. It is much quicker than using BINDFIX and requires no user intervention. Use this to back up user and security information.

FINFO.ARC: File Server Information

FINFO.EXE is a program that displays various information about the default file server. The program was originally written to provide the serial number from the DOS prompt, but then the other file server description strings were also added. Written in Microsoft C Version 5.10. The NetWare C library is used for NetWare function calls.

U-CHK.ARC: Source Code for LIB 10's USERIS

This file includes an example program that verifies that the shell is loaded and a user is logged into a server. It will take a command-line argument and verify that the name given is a valid login name on the current file server. The example is coded in TP5 and TC2 (Pascal and C). There are 220 previous downloads.

GRP.ZIP: Utility to Scan Bindery/Display Groups and Members

This file contains a utility to scan the bindery and display the group names and their members or to scan and display the user names and the groups to which they belong. Turbo C source included.

DETECT.ZIP: Utility to Listen to Server's SAP

This file contains a program using the NetWare C Interface to detect the server's Service Advertising Protocol (SAP) identification packets. The author is Mark Sadler.

USERS.ARC: A Sorted List of Users with C Source Code

USERS.ARC displays a sorted list of all user objects, either logged in or existing in bindery, and optionally gives the total disk usage on all volumes. C source code is included. It requires NetWare Version 2.1x.

John: Listing users by name rather than connection gives a new twist to an old favorite.

FLAGBI.ARC: Recursively Searches Directory

This file contains FLAGBIG, an example program that recursively searches a network volume for files over/under a certain size. Files oversized and indexed are listed; files oversized and not indexed are prompted by

FLAGBIG for index or not; files undersized and indexed are prompted by FLAGBIG to turn indexing off; and files undersized and not indexed are ignored by FLAGBIG. The indexing is Novell FAT indexing. The file includes Turbo Pascal Version 5.5 source and is ARCed using PKARC.

LASTDR.ARC: A Utility to Find Last Valid Drive, Source Included

LASTDRIV.ARC contains LASTDRIV.EXE and C source. This is a very simple program that uses DOS function calls to find out how many drives are installed. The program loops through all the drives until it reaches the last valid drive. This program is helpful in batch files where a user logs off the network and forgets to what drive the LOGIN directory was last mapped.

John: This one can help you eliminate needless workstation rebooting just to get back to a known state.

ENVP.ARC: Routines to Change Environment of Parent Process

This file contains routines to handle the environment of the parent process. A normal DOS process gets only a copy of the original environment. Any changes made to that environment are accessible only to the child programs (programs that the parent program runs). These routines may be used to change the environment of the parent. Usually, the parent process is COMMAND.COM. (©Cyco Software, the Netherlands, January 1989. Bart Mellink 76702,256).

> **John:** This gives you another way to manipulate the master environment. It's definitely worth a look!

ERRORC.COM: A Utility to Clear Pending DOS Error Levels

This file contains a program to clear any pending DOS error levels. This is a solution for those who are having a problem with pending error levels causing grief to the relinked Version 2.0a MENU program (MENU 1.02 in MENU.ARC) running under Advanced NetWare Version 2.1x. The program calls DOS functions 4C with error level 0. Use it at the end of batch files, just before the control returns to MENU.

PHANTM.ZIP: Phantom of the Console Version 1.58

The Phantom of the Console, latest version, enables network administrators to schedule any VALID NETWARE CONSOLE command to be executed at a specific date and time. This is a necessary utility for owners of server-based database products that must be unloaded before the nightly backup process can begin. This version does not require the btrieve database NLM to be loaded. This is uploaded by ZhofWare, Novell Professional Developer.

ICFOS2.ZIP: Inventory Capture Facility (ICF) Audits PCs

The OS/2 version of ICF identifies installed software and hardware on PCs, all status information including memory, CPU, and even physical items such as printers. Data is displayed on screen or saved to dBASE, Lotus or ASCII files. It's an automatic LAN and/or stand-alone configuration-gathering tool with more than 200 options. Read ICF.TXT for information (this is shareware, and the new version comes with full documentation).

ICFDOS.ZIP: Inventory Capture Facility (ICF) Audits PCs

The DOS version of ICF identifies installed software and hardware on PCs, all status information including memory, CPU, and even physical items such as printers. Data is displayed on screen or saved to dBASE, Lotus, or ASCII files. It's an automatic LAN and/or stand-alone configuration-gathering tool with more than 200 options. Read ICF.TXT first for information (this is shareware, and the new version comes with full documentation).

ICF.TXT: Inventory Capture Facility (ICF) Audits PCs

This one describes ICF for DOS and OS/2. ICF identifies software and hardware on PCs, all status information including memory, CPU and even physical items such as printers. Data is displayed on screen or saved to dBASE, Lotus or ASCII files. It's an automatic LAN and/or stand-alone configuration gathering tool with more than 200 options. ICFDOS.ZIP is the DOS version. ICFOS2.ZIP is the OS/2 version (this is shareware, and the new version comes with full documentation).

ZIPW31.EXE: ZIP/ZIPX Command Modules

Tired of waiting for PK? Wait no more, FlashPoint ZIP Tools for Windows are here! FP's ZIP Tools are 100 percent Windows applications that can create, modify, test, expand and otherwise manage ZIP archives. FP ZIP Tools are compatible with the PKZIP 1.1 ZIP file format, and support all PKZIP 1.1 compression methods. Any file created or modified with ZIP Tools for Windows remains fully compatible with PKWare's DOS ZIP utilities. ZIPW31.EXE is the COMMAND LINE ONLY version.

WIZ310.EXE: WIZIPER (Full Package)

FP's ZIP Tools are 100 percent Windows applications that can create, modify, test, expand and otherwise manage ZIP archives. ZIP Tools are compatible with the PKZIP 1.1 ZIP file format and support all PKZIP 1.1 compression methods. Any file created or modified with ZIP Tools for Windows is fully compatible with PKWare's DOS ZIP utilities. WIZ310.EXE is the three-dimensional, drag/drop WIZiper (full) version.

NCL.ZIP: NCL.ZIP NetWare Command Language NLM

The final version of AESPEP runs any NW console command plus 30 additional NCL commands at a specific time, period, or event (login, bindery access, mount, dismount, change security, and so on). It can test for the presence of network services (NLMs, gateways, routers) and can run any NCF file accordingly. It runs environment-variable tests and logs in any other server for backup and file transfer. 40K of help is included with the examples. It emulates most NetWare commands (NDIR, FLAG, NCOPY) and DOS commands (DIR, DEL, CD, MD, TYPE, and so on).

AWIN20.EXE: ARCHIVER for Windows Version 2.00

This new Version 2.0 of ARCHIVER for Windows is the most user-friendly archive management shell available anywhere. It has an easy-to-use point and shoot control screen, SmartFile sys, auto virus scan, launch pad, and more. It archives, unarchives, views, prints, provides archive information, converts formats, makes self-extract files, and much more. It supports ZIP, LHA, ARJ, ARC, ZOO, SCAN, VIRx.

VDT191.ZIP: VDT191.ZIP

This file contains VIDTYPE Version 1.91, and features description string(s) assigned to environment variable(s) (or you can choose an error level option) to represent detected video adapter, row/col mode, CPU, system type, keyboard type, DOS version, free environment space, total environment space, and disk type(s) on IBM/XT/AT, PS/2, 386 or clone. It automates work for network administrators who have different equipment among their PC workstations, and gives file server batch files the ability to do the choosing between various configurations of an application.

John: This one is useful for those antique programs that are not LAN-aware and are in need of LAN-based customization.

TMCFWR.ZIP: The Message Center for Windows Version 2.22 (Includes VBRUN)

The Message Center for Windows Version 2.22 is a comprehensive telephone messaging system for Windows 3.0 and 3.1. It features frequent callers, attached notes, multilevel password protection, telephone extension directory, extensive help, and hundreds of other functions. It includes the MONITOR, TMCFW's message watchdog and VBRUN100.DLL. If you have the Visual Basic runtime module, VBRUN, use D/L TMCFW.ZIP instead. This is shareware from Graphical Bytes, Inc.

TMCFW.ZIP: The Message Center for Windows Version 2.22 (Without VBRUN)

The Message Center for Windows Version 2.22 is a comprehensive single and multiuser telephone messaging system for Windows 3.0 and 1. It features frequent Callers, attached notes, extensive help, multilevel password protection, telephone extension directory and hundreds of other functions. It includes the MONITOR, TMCFW's message watchdog and requires Visual Basic runtime module, VBRUN100.DLL. If you need VBRUN, D/L TMCFWR.ZIP instead. This is shareware from Graphical Bytes, Inc.

ODIPKT.ZIP: ODIPKT (Version 1.2) Adapter for Packet Driver Over ODI

This is Version 1.2 of ODIPKT, and it allows the use of networking applications written to the Clarkson Packet Driver specification over existing ODI drivers. ODIPKT supports EtherNet, ARCnet, and token ring frame types. Please send any comments or bug reports by mail to Dan Lanciani at Harvard University (Internet: ddl@harvard.harvard.edu).

HOTMAX.ZIP: HotMax 1.0 Task Switcher Enhancer for DR-DOS

HotMax 1.0 is a DR-DOS TaskMax utility that enables you to assign hot keys to named tasks. In this way you can use Alt-M to bring up your mail program. HotMax also gives you command-line control over your TaskMax environment. If you're using TaskMax, you're going to want to download this program, written in MarxMenu script with source included. This is another Computer Tyme product.

WALKDI.ZIP: WALKDIR

WALKDIR is a shareware utility that "walks" through a disk's directory structure, pausing to run a user-supplied DOS command, DOS batch file, or executable program in each directory it passes through. It is great for LAN managers or anyone else who has to run the same command/process in several levels of a disk's or volume's directory structure. The ZIP file includes a fully functional version of the program, documentation, and registration information, and the documentation includes examples. This is a small program, written in Borland's Turbo C.

John: I like it! This one helps automate many processes and cuts down on the keystrokes.

(d)CLRK10.ZIP: Clerk Version 1.01 MHS File Requestor Gateway

CLERK Version 1.01 is a fully-configurable MHS gateway program that enables users of any MHS-based E-mail program to request file and textual information to be sent to them. It contains multiple levels of access, ability to password protect, administrative commands, two levels of activity logging, file searching, built-in help system for users, and too many other features to list here.

Rick: This file is actually quite useful if you want to set up a system in-house that, for example, has the lunch room menus, human resources announcements, policy statements, your baby pictures, and so on.

STRE25.ZIP: STREE 2.5 Beta

The latest version of STREE (Sorted Tree) is the perfect tool for reporting and cleaning up local and network hard drive subdirectories. Features include file size totals for entire directories, all subdirectories below a parent directory, file count, browse file list within directories, and delete entire directories including all directories below.

ONCALL.ZIP: Memory Resident "Chat" Utility for NetWare

OnCall! (Version 1.30) is a cool pop-up (memory resident) "chat" utility for Novell NetWare that runs in less than 2.5K of workstation memory. While still not Windows specific, this new version runs happily in a Windows environment. A 30-day trial version is available from Infinite Technologies at (410) 363-1097.

LK112A.ZIP: Locker Version 1.12 Metering Software for DOS and Windows

LOCKER Version 1.12 Metering Software for DOS and Windows is available for a 30-day trial use. It controls concurrent access to both DOS and Windows programs and is easy to use and install. It contains a management console. Version 1.12 is the same as Version 1.10 except that it has improved Windows metering.

IQUEUE.ZIP: I-Queue! Print Queue Utility for DOS and Windows

I-Queue! simplifies network printing and print queue management in the NetWare environment. For DOS workstations, IQueue! is a small TSR that runs in less than 2.5K of memory that enables users to easily change print queues and modify "CAPTURE" parameters. For Windows workstations, I-Queue! Windows (also included in this ZIP) automatically loads the correct Windows print driver for the queue that you select. It's PRINTCON/PRINTDEF compatible, has delete/reorder print jobs, hold/delay jobs, and more. Available from Infinite Technologies at (410) 363-1097.

DKALRT.ZIP: NetWare Early Warning System

DskAlert, by AlphaWare, is an early warning system for NetWare 2.x/3.x. It shows you all your disk drives on all attached servers in a color graphics format. You can set warning groups and send messages to people, files, or pagers. This is the shareware version, and it's uploaded by AlphaWare.

CASTAW.ZIP: Intercepts NetWare Broadcast Messages

CastAway! Version 2.12 is a better NetWare message trap. Get NetWare broadcast messages (for example, SEND) without your PC locking up unless you press Ctrl-Enter. You can be notified of new messages while you're in graphics-based applications, and you can send and reply to broadcast messages—all in a TSR that runs in less than 2.5K of conventional memory. (Note: Users with DIR problems, put GET LOCAL TARGET STACKS = 3 in your NET.CFG) Infinite Technologies 410-363-1097.

NDS110.EXE: Directory Sort, Version 1.10

This is a directory sort utility that works on network drives as well as local DOS drives. New in this version is full-screen interface with mouse support

331

for ordering files by hand, as well as simple command-line sort operation. Optional sorting criteria include filename, extension, date, time, and size. Any or all may be in ascending or descending order. This is a self-extracting archive.

TRASHM.ZIP: Trash Manager, The Trash Can For Windows

Introducing Trash Manager! TrashMan is a real, working trash can for Windows that works hand-in-hand with the file manager. Drag files to the trash where they'll be safely stored (even after exiting and restarting TrashMan, Windows, or the PC itself) until you restore or delete them. You can even associate WAV sounds with different events. Don't be fooled by low-grade, crippled knock-offs, this is the original and best trash can for Windows (shareware for Windows 3.1., Version 1.1).

BINDMP.ZIP: BindDump Version 1.0 Bindery Dump Utility

Do you want to see what's really in your bindery? BINDDUMP enables you to dump the contents of your bindery to a file or printer. This program lets you look into all those hidden goodies that various software packages leave behind. Written in MarxMenu, it's a product of Computer Tyme.

AUTOPI.ZIP: AutoPilott Menu System Version 1.1e

AutoPilott uses "SysCon-like" keystrokes to edit, and it has the same look and feel as NetWare. It allows one master menu, regardless of individual access rights, and uses AI to mask out commands to which each individual user does not have access. It works even after logging out or before logging in. With quick conversion from NetWare menu scripts, it uses no RAM or temporary files, and changes can be made while users are active. The easiest to use time-saver on the market, it now includes a screen saver.

John: You should check this out before committing to a commercial product. It's very nice.

PCNT12.ZIP: PCOUNTER1.2

PCOUNTER1.2 is a page-counting print server for NetWare Version 2.1 and up. It supports PostScript and HP LaserJet compatible printers, requires a dedicated CPU, converts text to PostScript, and updates a NetWare user's account balance after each print job. The registered version can handle 16 queues on 8 file servers, and the problems associated with previous versions have been corrected.

DMENU1.EXE: DOS Application MENuing Utility Version 1.2

DAMENU is an easy-to-use hard disk menuing utility that features no memory overhead (not memory resident), password protection, a built-in screen saver with user-selectable delay, and network compatibility. It features easy installation and an on-the-fly menu modification/addition. You can switch between applications with one keystroke. It requires an EGA or better monitor, DOS Version 3.3 or later, and a hard disk with at least 300K free. This program is a definite productivity enhancer. It's ASP shareware, the registration fee is $15, and Version 1.2 is uploaded by John Skurka.

LANPRT.ZIP: LANPrint 2.0

LANPrint 2.0 provides an easy Windows attach and detach of networked printers, without knowing the printers' network names or addresses or the syntax of attaching them. New features include configuration checking, automatic adjustment to the Windows printer configuration, and direct access to the Windows default printer setup screen. It has lower memory and FSR requirements, too.

I-MAST.EXE: Integrity Master Version 1.13: Data Integrity/ Anti-virus

Be sure both your file servers and workstations are operating correctly. IM provides complete, easy-to-use virus detection and data integrity functions. Do you have a flaky hard disk? Did someone illegally change a file? Are software glitches damaging your files? Find out for sure with Integrity Master. It recognizes known viruses, but does much more than just detect and remove viruses.

VTREE.ARC: Shows the Directory Tree Visually

This file contains VTREE.COM, which shows your directory structure.

USERS.EXE: Show the Number of Connections in Use

The program in this file indicates how many connections are currently in use.

USAGE.EXE: See Disk Utilization for Users

This file contains a program that determines the disk utilization of logged-in objects. The program uses the NetWare log function 14.

TSRSEL.ZIP: TSR-Select Version 1.06a—Run Any Program in Only 8K RAM

You can run Mail, Chat, SetPrint, and so on, without exiting the program that is running and free up to 525K for another program. TSRSelect allows up to 15 entries in a pop-up menu, enabling you to run any program from inside any other program and take only 8K of memory. A configuration program helps you create up to 15 fully configurable entries. Designed particularly for network environments.

TIMELO.ARC: Track User Activity

This file contains a method of creating user system-use logs using DOS's environment space and requiring Norton's TimeMark Program. A complete description, including example files, is included in TIMELOG.DOC after unarcing the file. The program tracks user login/logout, the physical station used, and times in/out of applications by application name. The program is currently running on SFT NetWare Version 2.1 and DOS Version 3.2.

TESTNE.ARC: A Utility Like PERFORM, It Tests Throughput

TESTNET.EXE is a network and stand-alone file I/O performance tester. It supports multistation tests. Documentation and examples are included.

> **John:** Benchmark your network and check it routinely—it might be revealing.

STAKEY.ARC: Stuffing Keys into Buffer

This file contains the STACKEY utility, which enables a user to exit Novell's menus to log out or return to DOS. The README file explains this use.

RB.ARC: Display Drive Table, Source Included

This program reads the drive table in AT compatible ROM BIOS. The program is written in Turbo Pascal and the file includes the source code.

> **John**: You might want to know what is hiding in your ROMs!

OR.ZIP: Outrider

Commercial software gone shareware, this one has received great reviews in *PC Magazine*, *LAN Times*, and other publications. It uses a traffic light metaphor to display disk space, directory entries, CPU utilization, connections, and so on. There are up to eight servers per screen in EGA mode. The data recording option outputs comma delimited file. A $20 registration fee gives access to BlueSky BBS for latest versions, support, user-defined sensors, documents, and so on. See the review in *PC Magazine* (October 30, 1990).

MEM.COM: Total Memory Checker

MEM.COM enables you to check available memory (RAM) in your PC. It is especially good for diskless stations or for those times when

CHKDSK is inconvenient. It is not archived, and it's ready to run once you download it.

John: Although it's extremely useful, DOS 5 users may find it redundant!.

MCATCH.ARC: Catches Up to Ten Messages

This file contains a new utility by Integrity Software called MCatch. It is a message-catching utility. As the name implies, it captures messages that are sent to you with the send (or like) command. It stores up to ten messages at a time (it can be expanded).

John: I had a hand in this one, but it hasn't been updated for some time. It's still useful, however.

LOGIT.ARC: A Simple Software Metering Utility

This file contains a simple login program for placing date- and time-stamped messages in the system log file. The program requires Turbo Pascal Version 4.0 and Turbo Professional to compile. See LOGIT.EXE for the executable version. The program can be called from a batch file or the menu system (that is, LOGIT STARTING LOTUS 123, then on program exit, LOGIT ENDING LOTUS 123 appends date, time, and username to message).

John: This one is too easy to defeat for all but the simplest of users.

IFCRC.ARC: Batch File Control Program (Checks CRC Values)

IFCRC.ARC enables you to control the execution of a DOS command in a batch file, based on the CRC value of that file. The program can also be used to display the CRC value of any DOS file. It can be used to check a daily transfer from a remote site or from computer viruses. Anyone with the intelligence to alter your COMMAND.COM without changing its CRC value probably wouldn't be wasting time writing a virus.

John: Too many new viruses can defeat this one.

HOME.ARC: Maps a Drive to a User's Mailbox Directory

This is a small program with MASM source that maps a drive to the user's SYS:MAIL\ID# directory. It can be used within a login script or at the DOS prompt. Usage is HOME x: where x is the letter of the drive you want to be mapped. You can also type HOME without any parameters and it maps the current drive, so be careful. Note that this only goes to the default server, so if you are on an internet, keep that in mind.

GTREE.ARC: Locate Files (Sources Included)

The two programs contained here are HUNT and GTREE. HUNT is used to locate a file anywhere on a disk that contains subdirectories. GTREE prints a graphical representation of the tree structure of a disk (source code is included).

GO-COM.ARC: Runs a Batch File from Within a Login Script

This file enables you to run a batch file from within a Novell login script. See the file CTRLBK.TXT in Library 12 for additional useful detail (uploaded by John T. McCann).

GI2B.ZIP: GATEWAY INTERPRETER Version 2.0b

GATEWAY INTERPRETER Version 2.0b is a maintenance release that adds one new function and several cosmetic changes. It interprets the LOG file that is created by the cc:Mail Gateway and provides statistics for LAN E-mail administrators. It includes several report formats including CONNECTION BREAKOUT, CONNECTION STATISTICS, ERROR REPORT, and MESSAGE STATISTICS. Reports include breakouts by post office, total number of messages, answer versus originate statistics, and more.

John: I recommend this one if you have cc:Mail.

DRVTBL.ARC: Erik Stork's DRIVE Bios Display Utility

This file contains a drive table program that displays all the drive types in an AT's drive type table.

DIAGS.ARC: Show the Internal Parameters of a PC

This file contains a utility that provides listings for virtually every internal parameter being used by the PC it is running on.

CWEEP.ARC: File/Directory Manager (Works With NetWare)

This is a public domain program that can tag files, display sorted directories, and copy or delete the tagged files. The program also enables you to browse a file in either hexadecimal or ASCII. The program works with Novell and all known versions of DOS above Version 2.0.

CHECK.ARC: Checks Error Levels (A Control Program)

This file contains a utility that is very useful for batch program control. The check returns error levels for video card type, keypress, disk space, file size, and so on. See *PC Magazine*'s February 10, 1987 article "PC Lab Notes" by Jeff Prosise for more detailed documentation than CHECK.TXT.

WINJOB.ZIP: Winjob for NOVELL Version 1.01a

The much-improved Winjob for Novell enables you to reboot, restart, and copy to and from any PC in the network. Send messages and wait for the answer, get a list of all logged-in users and all defined users from the bindery. This version supports from 1 to 255 users. It's fast and easy to use. You can install it on every PC, even if the user does not see it. It's great for the system administrator to have access to the PC. Look at file WINJOBD.ZIP for the full and newest DOC. Uploaded by the author, T. Stoll, this one is also shareware.

QSTAT.ZIP: Quick and Dirty Print Queue Managers

With the re-upload of QSTAT and QKILL, quick and dirty print queue managers, users can check job status and remove the job with QKILL. It ignores queues to which user has no access. Available in complete demo shareware versions (Novell Professional Developer).

WYWO3B.ZIP: While You Were Out 3.02

Version 3.02 of While You Were Out by Caliente International is a shareware Windows 3.0/3.1 office messaging system for any DOS compatible LAN. This version offers great new features such as user grouping, message forwarding, distinctive message search, object-sensitive pop-up menus, improved printing and much more.

WMDEMO.ZIP: AutoLogout Utilities

These NetWare utilities (Version 2.0 of MLOGOUT for DOS and WMLOGOUT for Windows) monitor a workstation for inactivity. When the workstation has been inactive for a predetermined amount of time, files are committed and closed, the user is logged out, and the machine is optionally rebooted. Both programs can be fully customized and offer many options. With more than 1,100 previous downloads, this one comes with free upgrades for a year, a special CIS user offer, and demos (Novell Professional Developer).

PAGEIT.ZIP: MHS to Alpha Pager Gateway

With an MHS gateway connecting MHS-based electronic mail systems (such as ExpressIT!, Notework, and DaVinci) to full-text alphanumeric pagers via the IXO/TAP protocol, PageIT! sends messages to an alphanumeric pager as simply as sending a message from your favorite MHS application. Call for a 30-day trial version from Infinite Technologies at (410) 363-1097.

MHSCED.ZIP: MHS Hub Scheduling Utility

The MHS Scheduler adds new control and flexibility to MHS hubs. Scheduler can drastically reduce long distance charges and CSERVE connect charges with flexible workday, weekend, and holiday hub scheduling. Gateways and internetwork connections can also be scheduled. RunIT!, a companion utility, makes it easy to run batch files as MHS gateways. Run your tape backup on the MHS server or respond to MHS messages. Call for a 30-day trial from Infinite Technologies at (410) 363-1097.

FATAL1.ARJ: FATAL-TSR Network Critical Error Handler

A TSR that traps critical network errors and tries to handle them in an intelligent way, it replaces the normal "Retry, Ignore, Abort" prompt and automatically attempts to retry failed operations. Written by Sam Smith (Sourceware), a registration fee of $10 includes source code. I'm currently testing this software with NetWare Lite.

4WARD.ZIP: MHS Message Forwarding Utility

ForwardIT! is an MHS mail agent used to automatically forward MHS-based electronic mail messages. ForwardIT! can forward (or copy) messages addressed to one MHS address to an alternate address (or multiple addresses). ForwardIT! is most useful in the MHS remote E-mail environment. Download this 30-day trial version and try it out. Available from Infinite Technologies at (410) 363-1097.

MRDOC.ZIP: Message Reader Version 2.0 Documentation

This ZIP file contains the 80-page user manual, formatted with page breaks for easy laser printing. Registered users receive a 100-page spiral-bound manual. This one is uploaded by the author, Richard Low at RLIB Software.

MR.ZIP: Forum Message Manager

Message Reader Version 2.0 streamlines message reading and management. The compose/reply editor writes TAPCIS <forum>.SND files, stores messages in thread order (even over multiple sessions), and lists thread titles only once for rapid thread scrolling. It also flags unread messages and shows new, waiting, and total message counts. It has powerful query, search, print, and delete options via pulldown menus or hot keys. This is uploaded by the author, Richard Low at RLIB Software (shareware: $49; documents included in MRDOC.ZIP).

MENU28.EXE: Mountain Menu 2.8.5

Mountain Menus 2.8.5 enhancements include an EXE file that has been reduced in size by almost 100K, which causes the menu to load noticeably faster. 286 and 8088 users will see a big difference in load time. Batch file naming now allows full paths. The Alt-S and F1 keys can be disabled. As always, it uses no RAM, and is Novell menu file compatible, mouse driven, Novell supported, and has had hundreds of previous downloads.

343

BSDEMO.EXE: The LAN Ideal Manager

This is a demo of BRAINSTORM Version 2.0 (The LAN Ideal Manager), and it illustrates BRAINSTORM's BBS-type message threads. If you would like to have CompuServe-type forum discussions between users on your LAN, check out this demo (uploaded by Mustang Software, Inc.).

LANHJS.ZIP: A Setup for LAN HIJACK Version 7.1C

This is an optional, but useful, setup program to maintain and install LAN HIJACK. See LANHJ7.ZIP. UL by KDS Software (CIS 70523,3047).

LANHJ7.ZIP: Control Other Network PCs

Use Version 7.1C of LAN HIJACK as a resident utility to control other PCs on your LAN or WAN. With LAN HIJACK you can access modems, fax cards, CD-ROMS, and other hardware in another workstation from your own station. LAN HIJACK is a small resident utility you can instantly use to help another station on the network, without leaving your word processor, spreadsheet or other software. It's uploaded by KDS Software (CIS 70523,3047).

NUTL6B.ZIP: Supplement (Updated) Files for Network Utilities

The update to NUTIL6.ZIP, this file contains files that are new and updated utilities of NUTIL6.ZIP. Most of the new utilities concentrate on the updating of workstation IPX files, NETx files, and other such information. Also, included are an MHS utility for documenting the host configuration, and an MHS Gateway file for automatically converting MHS

E-mail to a text file so that you can manipulate it (useful with Futurus's NotePad module). See NUTIL6.ZIP for all utilities. Use NUTIL6B.ZIP to update them.

PMSWAP.ZIP: Pegasus Mail Pop-up Program

Use this Pegasus mail program to allow pop-up of Pegasus mail into other programs, copy part of the current program to XMS or EMS or DISK, and load Pegasus mail in the freed space. It returns memory after exiting, uses about 2K of memory, and can be loaded high.

NS107.ZIP: Network Support System Version 1.07 by PaloByte

Network Support System Version 1.07, by PaloByte BubbaWare, is a computer service, support, and help desk information tracking system. Use this to track information for multisite installations including site, user, hardware, software, vendor and help desk service/support records. The new vendor database and upgrade utility are included. All completed features are active. This is uploaded by the author, Jerry Norman (550 previous downloads).

FLOGIN.ZIP: Fancy Login Utility for NetWare

The FLOGIN.ZIP Fancy Login for NetWare menu-driven LOGIN utility, user/password verification, and select file server acts as a front-end to LOGIN.EXE. This is great for multiserver environments. This is shareware, and it's uploaded by the author, D. Kelleher (©DAKWARE 1991, 1992).

QINFO4.ZIP: A Fantastic Disk Space Utility that Works with NetWare

Qinfo displays total/free/used disk space in a concise method with totals (huge NetWare volumes are supported). It also displays CPU type, speed, memory map, config.sys, autoexec.bat, environment, ports, DOS version, and more. This gives a great snapshot of a PC.

QINF42.ZIP: A Great Utility to Monitor NetWare Drives

Qinfo 4.2 is a utility for people who work with PCs and need a quick snapshot of the configuration. Included among its many features is the ability to see the used/available/total disk space on all specified drives with totals and percentages. Large NetWare volumes are supported fully as well as local drives. Other information includes CPU type, benchmark speed, a quick shot of config.sys/autoexec.bat, memory map, and much more.

PSPS11.ZIP: PSPS 1.1

PSPS 1.1 is a PostScript print screen utility that supports MGA/CGA/MCGA/EGA/VGA text and graphics modes. It requires less than 5K of RAM. Extended text modes, graphics characters, and output port choices are supported. This is an update to PSPS10.ZIP.

NCLASS.ZIP: NETCLASS— Network Demonstration/ Teaching Software

This program provides an electronic classroom environment on a Novell network by enabling an instructor to transmit "live" screens, including keystrokes and mouse pointer, to an unlimited number of students on the LAN. Students can also take notes online during a live session. NETCLASS can also be used for other purposes such as sales presentations, tradeshows, "store-front" displays, and so on.

LOCK.ZIP: METZ Lock 3.1b for Microsoft Windows

METZ Lock 3.1b is your key to Microsoft Windows security. It can be used to prevent unauthorized use of your PC and to disable Ctrl-Alt-Del, and it has several configuration options, as well as a customizable screen blanking feature. It also supports Novell passwords. See the included LOCK.TXT for additional details and features.

BOOT22.ZIP: Boot Selector Version 2.20 Allows a Multiple Boot Scenario

The new version of BOOT_SEL allows booting from drives other than C. Help alleviate RAM-CRAM by having a "boot menu" for different purposes.

John: This one makes life a little simpler.

MXPOP.ZIP: MarxPop Version 1.0 Pop-up Utility

MarxPop Version 1.0 is a little 7K TSR that lets you pop up ten of your favorite applications as if they were TSRs. Now you no longer have to exit what you are doing to run something else. When used with MarxMenu you can use MarxMenu script to write your own TSRs. This is uploaded by Marc Perkel, and it's another product of Computer Tyme.

ARCD25.ZIP: ARCnet Diagnostic Program, Shareware

This latest version (2.5) of ARCDIAG network monitor program includes support for 8- and 16-bit cards. All of the features are active.

COM306.ZIP: The Last Version of the Legendary Comment—3.06

The newest and last version of the legendary Comment, Version 3.06 adds still more weird comments and quotes, along with the elimination of a couple of minor flaws and inaccuracies found in previous versions. Install this in your system login and become a cult legend on your network. Previous versions totaled more than 3,000 downloads on CIS. Read the DOC file! This comes from Scott Wenzel/Galapagos Development.

> **Rick:** I downloaded this puppy and checked it out. It's cool stuff if you have the type of environment that likes this kind of thing. I have found that in some places, this does not go over well with senior management who are trying to get people to stop thinking that the PC/LAN stuff are all toys.

STOW17.ZIP: Stowaway Version .1.7!—A True PC Archival System

Move old or inactive files off your hard disk onto floppies. Stowaway maintains a library of files that keeps all files available for restoration almost instantly. You can free needed disk space by archiving old GIFs for

ZIPs and old documents and archive anything that is too valuable to delete, but not currently needed. It features data compression, formatting on the fly, a low price, and much more. This is uploaded by the author, Norm Patriquin.

John: This one is not NetWare specific.

ZEP12.ZIP: ZeppeLAN 1.2 NetWare Utilities

ZeppeLAN is a memory resident/stand-alone NetWare printer utility that includes a shared printer selection, a telephone dialer, network log off/on, and one-line message sending to other logged-on users or groups. It looks and feels much like Novell utilities. This is uploaded by Contact Plus Corporation.

TIM_SY.ZIP: Time Synchronization NLMs

The TM.NLM and TS.NLM are NetWare Loadable Modules to be used in a multiserver network. The two NLMs perform a constant time synchronization between the file servers. One file server is the master (the one that has TM.NLM, Time Master, loaded) and the rest of the file servers are slaves (TS.NLM loaded). This is shareware.

John: You should be careful about putting this on a large internetwork. Consult the author first!

XGATE1.ZIP: XGATE Version 1.40 MHS to SMTP Gateway

XGATE is a high-quality, intuitive, seamless message handling system (MHS) to standard message transport protocol (SMTP) gateway. It requires virtually no ongoing administration (that is, no look-up tables or user name aliases). Addressing on both sides is kept as simple as possible. One XGATE installation can service any number of MHS hosts.

SHOWUS.EXE: Showuser NetWare Bindery Information Utility

This is a great NetWare 2.x/3.x bindery management utility. It enables a supervisor or equivalent to get a quick listing of all users parsed by last login dates, name wildcards, and so on. It is especially useful for removing user accounts that have not been used in a long time. It also outputs user information in comma-delimited format. (Uploaded by 72441,2462, 162 DLs.)

FYI.ZIP: Network Messaging System

FYI.ZIP is a system used to display bulletin-board-type messages to network users at login or by selection from a menu. Messages are time-stamped by the system administrator to set beginning and ending dates for display. The messages are displayed automatically to users only on the days between the beginning date and the ending date. Messages consist of ASCII text files, created or designated by the system administrator. This is shareware.

UU-MHS.ZIP: UUCP-MHS GATEWAY

Both UUCP and MHS allow machines to exchange files and messages over modems, but they use completely different protocols. UGATE is a "gateway" task that connects the two. It allows MHS machines to call UUCP machines and exchange mail messages. It enables MHS users to think UUCP users are really MHS users, and vice versa.

> **Rick:** The important point here is that with E-mail systems and gateways, you are going to run into people who want to share more than just a recipe. Keep this kind of thing in mind.

SKEDUL.EXE: Daily Agenda Group Scheduling Program

Scheduler is a multi-user daily agenda organizer. Its features include automatic rescheduling of meetings (conflicts); a "to do action list"; assignable action items; and daily diary and additional meeting notes. This is a total network time management tool, and it requires DOS Version 3.3 or later.

UPDV13.ZIP: UPDATE Version 1.3

UPDATE Version 1.3 is designed to help administrators maintain updates to workstations across the network.

ISMEMB.ZIP: ISMEMB.ZIP

ISMEMB.COM enables you to check for group membership from within batch files without setting environment variables, and so on. This is uploaded as shareware by Compass Computer Services.

351

John: This returns an error level so that you can branch accordingly.

BATCHF.ZIP: BatchFiler, A Novell JobServer

BatchFiler is a program that enables the user to distribute heavy or time-consuming tasks to a dedicated workstation in the network. It's fully integrated with Novell NetWare (version 2.12 or later).

John: All jobs are spooled to Novell printer queues and the JobServer (which is a machine with BatchFiler running) serves those queues. This implies that Novell's Queue Management System can manipulate the jobs, set an execution, and so on.

PMI10.EXE: Phone Message Interface for PMAIL

This is a phone message interface to be used with Pegasus Mail.

386TST.ZIP: Burn-in for '386, '486, and '586 Servers

This is the "big brother" to CPUTST.ZIP in this library. Use this for 386, 486 and 586 servers. New tests are included that are specific to these machines, and there is a new, lower shareware registration fee. See CPUTST.ZIP in this library.

Rick: Burn-in is actually something you should insist upon from your PC vendor. Machines that fail normally do so within the first couple of startups. Make sure the machines you buy get a good burn-in.

NUTIL5.ZIP: The Latest Version of NetWare Utilities for 286/386

The replacement for JUNGNE.ZIP, this latest release has more than 35 utilities (highlights: report (document) your users, groups, queue, and print server configurations; manage and easily maintain the user's PRINTCON files and prr routing; automatically upgrade your IPX and NET shells; display statistics on workstation usage; and many more.

INB.ZIP: Electronic Personnel Management System

This small, simple-to-use program can be used as an electronic in/out board to keep personnel informed as to the whereabouts of others, and as an alarm to notify you when individuals "check-in." This is shareware. LAN software is required.

TSRBOO.ZIP: Reboot Your Computer

TSRBOOT automatically reboots a workstation or gateway at a given time. TSRBOOT (from the same authors of IDLEBOOT) is a TSR program that forces a system reboot at a specific time. It includes a utility titled BATTIME with which you can set up a workstation to perform various tasks at specific times of the day. It's great for forcing a cleanup reset after scheduled downtime for unattended workstations and gateways.

TL0411.ZIP: Security TSR Auto-locks Idle PC Keyboard

TimeLock 11Apr91 automatically secures idle PC by locking the keyboard and optionally locking a Microsoft-compatible mouse and blanking the screen. Written entirely in assembly language, this tiny TSR uses less than 3K RAM and is fast and efficient. It does not suspend foreground processing when locked, it simply secures the keyboard. This is an excellent security measure for PCs with network and/or mainframe access in corporate computing environments.

LSU.ZIP: Login Script Utility

This login script editing utility includes convenient side-by-side username/login script display. Find text in any script, pop-up users, groups, queues, script commands, and even add and delete users in groups while editing. This is an excellent shareware utility for network administrators (more than 120 previous downloads).

BSTNET.ZIP: BestNet Version 1.6 Boot Enhancement Utility

BestNet 1.6 is a utility that automatically selects the best network shell based on DOS version and the availability of XMS or EMS memory. It sets an environment variable NET=EMSNETX.EXE, for example, pointing to the best shell to load. It also sets NETD=F: or the first network drive. This utility makes loading the net shell easier when running a variety of computers. Uploaded by author Marc Perkel, it's another Computer Tyme product.

EASYMA.ZIP: Oxford Easy Mail (Version 3.4)—New Release

This new shareware release of Oxford Easy Mail (Version 3.4) gets your users hooked on E-mail. It uses Novell Bindery, and virtually no administration is required. Many features, including send, forward, reply, acknowledgments, file folders, import, and so on are included. This is affordable software in the best "Try before you buy" shareware tradition. Businesses, banks, schools, churches and many other companies across America are using it. Customers say it's the easiest to use E-mail system they've seen.

PRINTC.ZIP: PRINTCOP.ZIP

This utility is similar to PCON.EXE, but it has the ability to choose groups or users to which you copy printer definition files. It is easier to use to duplicate print jobs than the single-user method of PrintCon.

NCARD.ZIP: Display Workstation Network Card Statistics and Configuration

This one enables you to display remote workstation usage, statistics, and network card configuration. Compatible with NetWare 2.12 and later (including NetWare 386 3.x).

QM10.ZIP: NetWare Queues Manager

QManager Version 1.0 is a Windows 3.0 application for managing NetWare queues on NW386 and NW286 networks. It displays jobs by group or user, and supports VGA800x600 and Windows enhanced mode. This is the best queue manager I've ever seen.

APRITE.ZIP: Change User Rights During Program Execution

ApRite (Application Right) grants rights to applications. Based on bindery security and on the concept of job servers, a supervisor can allow selected users to run selected applications with pre-defined rights. The fully operational Version ApRite.EXE (time limit 61 days after installation) is written and uploaded by Wolfgang Schreiber.

WSMON.ZIP: WorkStation Monitor

The WS-Mon Workstation Monitor is just like Novell Console, except that it can be run from any workstation. This is shareware, so give it a try. It's very useful for monitoring the activity of other attached workstations, and includes file information, server information, detailed connection information, and so on.

SIZE.ZIP: Finds Total Size of Subdirectories

Size.exe displays the total size of directories including all subdirectories no matter how deep the subdirectories are.

FSP.ZIP: FLU_SHOT+ Version 1.83, Anti-Virus Program

FLU_SHOT+, Version 1.83 is a winner of *PC Magazine*'s editor's choice for anti-virus programs. This version includes a few bug fixes, some protection enhancements, and some new TSR virus traps. FLU_SHOT+ is a TSR that is triggered by suspicious or virus-like activities, stopping the virus dead in its tracks. It's table driven, so you decide how much protection you need or want. (ASP shareware, $19.) This is uploaded by the author, Ross M. Greenberg.

John: Watch for constant upgrades of this software. Ross is great about that.

RUNIT.ZIP: RunIt TSR File Executor PRACTICAL

RunIt is a TSR that enables you to run batch and other files from within other applications. It uses a menu and a mouse-driven interface. This demo is fully functional and is limited in that only the first listed file may be run. RunIt is great for printer redirection on networks.

QSWTCH.ZIP: Switch Queues Novell 2.1x Up

QSWITCH 1.22 is for users of NetWare Version 2.1x. QSWITCH is a pop-up, memory-resident program that enables the user to change or endcap the print queue from an operating program. To capture to the right queue, just select the new print queue from the pop-up menu. This version supports up to 20 queues on each of up to eight servers on the same network. QSWITCH was developed by Arnold Bailey and uses only 27K when memory-resident.

NETWAT.ZIP: Netwatch Diagnostic Utility

This is a shareware version of Netwatch, by Virtual Networks. It is a diagnostic and automatic inventory tool for Novell networks.

NMANPC.ZIP: Administer PRINTCON Files and Default Job Routing

A subset of NUTIL5.ZIP, this file enables you to manage your user's PRINTCON.DAT file and enable them to define printjob settings through their own default that activates automatically upon login. Create a report on user's printer configuration file. It includes three .EXEs.

WW.ZIP: Who's Where\Send Messages Utility

A NetWare 2.1 or later utility to show who is logged on where on the network and to send messages. It is available in two versions: a TSR (6K) and standalone. The TSR uses EMS or hard disk swapping. Two small bonus programs are included.

NETPAR.ZIP: NetWare Activity Analyzing Utility

This utility enables Novell NetWare administrators to track and report a wide variety of network activities, parses output of PAUDIT for import into any popular database for network activity analysis, makes it easy to spot problem trends, unauthorized activities, and so on. It's great for management and graphical reports.

John: Finally, a utility to use against that growing PAUDIT file!

DATENV.ZIP: DATENV 1.2

DATENV1.2 sets a DOS environment variable to a date-based value. This value is calculated from the current date. It also sets a variable based on file date comparison and is very useful for regular file downloading, creation, and audit files. This is for use in batch files, and samples are included. Version 1.2 offers choice of modifying the master or secondary environment or creating a batch file and minor document correction.

QFIL30.ARC: Qfiler Version 3.0b File Manager Utility

This file contains QFILER Verison 3.0b, a utility to aid the user in file management, and it performs various functions such as move, copy, and delete. QFILER works on NetWare and is good for sorted listing of directories. Originally uploaded by 76701,165 on February 26, 1990 (165 previous downloads).

MUTILS.ZIP: NetWare 286 Utilities

This contains four utility programs for NetWare 286, and it has an expanded USERLIST (called USERTYPE) showing the object type, another showing the number of files opened by the user, an optional list of those files, and a utility to show who has a specified file opened. This is for NetWare 286 only; the 386 version is in testing (166 previous downloads).

DFS.ZIP: Disk Free Space Version 1.3

This is a small utility to show the available free disk space on all local drives and on available NetWare volumes (this is freeware).

SINFO1.ZIP: Server Information Report Generator for NetWare 286 (Version 1.01)

This application is the Server Information Report Generator Version 1.01 (minor bug fixes). This program generates a report of statistics that appear in FCONSOLE under NetWare 286. It contains the printer drivers for several major brands of printers. (Code Masters, Inc.)

RBOOT.ZIP: RingBoot TSR ReBoot Utility

RingBoot is a 500 byte TSR that reboots your computer after a specified number of rings. It can be used to reset a modem that quits answering for some reason or to handle any remote reboot application. Distributed by Computer Tyme, it is written by Horizon Consulting, the same company who brought TSRBOOT to us (shareware $25).

KILLCO.ZIP: Controlled, Unattended Disconnector

KILLCONN enables flexible, controlled disconnection of workstations from batch file or in other unattended situations. Groups can be cleared. Users grouped by wildcarded usernames can be cleared. Users may optionally be warned at a timed interval prior to disconnection. A manual, confirmed mode is also implemented. It can have single-server or internetwork scope. A special group may be set up which KILLCONN will not disconnect.

LMAST.ZIP: Command Processor

This is a shareware product from Campbell's Software, Inc. It scans the bindery for user objects and processes up to ten command lines per user. This is useful when installing software, adjusting trustee rights, and most other user-related tasks. It allows for two substitution variables, HEXID and USERID. The appropriate value is inserted in the command line when these keywords (surrounded by %) are encountered.

UGRAPH.ZIP: Sliding Bar Graph of CPU Utilization Percent

UGRAPH Version 2.0 is a utility that displays a real-time sliding bar graph of file server CPU utilization, connection information, and Dynamic Memory 1 statistics. It also provides an auto-logoff security feature for unattended PCs.

TL.ZIP: TL.COM (Timeloop)

TL.COM is a utility for executing any program multiple times with a delay between executions. It was written as part of a network polling suite for one of our clients. It allows delay times up to 9 hours and as many as 32,000 iterations.

MSP202.COM: Print Server-like Printer Assist (Shareware)

This is a NetWare-compatible print server that works on one server. It was developed by BIX user Mark T. Van Ditta and is marketed as shareware (a multiserver version is available by registering). This is uploaded by Alan Medsker (AMEDSKER on BIX).

SHELLW.ZIP: Test for Windows-compatible NetWare Shell

This file contains a utility that checks to see if the NetWare shell is Windows-compatible. This is a batch file utility that sets a DOS ERRORLEVEL if the loaded shell is a Windows 3.x version. This can also be used to test the shell version for automated shell upgrades via a batch file.

CHOWN.ZIP: Change File/ Directory Owners for NetWare 286/386

CHOWN Version 1.11 is a utility to quickly and easily change file and directory owners on NetWare 286 and 386 systems. This version includes the ability to change entire directory trees at once. It is freeware!

MINY40.ZIP: Menu and Screen Saver/One Dozen DOS Utilities

MINY.EXE is a low-memory menu system with a busy screen saver. It can be set up to auto-select a menu option. Included are sample menu data files and documentation. Also included are 12 DOS utilities. MINY's menu data files can be shared and updated on-line.

JS12DE.ZIP: BobWare Job Server

This file contains information on Bobware Job Server by Campbell's Software, Inc. It is based on NetWare's Queue Management APIs. It allows any DOS command-line statement to be placed in a queue for execution by a dedicated job server machine on NetWare Version 2.1x networks, and it maintains the NetWare security, NetWare environment, and DOS environment of the client submitting the job. It has complete job and job-log monitoring and maintenance.

BATEXT.ZIP: Batch File Exit Utility

This file contains BatExit Version 1.0, the world's smallest useful program. It is used to exit a batch file. Batch files have never had a command to exit in the middle. Now they do! A product of Computer Tyme.

BUP.ZIP: Btrieve Update Process

This program enables you to update an "active" Btrieve file using an update file that is similar in layout to the BUTIL SAVE/LOAD format. It is a shareware program.

DS.EXE: DISK SPOOL I—the Finest Shareware Print Spooler

This is Mike Samuels' latest shareware (but fully functional) version of DISK SPOOL II. This version supports networking as well as DOS 5.0's load-high feature. This product is ideal for network situations where printer sharing is taking place. Your computer spools the data to a file on the disk where the printer is attached, and DISK SPOOL II on that computer takes care of printing files as they are received (and it's all done in the background).

John: This one needs extra disk space, but it can save time!

363

PSCREE.ZIP: PRINT SCREEN Utility—New Release Version 1.03

This file contains the new PRINT SCREEN utility (Version 1.03) that allows printing of the screen from the DOS prompt or from a batch file. It supports all printer ports, has an optional header with date and time stamps, and an optional top of form. It is great for printing the screen after a batch backup.

> **John:** Nice, but what about a hot key?

FIXPTH.ZIP: FixPath Version 1.0

FixPath reads your path and tests to see if the directories are still accessible. Any directory that isn't accessible is removed from the path. This is useful after logging off the network to eliminate "invalid drive in search path" errors. This is a product of Computer Tyme and is uploaded by the author.

> **John:** This one can be of use to those who inadvertently have inaccessible drive paths!

KBD10.ZIP: KBD Version 1.1 Keyboard Control Utility

This utility combines the functions of about ten other small utilities. It sets the Caps Lock, Num Lock, and Scroll Lock keys. It can also lock and unlock the keyboard, set the key repeat speed, and stuff and clear the keyboard buffer. This is uploaded by the author.

POSTTE.ZIP: Converts ASCII Text to PostScript On-The-Fly

This is a .PDF file for NetWare 386 Version 3.0 and 3.1, and maybe lower, for converting standard ASCII text to PostScript on-the-fly and sending it to a printer. It is a basic system that has quite a potential for expansion. It enables you to send data (text) from programs that do not support PostScript directly to a PostScript printer. (This is freeware!)

AGSDEM.EXE: AGSmenu-Multilingual Menu for NetWorks/Standalone

AGSmenu is a multilingual menu system that provides the user with an efficient, easily understood front end. AGSmenu has acceptable overhead and restricts the user from breaking out to DOS. AGSmenu is presented in English and French with support for most ASCII-based languages available from Diligence Software. Each menu selection can be protected by a password. AGSmenu allows complete user customization.

TESTIF.ZIP: Batch File Control Program

TESTIF, from the Computer Tyme DOS ToolBox, reads a variety of system status information and returns the results as error levels for batch file control. This program is handy for complex batch file processing, and is uploaded by the author.

VGARAM.ZIP: Use VGA Memory as DOS Memory (Up to 736K Free)

VGARAM is a utility that enables you to convert up to 96K of RAM on your VGA video adapter (and most EGAs) into usable DOS RAM for text-only applications. Stretch the 640K DOS limit up to 736K! No more insufficient memory errors in memory-hungry database managers like dBase! (This is shareware.)

QK0990.COM: Quickly Kill That Print Job

This file contains a demo of a print job deletion utility. This utility makes it easy to delete the last print job you submitted, and has multiple options.

NETPAK.ZIP: The Network Pack for Network Supervisors

NETPAK.ZIP contains the Network Pack for network supervisors. (Note that this replaces the previously uploaded NETPACK1.ZIP file.) This is a set of helpful utilities to make you a healthier, happier network supervisor. It is not written for any specific network, but merely for the shared environment.

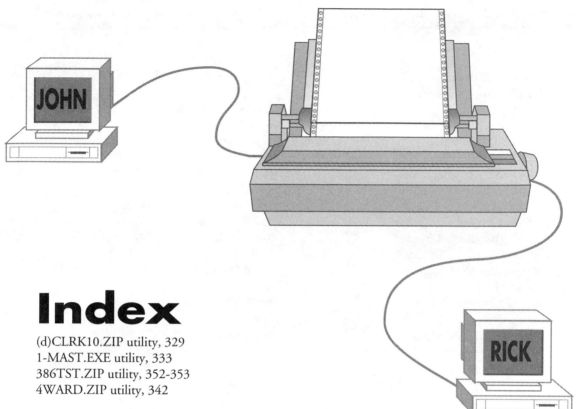

Index

F

J-K

V

If your computer uses 3 1/2-inch disks...

Although many personal computers use 5 1/4-inch disks to store information, some newer computers are switching to 3 1/2-inch disks for information storage. If your computer uses 3 1/2-inch disks, you can return this form to Sams Publishing to obtain a 3 1/2-inch disk to use with this book. Complete the remainder of this form and mail to

**NetWare LAN
Management ToolKit**

 Disk Exchange
Sams Publishing
11711 N. College Ave., Suite 140
Carmel, IN 46032

We will then send you, free of charge, the 3 1/2-inch version of the book software.

Name _____   Phone _____

Company _____   Title _____

Address _____

City _____   State _____   ZIP _____

Disk Information

The enclosed disk contains the following files:

ANS	COM	Answering machine
BRK	COM	Break.sys
SMAP	COM	System mapping program
DOPAIR	COM	Do Run and Don't Run programs
IDLE	COM	Idleboot program
KILLIT	COM	Station clearing program
VMODEM	EXE	Visual Modem
MXEXE	EXE	MarxMenu program files
MXHLP	EXE	MarxMenu help files
ALARM	COM	NetAlarm program
NOVBATCH	EXE	Novbat program
MAP	COM	RamMap program
BUGS	COM	Bug reporting program
TIMESYNC	COM	System Time sync program
WHO	COM	WhoIs program

All of the compressed files above are self-extracting programs. To use them, do the following:

1. Make a directory where you want the program to reside.

2. Copy the above program(s) to the desired directory.

3. Run the self-extracting program. This will decompress the program and any associated files.

   For example, to decompress the WHOIS utility:

   ```
   H:\TOOLS\WHO <return>
   ```

4. To save disk space, delete the self-extracting program files from your hard drive.

5. Keep the disk in a safe place— it should be your "just in case" backup.